Qualities of Mercy

Edited by Carolyn Strange

Qualities of Mercy:
Justice, Punishment, and Discretion

UBCPress / Vancouver

Printed in Canada on acid-free paper ∞

ISBN 0-7748-0584-6 (hardcover)
ISBN 0-7748-0585-4 (paperback)

Canadian Cataloguing in Publication Data

Main entry under title:

Qualities of mercy

  Includes bibliographical references and index.
  ISBN 0-7748-0584-6 (bound)
  ISBN 0-7758-0585-4 (pbk.)

  1. Punishment – Great Britain – History. 2. Punishment – Canada – History.
3. Punishment – Australia – History. I. Strange, Carolyn, 1959-

HV8693.Q34 1996   364.6'09   C96-910493-6

This book has been published with the help of a grant from the Humanities and Social Sciences Federation of Canada, using funds provided by the Social Sciences and Humanities Research Council of Canada.

UBC Press gratefully acknowledges the ongoing support to its publishing program from the Canada Council, the Province of British Columbia Cultural Services Branch, and the Department of Communications of the Government of Canada.

UBC Press
University of British Columbia
6344 Memorial Road
Vancouver, BC V6T 1Z2
(604) 822-3259
Fax: 1-800-668-0821
E-mail: orders@ubcpress.ubc.ca
http://www.ubcpress.ubc.ca

Contents

Foreword / vii
Douglas Hay

Acknowledgments / xi

Introduction / 3
Carolyn Strange

1 Civilized People Don't Want to See That Sort of Thing: The Decline of Physical Punishment in London, 1760-1840 / 21
Greg T. Smith

2 In Place of Death: Transportation, Penal Practices, and the English State, 1770-1830 / 52
Simon Devereaux

3 'Harshness and Forbearance': The Politics of Pardons and the Upper Canada Rebellion / 77
Barry Wright

4 Savage Mercy: Native Culture and the Modification of Capital Punishment in Nineteenth-Century British Columbia / 104
Tina Loo

5 Discretionary Justice: Political Culture and the Death Penalty in New South Wales and Ontario, 1890-1920 / 130
Carolyn Strange

Punishment in Late-Twentieth-Century Canada: An Afterword / 166
Anthony N. Doob

Select Bibliography / 176

Contributors / 179

Index / 180

Foreword

This collection of essays deals with the history of mercy, the remittance of punishments in the criminal law. It is published at a singular time in the histories of all the principal common law jurisdictions. We appear to be living through a great transformation in political and popular attitudes towards legal retribution, one of the recurrent sea changes in the politics of crime and punishment that historians studying the last two centuries have charted more precisely in recent decades. The shifts between retribution and reformation, punishment and reform, fixed penalties and administrative discretion, are recursive. Those pairs of tendencies often, not always, have moved in parallel. And the regressions are never exact replications. The turn towards or away from punitiveness is always highly specific, encoding the ambiguities, hopes, and (mainly) fears of the wider public, and embodying them in complex bureaucratic structures that may generate unanticipated and unintended consequences.

The contribution that historical studies can make to public policy debate on these issues is immense, and not only because the principal alternatives – in the corpus of criminal law and in administrative practice – have been substantially the same ever since the adoption of imprisonment as the paradigmatic punishment over 150 years ago. For historians of the criminal law are also familiar with the persistent belief in our societies, now and in past decades, indeed past centuries, that there was once (not so long ago) a wholly different world. It was radically better, a golden age; or it was radically bad, a time of barbarities. Most citizens alarmed about crime tend to use a not-so-distant idealized past as the measure of current depravity. Yet it is also true that sharp political differences often lead to opposite conclusions about recent history. We see extreme versions of such contradictory accounts in the current politics of crime. The class interests, the view of the state taken by protagonists, are crucial to their conclusions.

Although always grounded in supposed histories, these popular political debates about crime, law, and punishment are usually such gross misrepresentations of the historical record that they hardly deserve to be called debates at all. A vague meliorist picture of long-term 'reforms' of former barbarities of state punishment was found in many general accounts published in the middle decades of this century, and broadcast in legislatures and editorials. It was a complacent caricature of the long-term evolution of punishment in our societies, one that ignored the uneven weight of retribution and forgiveness according to class, gender, and race, and that often exaggerated the punitiveness of our ancestors. The current retributivist movement from the political right now seeks with greater stridency, and even less evidence, to convince electorates that before the moral dereliction of governments in the 1960s, fixed penalties, minimal discretion, and capital punishment ensured social peace and personal security. And both kinds of accounts largely ignore the changes in social structure, age distributions, economic opportunity, and political agendas that probably have most to do with the real and perceived incidence of crime, and punishment, at any given time.

The only cure for bad history is good history. The essays in this volume are an important contribution not only to the recent, vastly expanded professional historical literature on criminal law and punishment over the last three centuries and a good survey of much of that literature. They are also an important contribution to current public policy debates. For only by thinking hard about the complexity, irony, and wide social resonance of state punishments can we hope to escape the closed rhetoric of ignorant moral entrepreneurs. And we can only think hard with evidence. Evidence of past practice and its results. In short, history.

The current debate is one with very high stakes. Our collective societal capacity for punishment is more developed (in terms of prisons, courts, and police) than it has ever been before. Almost one-third of British men born in 1958 had a serious criminal conviction by the age of twenty-eight; a very high proportion of young men in the United States and Canada are entangled with the criminal law, particularly if they are black or aboriginal; many of the social conditions that have historically exacerbated both crime and punitiveness are apparently endemic in the late twentieth century. Our societies' ability or willingness to provide work, social relationships of full citizenry, and economic justice, have greatly declined in the last two decades. So too has our capacity for providing, in the criminal law, for outcomes other than mere retribution.

This volume throws that fact into sharp relief by its emphasis on the role of remission, mercy, and executive and administrative discretion, all of which have profoundly characterized the working of the criminal law in past centuries. It is the other side of the criminal law, often ignored or distrusted because the distinctions between mercy and corruption, discretion and administrative chaos, humanity and systemic bias, so often have been fine ones. But this other side of the criminal law is integral to it, an inescapable part of it. The apparently contradictory but always coexisting antinomies of rigorous law versus equitable balancing of interests, condign punishment versus reclamation of individuals and relationships – in short, of what we sometimes call justice and mercy – are inherent in all social arrangements, all personal relationships. These detailed historical studies of instances in which mercy, in the widest sense, also structured criminal law in past centuries, are a stimulating invitation to move beyond the simplicities of our current public debate.

Douglas Hay
Law and History
York University, Toronto

Acknowledgments

This collection began as an idea for a special issue of the *Canadian Journal of Law and Society/Revue Canadienne Droit et Société*. Historical approaches to the subject of mercy sounded interesting, my fellow board members told me, but my suggestion sounded more like a book proposal. Voilà: the idea became a reality.

Mercy in the context of criminal justice tends to be neglected not only by historians but by political scientists, sociologists, and criminologists. It occurred to me that many of the brightest historians working on the subject were people I knew. As an editor I was extremely lucky to work with a group of scholars who are not only experts in their fields but also cooperative and dedicated contributors. One of the goals of this collection was to address several questions about justice, punishment, and discretion in each chapter, and every contributor proved willing to modify her or his essay accordingly.

I am indebted to Douglas Hay for providing the book's foreword. Professor Hay's earlier work on mercy in eighteenth- and early-nineteenth-century England still sets the standard for historians (and scholars in a variety of disciplines) who continue to puzzle over the administration of punishment. His interest in the project is an honour.

Anthony Doob's afterword is equally appreciated. As a leading criminologist and policy adviser, as well as a warm and supportive colleague, he has confirmed my conviction that this collection has something to say to social scientists involved in contemporary criminal justice debates.

Qualities of Mercy was ferried in its early guises by two able editors. Laura Macleod set the project in motion. Her infectious enthusiasm was shared by Camilla Jenkins, who confidently took the helm halfway through the manuscript review process. What could have been an awkward transition was made effortless thanks to my press. Two astute assessments by anonymous reviewers made the revision process edifying and painless.

The often invisible support of friends and colleagues is a pleasure to recognize as well. Clifford Shearing, the Director of the Centre of Criminology, has encouraged me to see this collection as one of my 'normative projects.' Conversations with Mariana Valverde have assured me that the collection crosses disciplinary boundaries. And Lorna Weir, with her quiet wit and gentle guidance, continues to reassure me that history matters.

Qualities of Mercy

Introduction
Carolyn Strange

This collection treats mercy not as a theological subject but as a facet of criminal justice. Like Shakespeare's Portia, we probe the discretionary use of power and inquire how it has been exercised to spare convicted criminals from the full might of the law. This approach sets us apart from most students of punishment, who focus on its strict application rather than on its modifications and periodic suspension. Drawing upon the history of England, Canada, and Australia in periods when both capital and corporal punishment were still practised, we show that the past (contrary to common assumptions) was not a time of unmitigated terror; in fact, the full array of potential criminal sanctions has never been imposed, not even during periods renowned for their bloodiness. What motivated criminal justice actors to behave mercifully in these historical contexts, and what inspired restraint in punishment? In answering these questions, we arrive at the same conclusion that Portia grudgingly reached: the quality of mercy in criminal justice systems is, indeed, strained.

Although it is naïve to equate mercy to pity or forgiveness, we actually know very little about the various qualities of mercy. Content to leave the subject to religious thinkers, most social scientists and secular philosophers have dismissed it with an implicit binary logic: mercy is soft-hearted and compassionate, whereas justice is hard-headed and unyielding. Since the eighteenth century and the decline of monarchies, mercy has acquired an increasingly old-fashioned ring, reverberating with the archaic tones of royal prerogative. Justice, although an equally ancient concept, receives greater attention because it is more readily associated with the rule of law and modern systems of governance. Exercising mercy depends upon discretion, whereas dispensing criminal justice is apparently determined by the enforcement of rules. Depending upon where scholars stand on soft-heartedness, old-fashionedness, and discretion, their evaluations of mercy are predictable;[1] not surprisingly, few contemporary analysts consider the topic worthy of study, particularly since political compasses across the Western world point towards law-and-order solutions to social problems.

Secular analysts would do well to learn from discussions of justice in religious circles, where mercy is not subject to such neglect. Judeo-Christian philosophers (among others) value the personal virtues of forgiveness and compassion, and they are less prone than criminal justice scholars to draw sharp distinctions between justice and mercy. Considering the central texts that inform Judeo-Christian philosophers, their harmonized approach is apposite: 'Merciful the Lord is, and just, and full of pity' (Psalms 116:5). Throughout the Hebrew Bible and the New Testament, followers are told to place their faith in the mercifulness of God's justice and in the justness of God's mercy – if not in their lifetimes, then in the afterlife. But in these theological frameworks mercy is a worldly practice and not merely a utopian vision of justice. According to the prophet Micah, the Israelites are commanded to imitate Yahweh, 'to do justly, and to love mercy' (Micah 6:8). In the New Testament, Jesus instructs his disciples by performing numerous merciful acts, particularly for the least of his brethren. His parables of the good Samaritan and the prodigal son's redemption, for example, are meant to inspire compassion and forgiveness where harsh judgment might otherwise rule.[2] Yet Jesus also acts as a stern judge when he harshly condemns hypocritical moralists and throws moneylenders out of the temple. Thus, in the Judeo-Christian tradition, mercy is a virtue hinged to the unshakeable principle of justice.[3]

The common law tradition secularized these religious notions, both by prescribing punishment and by providing mechanisms for its modification. The royal prerogative of mercy derived from the ancient notion of the divine right of kings or a direct link between God and temporal powers. Religious radicals preached that God alone could forgive, but kings, eager to solidify their claims to power, asserted that their semi-divine stations rightly equipped them to decide who lived and who died. Although the Glorious Revolution and the French and American Revolutions undermined royal claims to political power, the royal prerogative was remarkably resilient. Even after democratic upheavals, England and its colonies retained the royal prerogative (in practice delegating pardoning privileges to cabinet members), whereas republics such as France and the United States invested executive members of government with the power to modify punishment. Although the prerogative was an outmoded monarchical or executive privilege, it was reconstituted as a beneficent adjunct to democratic rule. As one English judge put it to grand juries in the early nineteenth century, the prerogative of mercy was 'the brightest jewel in the British crown, and the most precious of the rights of the people.'[4]

When mercy was expressed as a democratic right and wielded benevolently by sovereigns, its capacity to reinforce political power was obscured, although never invisible. Punishment is altered and penalties are lifted for a host of reasons, but officially sanctioned mercy, like severity, ultimately expresses the politics of rule. This is not to say that intentions necessarily produce anticipated results. David Garland observed that punishment 'is not explicable in terms of its purposes because no social artefact can be explained in this way ... Punishment has an instrumental purpose, but also a cultural style and an historical tradition.'[5] Similarly, mercy cannot be interpreted simply as a technique for the alleviation of punishment. The royal prerogative of mercy and judicial recommendations of reduced sanctions fit the 'style' of British justice, whose traditions stretched from England to its colonies. Modified punishments certainly saved necks from the noose and backs from the lash, but the ineluctable point was that the bodies saved were ones that power-holders chose to save.[6]

Each of the articles in this collection illustrates this central point from different angles and from different periods and places. Simon Devereaux explains that the substitution of transportation for capital punishment in late-eighteenth- and early-nineteenth-century England was an option that suited the administrative requirements of an overburdened criminal justice system. In tracing the demise of corporal punishment in late-Georgian England, Greg T. Smith shows how class-based designs for urban order and emerging bourgeois sensibilities about pain inspired modifications of punishment. Barry Wright adds that the politics of mercy are most stark when governments decide to pardon rebels. But his essay also stresses that the granting of conditional pardons in the wake of the Upper Canada Rebellion of 1837-8 should not be confused with sympathy or forgiveness. Tina Loo's article on the 'cultural defence' of Aboriginals who were condemned in late-nineteenth-century British Columbia illustrates how colonial visions of Native 'savagery' could be translated into exculpatory narratives. Similarly, Carolyn Strange analyzes contrasts in political culture to explain why executive discretion spared more condemned persons in New South Wales than in Ontario at the turn of the twentieth century. Together, the articles remind us that officially sanctioned mercy is exercised by those empowered to be merciless, should they opt to be so. At the same time, the articles underline the double meaning of mercy by showing that those who appeal for mercy are necessarily *at* the mercy of power-holders. Anatole France's famous gibe about the rich and the poor being equally vulnerable to arrest for sleeping under bridges applies to the exercise of mercy: while theoretically available to all, mercy is nevertheless 'more likely to be needed by the poor and weak than by the rich and powerful.'[7] Mercy, it seems, comes at a price.

Although scriptures are important reminders of the organic link between mercy and justice, it is jejune to assume that mercy is inspired by compassion, even though sovereigns and politicians typically adorn their decisions in the language of pity and forgiveness. The essays in this volume record judges' and justice ministers' claims to mercifulness, but the authors do not take the men who granted pardons and who commuted sentences at their publicly declared word. Personal correspondence, unknown to most contemporaries but unearthed by historians, often exposes the colder logic of political calculation. The motivations of those who advocated restrictions on physical punishment, both through public lobbying and private letters of appeal, are also scrutinized sceptically. Appellants aimed above all to inspire mercy, and they consciously crafted their commutation requests in rhetoric that they believed would be effective. That England's miscreants were eventually put into prison rather than whipped in public squares, that British criminals were transported to Australia rather than executed, that Upper Canadian political rebels were offered conditional pardons, that Aboriginal murderers in British Columbia could escape the gallows, that differences in political culture and history accounted for distinctions between Canadian and Australian commutation practices – in short, that convicted people were never subjected to the full range of criminal sanctions in history illustrates the politics of mercy.

Motivations to modify punishment are variegated and so are its effects: mercy can be kind, but when it is cruel and calculating, it may entail great suffering. It would stun the senses and defy the imagination of early transportees to Australia (*terra nullius*) to hear that forced expulsion to the outer reaches of civilization amounted to kindness. Kings and governors pardoned prisoners but they often attached conditions of various sorts, including banishment, fines, or the forced renunciation of political principles. Men and women who were spared the death penalty through commuted sentences faced the gloomy prospect of imprisonment, not just for years but for decades. If the recipients of mercy were grateful that they did not suffer death or torture, they were also deeply conscious that mercy did not translate into forgiveness but, more often than not, into modified forms of punishment.

Mercy's Histories

The essays in this volume take off from historian Douglas Hay's groundbreaking work on terror, mercy, and the majesty of the criminal law. Hay's provocative argument was that in late-eighteenth- and early-nineteenth-century England, a context associated with untempered brutality in punishment, mercy played a key role in legitimating class rule. Refining E.P. Thompson's arguments that the law appealed not only to power-holders but to the ruled,[8] Hay declared that mercy spared the poor while simultaneously reinforcing their obligations to aristocrats. Furthermore, the judicious dispensation of mercy to humble subjects and the sporadic hanging of gentlemen upheld popular faith in the law's legitimacy. Because a wide range of bodily punishments, from stocks and pillories to drawing and quartering and burning alive, were imposed overwhelmingly on the poor and friendless, well-chosen acts of mercy maintained the fiction that the law could be compassionate and not merely terrifying. This top-heavy version of criminal justice, in which trials were swift and defendants had virtually no legal representation, teetered dramatically between extreme severity and unfettered executive discretion to modify punishment. But Hay took a cynical view of the benevolence of the rich, arguing that a recommendation was never a 'simple positive act: it contained within it the ever-present threat of malice.'[9] In other words, the most compelling characteristic of benevolence was not its generosity or virtue but its contingency. The ruling class dispensed mercy because it had the power to do so, and it did so only as long as it suited its interests. In a country where notions of the free-born Englishman's rights and of British justice were deeply ingrained, restraint in punishment amounted to canny political management.

Although Hay's analysis of mercy provoked debates between conservative historians, who dismissed his argument as Marxist conspiracy theory, and leftist historians, who defended his characterization of ruling-class Machiavellianism, few historians (who should not be put off by old-fashioned concepts) have seriously studied mercy in the twenty years since Hay's essay was first published. John Beattie and Jim Phillips, who have examined mercy in the context of the wider operation of the criminal justice system, stand out as exceptions to the rule that historians of criminal justice tend to write about executions, torture, and imprisonment.[10] Like criminologists, historians have focused on the infliction of punishment, while overlooking its suspension or commutation. This is partly a matter of evidence: it is much easier to find pamphlets, ballads, newspaper stories, or legislative debates about hangings than it is to find records of the procedures that led to commutations, alleviated physical torture, or reduced prison terms. The explanation goes deeper than that, however. Professional historians are no different from their amateur counterparts in favouring drama over the banal – punishing less or not punishing at all. Criminal justice scholars seem to have wrongly construed mercy as an absence or lack, instead of an ontological subject: a political act. In this collection, we remedy historians' relative neglect of mercy on the basis of our conviction that analyzing justice is futile if one concentrates on punishment yet neglects its modifications.

Crime and punishment have always paid. As 'true crime' sections consume increasing shelf space in popular book stores, professional historians continue their tradition of writing about notable crimes and frightful punishments. For example, there are many more serious histories of Australia's convict past than its subsequent criminal justice history, and it is no surprise that Robert Hughes's bestseller *The Fatal Shore* deals with that same period of officially sanctioned brutality.[11] In British history, Peter Linebaugh's *The London Hanged* and V.A.C. Gatrell's *The Hanging Tree* are two recent examples of studies that passionately recount the 'grim chronicle' of law's violence.[12] Although both discuss mercy, their overriding sense of legal injustice prompts them to focus on the infliction, rather than the modifications of punishment. Gatrell stoutly faces accusations that his interpretation is anachronistic: 'English punishments ... delivered an offence against humanity, and ... the scaffold and the justice which sent people to it were monstrous devices of power.'[13] Little wonder that popular perceptions of past criminal justice are slanted so sharply towards the terrible penalties inflicted on criminals. With so many critics of injustice writing about executions and torture, the serious study of mercy is set up as a preoccupation worthy of conservative apologists for old regime justice. As John Langbein stoutly declared in his famous rebuttal of Hay's thesis, the law was merciful whenever criminals deserved to be spared; when it was merciless, it operated in the service of crime victims (mainly the poor) not the elite. Consequently, Langbein concluded, historians like Hay and Linebaugh had unwittingly proved that British justice was not nonsense after all.[14]

Rejecting this false historiographical dichotomy between critics and apologists of punishment regimes, the contributors to this volume pursue the history of mercy as an expression of culture and politics. Natalie Zemon Davis's analysis of 'pardon tales' in sixteenth-century France is particularly inspirational. *Fiction in the Archives,* more a literary study of pardon letters than a legal history of commutation, has not yet received the attention it deserves from criminal justice historians.[15] Without dwelling on the ultimately conservative effect of the king's dispensation of mercy, Davis stresses that the pardon was commoners' sole avenue of hope. Of course, inspiring mercy required 'playing by the King's rules' – presenting oneself as a supplicant, exposing oneself to the sovereign's benevolence, and spinning a narrative that obscured moral culpability. In granting mercy, the king could enhance his glory and cast himself as the very embodiment of divine mercy. But Davis thinks that pardoning offered benefits to a wider audience. 'Pardon often brought peace among equals and sometimes assisted the poor against the rich. The most consistent winner was probably monarchical authority, but in a way that did not erase the subjects' understanding of how pardons were crafted.'[16]

For Davis (unlike Langbein), the royal pardon process propped up relations of rule, but what impressed her was that it also gave otherwise powerless people the opportunity to write their own escape clauses. As she bluntly asked, 'How else could a carpenter who had killed a seigneur have ever been forgiven?'[17] In a period when defendants had poor or no legal representation, when appeal courts were still centuries away, and when guilt – not innocence – was presumed, the answer to Davis's rhetorical question is obvious.

Historians who have studied the history of mercy and the pardon in Canada, Australia, and Britain have been equally suspicious of the motivations that animate penal restraint. Although recent empirical work has enriched our knowledge of modifications of punishment, it has thus far failed to provoke cross-disciplinary debate, even though historical evidence might well refine theoretical formulations. For instance, the profile of pardoning in the past strips mercy to its barest political guise, as Barry Wright argues in his study of political rebels' conditional pardons after the Upper Canada rebellions. Writing about British Columbia when white colonial rule was being actively consolidated, Tina Loo reaches similar conclusions. Mounting successful cultural defences of Aboriginal offenders depended upon portraying them as savages who could not be judged by the norms of 'civilized' white men. Only by reinforcing hegemonic social relations did legal narratives inspire mercy. The most striking aspect of pardoning is that rates of commutation differed between jurisdictions and varied over time within jurisdictions. As Simon Devereaux shows, the English criminal justice system was transformed over the eighteenth and nineteenth centuries from one in which mercy was enacted relatively infrequently into one in which the volume of pardoned felons threatened to collapse the system. In this context, transportation of criminals was a bureaucratized means of ensuring severity while modifying punishment.

Patterns of commutation were often politicized in the context of struggles to overthrow regimes, but historians have documented what contemporaries recognized – that mercy seemed both arbitrary and predictable. On the one hand, pardons were frequently granted for no discernable reason, as if some were spared through the luck of the draw;[18] on the other, certain types of crimes and offenders have consistently inspired either sympathy or intolerance. John Beattie's and Peter King's work on early modern England confirms that profiles of mercy and severity were consistent with cultural values and political objectives: condemned persons without respectable friends to vouch for their good character, persons convicted for crimes that communities feared most, and obdurate, seasoned offenders were always the most likely to be executed.[19] Pursuing Beattie's and King's attention to administrative processes, Carolyn Strange's essay focuses on decision-making by stressing that executives gauged their choices not only on the facts of cases and on expressed demands for severity or mercy, but also according to their perceptions of British justice and fairness. From a different angle, one that examines shifting notions of physical suffering, Greg Smith connects the decline of corporal punishment to emerging arguments about the supposed civility of the English people. In this sense, officially sanctioned modifications of punishment were attempts to impose shifts in sensibility or to advance what Norbert Elias termed 'the civilizing process.'[20]

Empirical studies of pardoning in the past suggest that theories of mercy must take into account the peculiarities of time and place. The essays in this volume look exclusively at England and its colonies, and thus they explore distinct manifestations of Anglo culture in its imperial and colonial guises. Nonetheless, our analyses are informed by US and European historians, some of whom have argued the contemporary relevance of their findings.[21] US historians, for instance, have provided overwhelming evidence of the persistently racist character of mercy. Well into the twentieth century, white men could murder, rape, and rob blacks with relative impunity, while accused black men were vulnerable to the full force of the law, not only through the state but also through the extra-legal mechanism of lynching. Historical evidence was instrumental in urging the US Supreme Court to rule in *Furman* v. *Georgia* (1972) that the systematic severity towards blacks and unwarranted leniency towards whites compromised the administration of justice. Even in the US, however, the history of punishment is more complicated than a stark story of racist injustice would suggest, since other factors (such as shifting rates of unemployment, rural-urban migration, and war) also shaped the changing contours of mercy and severity.

Historical evidence from other jurisdictions further suggests that mercy and severity are incomprehensible outside their cultural and political logics. As Jim Phillips has noted in his study of late-eighteenth- and early-nineteenth-century Nova Scotia, the pardon system 'involved socially and politically significant decisions, not merely formal legal ones.' In this colonial context, military men of all ranks benefited from high rates of commutation largely on account of the military's critical role in imperial defence. English administrators routinely persuaded colonial governors to exercise restraint in punishing military criminals – even murderers.[22] In eighteenth-century England, a different array of considerations seems to have inflected pardoning decisions. In John Beattie's estimation, factors not directly linked to class, including the offender's respectability, sympathy for the criminal's family, and disdain for the victim, could move a king to commute. Of course, the anticipated popularity of a pardon, like the perceived utility of an execution, was ultimately an expression of rule. As Beattie concludes, 'The management of death was a crucial aspect of the administration of the law ... There is no doubt that the level of capital punishment was manipulated.'[23] Although Beattie and others have questioned Hay's characterization of mercy as an expression of class rule, historians and theorists of punishment remain intrigued by his principal insight: mercy spares in a politically and culturally characteristic fashion.

The Politics of Discretion

Unlike historians, who preoccupy themselves with contingency and context, political theorists and social scientists have devoted more energy to searching for general laws that determine punishment patterns. Consequently, contemporary policy-makers tend to turn to research and theories from the latter, rather than to historians' findings. For the most part, social scientific and philosophical work on crime and punishment has spared little room for mercy. Rousseau was convinced that legal advantage inevitably accrued to the wealthy, although he envisaged the social contract, not the eventual withering away of the law, as a solution: 'The universal spirit of Laws, in all countries, is to favour the strong in opposition to the weak, and to assist those who have possessions against those who have none.' Marx was neither the first nor the last philosopher to observe that the poor are the pawns of the rich in whose interests law operates. He theorized that the inequity of capitalism breeds pauperism and crime, from which bourgeois society inevitably must defend itself by hiring hangmen. Durkheim's laws of penal evolution rejected materialist perspectives in favour of a psycho-cultural explanation of punishment. Since crime violates deeply held, quasi-religious sentiments about the sanctity of social order, the state violates the *conscience collective* if it modifies or withdraws punishment. Rusche and Kirchheimer did not grant a meaningful role for mercy in their sweeping Marxist account of penal change. For them, punishment reflected and inexorably reproduced economic and social inequality. In the 1970s, Donald Black theorized a direct link between social stratification and the behaviour of law. Only the respectable, the socially integrated, and the higher-ranked receive lenient treatment because law values what society values. In M.P. Baumgartner's recent application of Black's theory, apparent acts of mercy towards low-status persons demonstrate that discretion invariably upholds prejudicial notions of status, even if the underlying sociological laws at work cannot be identified. Similarly, Ericson and Baranek argue that the mystical aura of the courtroom and the judge's magisterial appearance raise defendants' hope that they might be treated mercifully. But whether or not the accused is treated harshly or leniently, '[he] is ordered to do what others say is best for him and is used to reproduce the order of things.'[24] According to these various theoretical formulations, then, mercy is structurally impossible, dysfunctional, mythical, or a ruse.

Criminologists and penologists subsume their interest in mercy under their primary concern about punishment. Nevertheless, their studies of discretion in criminal justice processes have enriched our understanding of modification in punishment. Because punishment is modified by persons legally empowered to inflict penalties (although not invariably, as Greg T. Smith's essay on cultural sentiments illustrates), analyzing how discretion operates exposes the bureaucratic mechanisms of mercy to scrutiny. But penological and criminological theories of discretion have historically emerged in the context of normative philosophy about the aims of punishment while neglecting the administrative practices that inflict or suspend sanctions. Studying how discretion works in the context of criminal justice calls for political analysis.

Criminologists were hardly the first to analyze discretion in the criminal justice system. From the late eighteenth century, beginning with Beccaria and Bentham, political philosophers and criminal justice reformers argued that discretionary justice was both ineffective and unjust because it yoked unchecked cruelty to unbounded mercy. Revolutionary rhetoric at the time, inflamed by attacks on the arbitrary rule of kings, was passionate in advocating the rule of law. Thus by the mid-nineteenth century, the political climate was ripe to implement utilitarian principles of uniformity and predictability of punishment. But most historians agree that utilitarianism was quickly overwhelmed by a consequentialist philosophy of punishment, the idea that imprisonment, psychiatric treatment, or re-education could 'correct' criminality. In the Victorian era, this notion of corrections as self-improvement flowered and inspired a flurry of institution building. Discretionary justice enjoyed freer reign than ever before in the guise of indeterminate sentencing, probation, and juvenile justice. Social workers and psychiatrists numbered among the new arbiters of punishment, both its imposition and its modifications. But the cycle began to turn again in the 1950s, as political theorists charged that discretionary justice was an inappropriate means of exercising power in modern, democratic polities. Led by Kenneth Culp Davis, critics of discretion drew on the central tenet of liberalism – that power ought to be exercised through the rule of law rather than at the whim of officials, be they sovereigns or social workers. Although Davis considered discretionary abuses to be more troubling than unstructured decision-making per se, many subsequent critics tried to eliminate discretion altogether, in the hope that it might be swept away as a thing of the past.[25]

From the once-dominant therapeutic model, with punishment tailored to suit the offender, penal theory has recently taken a retributivist turn, with policy-makers designing punishment to fit the crime. Disbanded parole boards, restrictions on judicial sentencing options, mandatory charging policies, and the erosion of juvenile justice are all products of this shift. Two centuries ago, criminal justice systems based on the discretionary infliction of capital and corporal punishment were dismantled in the name of moderate but uniform justice. At another fin-de-siècle, we now see discretionary therapeutic justice under siege in the name of stricter, more predictable punishment.

Ironically, criticism of discretion in the 1960s and 1970s began with calls for prisoners' rights. Advocates claimed that 'corrections' was a euphemism for arbitrary and inconsistent punishment. Those who felt they had suffered at the hands of discretion, enduring indeterminate sentences that stretched inordinately until they were deemed to be 'cured,' were among the most vocal protesters. Leftists and prisoners' rights advocates argued that corrections medicalized the political and economic roots of crime, leaving individual offenders to pay for social injustice. To these critics, reform-oriented corrections had failed to uphold its own ideals in that it had allowed power-holders too much scope to act out their prejudices. Predictably, the most disadvantaged – indigenous peoples, the poor, and minorities – tended to serve the longest sentences.[26] Gender-based discrimination was evident as well. Feminist criminologists showed that women, although under-represented in the prison population, were routinely given court-ordered treatment 'for their own good.'[27] In the US case that led to a moratorium on capital punishment in 1972, arguments alleging racist injustice were based on evidence of unchecked discretion in policing and prosecution, in the selection of jurors, in the assignment of defence counsel, and in the deliberation of appeal courts.[28] According to these arguments, discretion amounted to a gloss for discrimination in its manifold guises.

Disenchantment with consequentialist principles of punishment spread across the political spectrum and soon gained a firmer hold in conservative camps.[29] If the aim of penal reform had been, as Foucault quipped, not to punish less (than had been the case in ancien regime Europe), but to punish better, most criminologists and practitioners agreed that therapeutic corrections had punished worse. In the wake of attacks on welfarism, individual responsibility – rather than prisoners' rights – has become the central concept in penal reform since the 1970s and 1980s. Garland and Duff characterize disenchantment with reformism as a sea change from unrealistic optimism (the hope that individually oriented sentences would correct anti-social behaviour) to unwarranted pessimism (nothing works).[30] Not only had therapeutic corrections led to administrative abuses, such as gross discrepancies between sentences, but it had failed to fulfil its own objectives. Rising crime rates in the post-World War II era left reformist penal philosophy vulnerable to right-wing calls for stricter punishment. Pointing to high recidivism rates, conservative critics concluded that the discretionary therapeutic system of corrections had been *too* merciful. If prisoners thought that waiting for years behind bars – wondering if they would be granted parole and never knowing why they had been turned down – was arbitrary and cruel, law and order campaigners countered that plea bargaining, early releases, and sentencing discretion were irresponsible and dangerous.

The reception of Andrew von Hirsh's *Doing Justice* illustrates how easily criticism of discretionary justice was translated into political demands for uncompromising punishment. Von Hirsh believed firmly in individual responsibility, but he also called for an overall reduction in punishment in favour of a standardized scheme of proportionate penalties.[31] Like Beccaria, he believed that systematic moderation would obviate discretion; above all, he advocated remodelling the criminal justice system to eliminate disparities. But when public policy bureaucrats and politicians listened to theorists' calls for retributivism, they ignored the call for moderation, hearing only the necessity to punish without compromise. The climax of retributivism was reached in 1993 when several US states and the federal government passed laws imposing mandatory life sentences for 'three-time losers.'[32] Complex and politically diverse critiques of reform and therapeutic corrections seem to have devolved into single-minded (not to mention simple-minded) formulae: punish more, forgive less.

History and the Future of Mercy

In the 1990s 'get-tough' politics have become everyday politics as crime and justice receive unprecedented levels of media coverage.[33] Popular calls for draconian measures against criminals fuel a climate of punitiveness that politicians find irresistible for fear of appearing soft on crime. In the United States, for instance, over 260 people have been executed since capital punishment resumed in 1976, and over 3,000 people on death row currently await their fates. In countries such as Canada, Australia, and England, demands for a return to the death penalty are backed by overwhelming support in public opinion polls. The acceptance of corporal punishment appears to be on the rise as well. In North America, several states and provinces have established boot camps, complete with ruthless drills, privation, and physical intimidation, not for seasoned criminals, but primarily for male youthful offenders.[34] Even traditionally left political parties, such as the Australian Labor party, have embraced 'truth in sentencing' legislation and mandatory imprisonment policies in response to public demands for effective crime-fighting techniques. To call for mercy or penal restraint in such a climate is political suicide; in contrast, demanding stricter punishment generates political capital, certainly enough to win elections and sustain voter confidence.[35]

History has been introduced into these debates about the revival of physical punishment, not by historians but by politicians eager to manipulate public opinion on the new motherhood issue: law and order. A nostalgic view of 'the past,' a time when law-abiding citizens supposedly lived in peace, animates calls for old-time retributivist punishment. In the olden days (so the argument goes), we used to be tough on criminals; we whipped them when they misbehaved, and we hanged them when they committed serious wrongs. The result? Potential miscreants thought twice before breaking the law. Back when we had the death penalty and executed convicts in public, people rightly feared the law and treated it with more respect. Justice used to be uncompromising before social workers, probation officers, and parole boards got involved in trying to 'correct' wrongdoers. Populists, like Canada's Preston Manning, leader of the Reform party, call for binding referenda on capital punishment, arguing that because most people *believe* it deters criminally minded people from killing, it must, in fact, deter killers.[36] Thus, political demands to restore corporal and capital punishment masquerade as history lessons.

And what odd history lessons they are, grounded in fantasy rather than evidence. In view of the misapprehension and misappropriation of history in political discourse, what can historians contribute to policy debates? The obvious corrective is to counter myths that the past was somehow crime-free because the law was apparently more severe. Once again, Douglas Hay has led the way. He observes that we have for some time now been 'tough' on crime; in fact, current levels of incarceration in Western democracies are historically unprecedented. Since the nineteenth century – and World War II especially – police resources have become extraordinarily capable of suppressing the criminal and the poor. Thus, Hay concludes, 'It is highly unlikely that, at any time in the past of English-speaking societies, we have stigmatized such a large proportion of our populations.'[37] While some lawbreakers were certainly subjected to physical torment and death prior to the ascendency of penitentiaries in the early nineteenth century, many emerged from the criminal justice process without a scratch. The articles in this collection venture beyond documenting barbaric punishments because convicted criminals have never suffered the full force of the law.

Criminal justice sanctions were certainly harsher in the past, yet historic forms of punishment did not always involve inflicting pain (as the imposition of banishment and fines confirms). More important, no matter how bloody the form of punishment available in any historical period, provisions were made for modifications of punishment. Tina Loo's discussion of the cultural defence for Aboriginals reminds us that oppressed and/or exploited people, including women and children, have sometimes benefited from their characterization as inferiors to adult white males. In most cases men in power acted mercifully through jury nullification, partial verdicts, or executive discretion, but more formal practices emerged too. For centuries, pregnant women 'pled the belly' in order to put off and, in some cases, avoid altogether the prospect of hanging. In common law jurisdictions, prosecutors did not regard infants under the age of seven as criminally liable, and pre-teen children were usually spared harsh criminal sanctions. Benefit of clergy (the buffering of religious personages from criminal sanction) was available to any priest by right, although literate people also argued their way out of tight spots under this means. Friends of the powerful (and those beholden to them) have modified punishment informally to protect the rich and privileged. The introduction of penal codes dictated that all were equal under the law, but aristocrats, the wealthy, and the powerful rarely saw the inside of a jail cell let alone stood atop a gallows. More flamboyant (and, from a legal point of view, groundless) acts of mercy were favoured by kings who periodically freed criminals to commemorate battles or to mark coronation anniversaries. Until the mid-nineteenth century, offenders could face sanctions (including torture, burning, drawing and quartering) that we would now consider barbaric, but the scope for discretion meant that judicially imposed sentences of corporal and capital punishment were imposed selectively, not routinely. As Greg T. Smith shows, punitive discretion prior to the early nineteenth century was measured largely in increments of pain and physical suffering; by the late nineteenth century, it was marked by units of time spent behind bars.

The historians who contributed to this collection challenge theorists to accommodate evidence that criminal sanctions have varied widely, not only over time, but also within and between jurisdictions. Foucault himself admitted that his grand schema for the transition from the punishment of the body to the punishment of the soul was ripe for refinement.[38] Thus, to speak of 'old-style' or 'ancien regime' justice is nonsensical unless one specifies times, places, offences, and offenders. Patterns of punishment and pardon have clearly varied by cohort, and qualified generalizations are possible: policies that have historically applied to strikers, rioters, and rebels were different from those that applied to infanticide killers, rapists, and highway robbers. Commutation rates for men have never been the same as for women; similarly, Aboriginals and racial minorities have fared differently than whites. However, by focusing here on modifications of punishment, we establish that marginalized peoples have sometimes been candidates for mercy, even as they have suffered great injustice. In particular political and economic climates, justice administrators have spared even the poorest and the most reprehensible from the full severity of the law. To attribute their actions *either* to sentimentalism *or* to Machiavellianism misses the mark. As these essays suggest, the motivations to moderate punishment are as complex as the rationales that underlie its infliction.

How do we, as historians, contribute to the theorization of mercy? As we suggest in this collection, merely describing the past is less valuable than probing it with questions that penologists and philosophers also grapple with. Barry Wright, for instance, asks what the pardoning of expressly political criminals can tell us about the wider politics of mercy. Simon Devereaux's study of transportation considers how the impulse to spare individuals is always in tension with wider goals connected to the common good. Carolyn Strange asks how discretionary justice is rationalized in contexts where the rule of law is exalted, and Tina Loo questions mercy's role in the perpetuation of racial inequality. Finally, Greg T. Smith explores how civility modifies punishment and considers what prompts and even reverses the civilizing process.

Mercy is hardly in vogue, either in academic or in political circles. As Canadians, Britons, and Australians contemplate the resumption of corporal and capital punishment, and US citizens watch the state-executed death toll rise, we would do well to recall that the recent turn to retributivism was originally inspired by concern over the variable quality of justice. As Kathleen Moore remarked in her study of the history of pardoning in the United States, the attack on administrative pockets of discretion (most notably through the institution of uniform sentencing tariffs and the dismantling of parole boards) means that 'pardon may end up as the only means of individualizing sentences.'[39] In the United States, Moore's point is especially urgent, yet it is equally relevant to other jurisdictions where increasingly punitive approaches to law and order are finding favour. As old prisons are closing, new ones, including private penitentiaries and 'home' detention, are multiplying to keep pace with unprecedented numbers of prosecuted persons. Throughout the Western world, the call is for more punishment and less discretion.

But the history of modified punishment should also urge us to question policy-makers who see mercy as a possible way out, having painted themselves into a retributivist corner. Because it is exercised through discretionary means, the modification of punishment can be arbitrary, unaccountable, and unfair. Mercy can be inspired for all the wrong reasons – to overlook racist killings or to repay political debts, for instance – and it has never guaranteed remedial justice for those routinely disadvantaged. Indeed, Jeffrie Murphy argues that relying on mercy gives the state a perfect excuse to leave structural injustice unaddressed. What we commonly interpret as mercy should, by right, be fairness: 'To avoid inflicting upon persons more suffering than they deserve, or to avoid punishment of the less responsible as much as the fully responsible, is a simple, indeed obvious, demand of justice.'[40]

It is tempting to hope, as Moore does, that executive pardons might pad the bare cell of retributive justice. Discretionary mercy has always saved a few from the harshest penalties in the state's arsenal of sanctions, but its standards have never consistently passed the test of equity or 'natural' justice. If the move towards unyielding and harsher punishment, including campaigns to reinstate capital punishment, proceeds, mercy alone will fail to neutralize the inequities of criminal justice.[41] Only profound cultural shifts and transitions of sensibility have the force to stem the tide of unprecedented punitiveness. As Douglas Hay argues, the 'violence of the law' is accomplished not only through its word and its imperative that pain be imposed, but through its silence: 'much of the power of the word was always partially based on its silencing of the dissentient voice of the lawbreaker, and of those who would criticize the violence of the law.'[42] In the 1980s, the loudest voices in criminal justice debates spoke only for the victims of crime. At the turn of the twenty-first century, in an era when alternative accounts of injustice are rarely heard, these historical essays speak in a different voice – about mercy and the modifications of punishment.

Notes

1 Joshua Dressler paints advocates of strict justice as masculinist thinkers, in his review of Jeffrie Murphy and Jean Hampton's, *Forgiveness and Mercy* (New York: Cambridge University Press 1988). See Dressler, 'Hating Criminals: How Can Something That Feels So Good Be Wrong?' *Michigan Law Review* 88 (May 1990):1448-73. On contrasts between women's and men's inclination towards mercy, see Carol Gilligan, *In a Different Voice* (Cambridge, MA: Cambridge University Press 1982).
2 Harold A. Buetow, *The Scabbardless Sword: Criminal Justice and the Quality of Mercy* (Tarrytown, NY: Associated Faculty Press 1982), 327.
3 Philosopher Jeffrie Murphy also reinterprets mercy *as* justice. Murphy and Hampton, *Forgiveness and Mercy*, 171.
4 E. Christian, *Charges Delivered to Grand Juries in the Isle of Ely* (1819), 283, quoted in V.A.C. Gatrell, *The Hanging Tree: Execution and the English People, 1770-1868* (Oxford: Oxford University Press 1994), 200.
5 David Garland, *Punishment and Modern Society: A Study in Social Theory* (Chicago: University of Chicago Press 1990), 19.
6 On the physicality of punishment, see Randall McGowen, 'The Body and Punishment in Eighteenth-Century England,' *Journal of Modern History* 59 (December 1987):651-79, and Thomas Laqueur, 'Bodies, Details, and the Humanitarian Narrative,' in *The New Cultural History,* ed. Lynn Hunt (Berkeley: University of California Press 1989), 176-205.
7 Murphy and Hampton, *Forgiveness and Mercy*, 181.
8 Edward P. Thompson, *Whigs and Hunters: The Origins of the Black Act* (Harmondsworth: Methuen 1975).
9 Douglas Hay, 'Property, Authority and the Criminal Law,' in *Albion's Fatal Tree: Crime and Society in Eighteenth-Century England,* ed. Douglas Hay, Peter Linebaugh, John G. Rule, E.P. Thompson, and Cal Winslow, 17-63 (London: Allen Lane 1975), 62.
10 John Beattie, *Crime and the Courts in England, 1660-1800* (Princeton, NJ: Princeton University Press 1986). See also Beattie, 'The Cabinet and the Management of Death at Tyburn after the Revolution of 1688-1689,' in *The Revolution of 1688-1689: Changing Perspectives,* ed. Lois G. Schwoerer, 218-33 (Cambridge: Cambridge University Press 1991) and Jim Phillips, 'The Operation of the Royal Pardon in Nova Scotia, 1749-1815,' *University of Toronto Law Journal* 42 (1992):401-49.
11 Robert Hughes, *The Fatal Shore: The Epic of Australia's Founding* (New York: Vintage Books 1986). More scholarly studies include Michael Sturma, *Vice in a Vicious Society* (St. Lucia: University of Queensland Press 1983); David Neal, *The Rule of Law in a Penal Colony: Law and Power in Early New South Wales* (Cambridge: Cambridge University Press 1991); and Paula Byrne, *Criminal Law and Colonial Subject, New South Wales, 1810-1830* (Melbourne: Cambridge University Press 1993).
12 Peter Linebaugh, *The London Hanged: Crime and Civil Society in the Eighteenth Century* (London: Allen Lane 1991); Gatrell, *The Hanging Tree.*
13 Gatrell, *The Hanging Tree,* 55.
14 John Langbein, 'Albion's Fatal Flaws,' *Past and Present*, 98 (1983):96-120.
15 Natalie Zemon Davis, *Fiction in the Archives: Pardon Tales and Their Tellers in Sixteenth-Century France* (Stanford, CA: Stanford University Press 1987). A recent Canadian adop-

tion of Davis's approach is Joan Sangster's '"Pardon Tales" from Magistrate's Court: Women, Crime, and the Court in Peterborough County, 1920-50,' *Canadian Historical Review* 74, 2 (1993):161-97.

16 Davis, *Fiction in the Archives*, 58 (n).

17 Ibid., 57.

18 The good-luck, bad-luck scenario remains evident in US states that retain the death penalty. See Sanford J. Kadish, 'Foreword: The Criminal Law and the Luck of the Draw,' *Journal of Criminal Law and Criminology* 84 (Winter/Spring 1994):679-702, and Kimberly D. Kessler, 'The Role of Luck in the Criminal Law,' *University of Pennsylvania Law Review* 142 (June 1994):2, 183-237.

19 Beattie, 'Cabinet and the Management of Death'; Peter J.R. King, 'Decision-Makers and Decision-Making in the English Criminal Law, 1750-1900,' *Historical Journal* 27 (1984):25-58.

20 Norbert Elias, *The Civilizing Process*, vol. 1: *The History of Manners* (1939; reprint, Oxford: Oxford University Press 1982), and *The Civilizing Process*, vol. 2: *State Formation and Civilization* (1939; reprint, Oxford: Oxford University Press 1982). The most influential application of Elias's theories to the history of punishment is Pieter Spierenburg, *The Spectacle of Suffering. Executions and the Evolution of Repression: From a Preindustrial Metropolis to the European Experience* (Cambridge: Cambridge University Press 1984).

21 Peter Linebaugh is particularly active in this area. See his 'Gruesome Gertie at the Buckle of the Bible Belt,' *New Left Review* 209 (January/February 1995):15-33. Gatrell hopes that *The Hanging Tree* will prompt readers to question whether or not they have become more civilized than historical figures who condemned the poor and friendless to death.

22 Phillips, 'The Operation of the Royal Pardon,' 441-2. Seventy-two per cent of soldiers and sailors were pardoned compared with 47 per cent of civilians.

23 Beattie, 'Cabinet and the Management of Death,' 222.

24 Karl Marx, 'Capital Punishment,' quoted in *Marx and Engels on Law and Laws*, ed. Paul Phillips (1850; reprint, New York: Barnes and Noble 1980); Jean-Jacques Rousseau, *Emilius and Sophia: Or, a New System of Education*, vol. 2 (London: T. Becket and P.A. de Hondt 1763) 200; Emile Durkheim, 'Two Laws of Penal Evolution,' *Année Sociologique* 4 (1902):65-95; Georg Rusche and Otto Kirchheimer, *Punishment and Social Structure* (New York: Columbia University Press 1939); M.P. Baumgartner, 'The Myth of Discretion,' in *The Uses of Discretion*, ed. Keith Hawkins, 129-62 (Oxford: Oxford University Press 1992); Richard Ericson and Patricia Baranek, 'The Reordering of Justice,' in *The Social Dimensions of Law*, ed. Neil Boyd, 41-65 (Toronto: Prentice-Hall 1986), 59.

25 Jeremy Bentham, *An Introduction to the Principles of Morals and Legislation*, ed. and intro. Wilfrid Harrison (Oxford: Basil Blackwell 1967); Becarria, *On Crimes and Punishment* (Indianapolis, IN: Hackett Publishing 1986); Kenneth Culp Davis, *Discretionary Justice* (Baton Rouge: Louisiana State University Press 1967). For an excellent review of recent trends in punishment philosophy, see Antony Duff and David Garland, eds., *A Reader on Punishment* (Oxford: Oxford University Press 1994). For claims that strict rule-of-law advocates are naïve, see David J. Galligan, *Discretionary Powers: A Legal Study of Official Discretion* (Oxford: Oxford University Press 1986).

26 An influential account of these claims was written by J.B. Jacobs, *New Perspectives on Prisons and Imprisonment* (Ithaca, NY: Cornell University Press 1983).

27 Hilary Allen, *Justice Unbalanced: Gender, Psychiatry and Judicial Decisions* (Milton Keynes: Open University Press 1987).

28 *Furman* v. *Georgia*, 408 US 238 (1972). The moratorium expired after *Gregg* v. *Georgia*, 408 US 153 (1976), when the Supreme Court allowed the resumption of capital punishment, provided that states imposed safeguards to reduce arbitrariness. Since 1976, the Supreme Court has gradually relaxed its requirements in this regard. See the special issue on the death penalty in *Law and Society Review* 27, 1 (1993).

29 F.A. Allen, *The Decline of the Rehabilitative Ideal* (New Haven: Yale University Press 1981).

30 Garland and Duff, *A Reader on Punishment*, 10.

31 Von Hirsh, *Doing Justice* (New York: Hill and Wang 1976). Von Hirsh's theories were woven into the 1987 review of sentencing in Canada. Canadian Sentencing Commission,

Sentencing Reform: A Canadian Approach (Ottawa: Supply and Services 1987). In the wake of the report, government policy has generally drifted towards greater punitiveness. See Canada, 'An Act Respecting Firearms and Other Weapons,' Bill C-68 (passed 13 June 1995). Parts of the act that imposed higher minimum penalties came into effect 1 January 1996.

32 This phrase plays on the infamous 'three strikes, you're out' shorthand used to describe mandatory minimum sentencing for persons convicted of three supposedly serious offences. In November 1993, Washington became the first state to enact a 'three-time-loser law' for such crimes as drunk driving, promoting prostitution, and petty theft. Wendy Kaminer, 'Federal Offense,' *Atlantic Monthly* 273 (June 1994):102, 102-14.

33 Richard Ericson, Patricia Baranek, and Janet Chan, *Visualizing Deviance: A Study of News Organization* (Toronto: University of Toronto Press 1987).

34 Doris Layton MacKenzie and Claire Souryal, 'A "Machiavellian" Perspective on the Development of Boot Camp Prisons: A Debate,' *University of Chicago Roundtable* 2, 2 (1995):445-53.

35 In March 1995, the New South Wales Australian Labor party squeaked past the Liberals, largely on account of leader Robert Carr's willingness to promise strict law-and-order policies once elected. *Weekend Australian,* 4-5 March, 1995, 10. On the 'truth in sentencing' provisions of the New South Wales Sentencing Act, see Patricia Gallagher, 'Why does NSW have a higher imprisonment rate than Victoria?' *Crime and Justice Bulletin,* 23 (May 1995).

36 Preston Manning, 'Why we need a binding referendum on the death penalty,' *Globe and Mail,* 4 July 1995, A13. His argument is stunningly circular: 'If 50 to 60 per cent of the population of a country ... were to declare their conviction that the death penalty is or could be made such a deterrent, presumably this penalty has some deterrent effect, at least among those who so believe.'

37 Douglas Hay, 'Time, Inequality, and Law's Violence,' in *Law's Violence,* ed. Austin Sarat and Thomas Kearnes, 141-73 (Ann Arbor: University of Michigan Press 1993) 172.

38 Historians have generally been wary of adopting Foucault's formulations, originally expressed without qualifications in *Discipline and Punish: The Birth of the Prison* (London: Allen Lane 1977). For a neglected but deft application of Foucaultian perspectives, see John Pratt, *Punishment in a Perfect Society: The New Zealand Penal System, 1840-1939* (Wellington: Victoria University Press 1992).

39 Kathleen Dean Moore, *Pardons: Justice, Mercy, and the Public Interest* (New York: Oxford 1989), 7.

40 Murphy, 'Mercy and Legal Justice,' in *Forgiveness and Mercy,* 171.

41 This theme is taken up in Philip Stenning, ed., *Accountability for Criminal Justice: Selected Essays* (Toronto: University of Toronto Press 1996).

42 Hay, 'Time, Inequality, and Law's Violence,' 161.

1

Civilized People Don't Want to See That Kind of Thing: The Decline of Public Physical Punishment in London, 1760-1840

Greg T. Smith

> There is nothing we can learn from the penal code of [the eighteenth century] except that we are well rid of it.[1]

At a time when anxiety about crime and the need to 'get tough' on criminals capture headlines and dominate television news and entertainment, when popular opinion polls show strong support for the reintroduction of the death penalty, and when history is casually invoked to support calls for a return to 'old style' punishment, comments such as that quoted above stifle historical inquiry and leave the contemplative reader dumbfounded. In spite of assertions that criminal justice history is irrelevant, penal codes and penal practice do offer a point of entry into the rich cultural, social, and political worlds of the past and also provide the foundations for an understanding of who we are today.

Ironically, many of the penal strategies being considered casually and uncritically in present-day penal reform discourses hearken back to the variety of punishments available to the courts in eighteenth-century England. The difference is that over the course of the late eighteenth and early nineteenth centuries, those punishments were severely circumscribed or eliminated altogether. Between 1760 and 1840 there was a remarkable change in the techniques of criminal punishment in England. Historians have thus far concentrated on changes to the capital code, specifically the movement to repeal or at least restrict the death penalty, and the campaign to eliminate public executions.[2] But other reforms to penal practice were also undertaken in this period and, in particular, we can point to the restriction or abolition of such corporal punishments as the pillory and public whipping, which had long served the needs of English justice.

It is astonishing how swiftly, in relative terms, these changes in penal practice came about. Social historians and historians of English law reform have often described what happened as indicative of a general 'humanitarian' trend, sparked by reformers sensitive to the suffering of the criminal and the poor. Since brutal sanctions are no longer legitimately employed in England today, it might be useful to reconsider why the English penal system underwent such extensive modification in the period between 1760 and 1840. In doing so, we must remember to situate these punishments within their cultural and social context. As we will see, it is important to understand punishments not simply as administrative adjuncts to a dry legal system. We must recognize that punishment manifests repression and that the particular coercive models adopted by any one society are, as David Garland has said, 'social artefacts embodying and regenerating wider cultural categories' that are historically grounded in time and place.[3]

One of the aims of this essay, then, is to show how the 'civilization' of punishment reflected and reinforced changing attitudes towards violence and towards the public presentation of the physical body. Such ideas, connected with emerging notions of the self, with new understandings of class and gender roles, and with bourgeois sensibility, informed the nineteenth-century discourse of Victorian morality and still continue to animate our late-twentieth-century conceptions of acceptable levels of violence and coercion in judicial punishment.[4] The close connection between punishment and these broad cultural dispositions urges us to recollect the complexity and frequent contradictions embedded within culture, and to remain cautious of any single explanation that may depend upon a kind of contrived determinism. What I am suggesting, then, is that one way of exploring what some literary scholars have characterized as an emergent 'culture of sentiment' or 'sensibility' in this period is through an examination of the cultural context of violence, through both its experience and its prosecution at law.[5] In particular, if we focus on the changing attitudes to corporal punishment, we may discern the complex relationship between violence, punishment, humanitarianism, civility, and law reform. As we will see, the exercise of mercy and the modification of punishment in eighteenth-century London was influenced as much by execution rates, humanitarian sympathy, concern for public order, and the fear of rising crime as by such apparently unrelated factors as street maintenance, commercial trade, and evolving gender roles for the 'civilized' individual.

The Norms of Penal Practice
Sociologists, social theorists, and historians have often noted the implicit links between sentiments, values, and attitudes, and the logic of penal institutions and punitive strategies within societies without exploring how such cultural patterns fashion the ways in which punishments were legitimized or at least tolerated within their distinct historical context. The

'cultural defence' that Tina Loo speaks of in her chapter and the politics of executive discretion discussed by Carolyn Strange in hers offer examples of culture's place in the mitigation of punishment. This essay provides further evidence that the modification of punishment is more than an administrative decision. Cultural norms have been employed in all ages to rationalize and justify certain punishments and to prohibit others.

The case of the American student Michael Fay, convicted of vandalism in Singapore in 1994, is a recent example of how the close scrutiny of particular penal strategies can expose what Norbert Elias styled the culturally imposed 'thresholds of repugnance.'[6] Fay was sentenced to a fine and a term of imprisonment along with six lashes with a rattan cane. Since his culpability was beyond doubt, public opinion was focused narrowly upon the suitability of corporal punishment. However, the controversy that erupted in the aftermath of his sentencing, particularly in the United States, touched a much deeper chord than expected. While many Americans applauded the caning, others condemned it as barbaric and the ensuing public debate exposed the deep tensions inherent in penal practice and the ambivalence in the social and cultural predispositions of penology in Western society today.

The Singaporean authorities defended the penalty, maintaining that such strict punishments rendered Singapore a safe place to live in and visit. Indeed, the argument went, Americans protesting the use of corporal punishment in Singapore and other Asian countries were not only hypocrites, given the strong popular support for the death penalty and the apparent glorification of violence in 'Rambo-style' movies, but were guilty of 'cultural arrogance' or 'cultural imperialism' in trying to impose their belief systems on a legal case in a foreign country. But the outrage against the Fay sentence was far from universal. Many Americans, 38 per cent according to a *Newsweek* poll, approved of the caning and many other North Americans shared in the view that 'if we caned all those punks out there stealing cars and causing trouble, you'd see the crime rate go down.' What the Fay case revealed was the profound uncertainty about and dissatisfaction with therapeutic corrections systems in Western societies generally. But perhaps more disturbingly, it highlighted the power of the fear of crime to excite the appetite for brutal punishments that rely upon physical pain and torture to achieve their ends.[7]

The Fay affair was not about whether corporal punishment was appropriate in this case for this particular offender; rather, it forced a re-examination of the cultural norms of penal practice by throwing the issues of punishment and the administration of justice into high relief. It forced 'civilized' Western countries to face the vexatious question of whether painful, physical punishments might not, in fact, retain a place in our societies. As well, it reminded us not only that penal systems are constructed around cultural norms and social orders, but also that supposedly universal notions of 'civility' and 'inalienable human rights' are products of the eighteenth-century Enlightenment and Western, liberal-democratic concepts of individuality and economic and political self-determination. The former prime minister of Singapore, Lee Kuan Yew, identified this fundamental difference early in the Fay debate by pointing out that Asian cultures put the good of society before individual liberties, prompting the *Washington Post* to counter: 'The whole point of upholding human rights across borders and cultures is that certain standards are universal.'[8] Conversely, those Americans who employed the social-structure argument expressed their opposition to corporal punishment in terms of their own culturally bound notions of propriety and manners – in precisely the form that Elias outlined in his study of Western civilization. Thus, opponents to corporal punishment asserted that stability and social order, or what Ellen Goodman identified as 'a livable society,' could be achieved only by 'balancing freedom and discipline, internalizing values, [and] making sure everyone has a stake,' and not by introducing a three-strikes-you're-out rule or by raising bloody welts on someone's backside.[9]

The perplexing question in the Fay case – Is there a role for violent, corporal punishment? – also confronted English people at the turn of the nineteenth century. By the last decades of the eighteenth century, most corporal punishments were falling into disuse as judges and magistrates employed other penal strategies not intended to be violent. But these changes in penology were not just the result of administrative changes or campaigns for law reform. Rather, I would suggest that reforms to the penal code of England in the late eighteenth and early nineteenth centuries were products of concurrent, but not necessarily related forces. Humanitarian sentiment, for example, was only one strain of argument enmeshed in a whole series of movements and ideas, ranging from the commercial and administrative to the pragmatic and expedient. Modifications to the penal repertoire occurred both through intentional interventions and as unintended consequences of social, intellectual, economic, and administrative change. The process was marked by unevenness, flux, regression, and progress, caused in part by the different trajectories of evolving gender roles, class relations, political pragmatism, economic opportunism, and the unevenness of social change generally. Most of the evidence I present here reveals the specificity of attitudes towards punishment and the unevenness of change. The project as a whole is, perhaps, best viewed as an example of cultural interpretation, specifically as it relates to the way in which penal strategies were constrained, conciliated, modified, or abolished altogether.[10]

Punishment in Early Modern England

Penal reformers' arguments about the humanitarian treatment of criminals in the late eighteenth century focused on the broad array of punishments available to the English state. The fact that over 200 capital offences existed in England at the turn of the nineteenth century has launched many discussions of the brutality of English criminal law. This view has been substantially revised by recent scholarship, but the study of mercy in the English penal system has usually centred on the mitigation of the death sentence. If we look at trials at the Old Bailey, the principal court for the City of London and the county of Middlesex, we can see that judges were also willing to mitigate non-capital sentences for reasons similar to those applying in capital cases, most likely because the law permitted their exercise of discretionary power in such cases and because they had recourse to a wider range of secondary punishments. In the mid-eighteenth century the range of punishments open to judges and magistrates would not have looked terribly unfamiliar to their colleagues from one or even two centuries earlier. For most capital offences, hanging in public was the means of imposing the death penalty. Disembowelling and burning at the stake for men convicted of treason, and burning at the stake for women convicted of petty treason (which included coining), was a more grisly form of execution for what lawmakers deemed the most serious crimes. Capital sentences, as Simon Devereaux and Barry Wright discuss, could be commuted to transportation to the American colonies and later to Australia for a fixed time; after 1718 transportation became a common sentence for non-capital offences. Other non-capital sentences included imprisonment, whipping, branding, a stint in the pillory, fines, or a combination of these. And although the printed trial accounts from the Old Bailey or other London courts do not reveal whether such punishments were actually carried out in every case, there exists a good deal of newspaper and other ephemeral evidence to shed some light on the popular reactions to those punishments that were administered.

A common feature of all of these punishments was their spectacular appeal; by this I mean that their evocative, disciplinary power relied upon the theatrical and public infliction of pain and physical harm for their moral and punitive effect. The procession of condemned men and women to Tyburn, the floggings through crowded city streets, and the pillories erected in public squares on market days were all public exercises intended to display order. For a very long time, these punishments were thought to be effective because they shamed and humiliated the offenders before their community and reasserted the power of the state. Crucial to bear in mind, though, is the fact that these degrading corporal punishments were constructed around particular acts of brutality that, when recast within a frame of judicial and legal legitimacy, sanctioned violence itself as an acceptable disciplinary tool.

There is significant evidence, however, throughout a wide range of sources, from newspapers, popular prints, and pamphlets to judges' reports and new legislation, that attitudes towards violence and sensitivity towards the individual's experience of pain and suffering began to be re-examined and reconstructed in this period. And as these sentiments changed, it became harder for judges and magistrates to see the utility in sentencing people in the conventional ways. People still wanted criminals to be punished, but increasingly they did not want them to be punished in the same kinds of ways as in the past. There was something unacceptable about the forms and functions of the secondary punishments available until the end of the eighteenth century. Brutality and cruelty, which in former times had been thought to intensify the sting of correction, were now seen as excessive and incongruous with the new aims of punishment, which favoured deterrence and reform. As one anonymous contributor to the *London Magazine* put it, 'It is not the Intenseness of Pain that has the greatest Effect on the Mind, but its Continuance; for our Sensibility is more easily and more powerfully affected by weak but repeated Impressions than by a violent but voluntary Impulse ... The Death of a Criminal is a terrible but momentary Spectacle, and therefore a less efficacious Method of deterring others than the continued Example of a Man deprived of his Liberty.'[11]

This anonymous author, in fact cribbing the work of Cesare Beccaria whose essay *On Crimes and Punishments* was translated and published in English in 1767, captured the essence of what historians, with the benefit of hindsight, are now beginning to discover: that for many complex reasons, punishments employing violence to effect their disciplinary ends no longer provided appropriate solutions to the larger problem of crime. Moreover, the author implies that punishments inflicted on the body of the offender and causing only some short-term physical discomfort would never be as successful as measures that instead undermined his very identity as a free-born Englishman and circumscribed his rights and liberties.

Historians and social theorists have continued to puzzle over the meaning of this shift in penal practice and, consequently, no satisfactory explanation for the end of public punishment has emerged. The ineffectiveness of public executions was the focus of Michel Foucault's *Discipline and Punish,* in which he argued that the end of the spectacle of punishment, with its focus on the physical body as the vital target for discipline and deterrence, was linked to larger changes in the relationship between the individual and the state's ability to exert power over all its subjects.[12] But Foucault's focus on the functionalist relationship between the state and the individual, although insightful and instructive, inadequately explains the relationship between individuals in society. In Foucault's view, when human bodies are reduced to symbols and metaphors for power, the fact that real, sentient humans are being pained and tormented is often lost, thus minimizing the offenders' experience and obscuring the relationship between their pain and suffering and the feelings and sensibilities of the crowd that surrounds them. Like vulgar Marxist accounts of class control, Foucault's explanations fail to account for the full range of human motivation, action, and reaction. Unidimensional explanations thus offered for the reform of punishment ignore the precipitating conditions – social, psychic, environmental as well as economic and political forces that play upon the minds of those advocating or effecting change. As well, such models make no allowances for the results of diverse intentions or the proclivities of unintended consequences.

On the other hand, the work of Norbert Elias on the sociogenesis of civility encourages the consideration of a wide scope of influences and factors that may be included in our study of changing penal practices. My allusions to a 'civilizing process' are in keeping with the kinds of changes Elias began to elaborate in his study of broad shifts in sensibilities, manners, and social structure in Western society since the late medieval period. Elias's seminal project did not deal with changes in forms of punishment as an explicit example of the civilizing process at work, but others have shown that Elias's work offers a heuristic model suitable for the study of the cultural underpinnings of penal institutions and penal practice.[13] In particular, Elias's methodology, which involves a close study of the minutiae of table manners and the translocation of all bodily functions to the realm of intimate experience, reveals how modifications to patterns of conduct regarding the everyday rituals of life relate to significant transformations in more general phenomena. Similarly, this article suggests that through a close study of the techniques of privatization, suppression, and modification of certain penal strategies, we can see how 'civility,' or what Elias identified as the later eighteenth-century manifestations, *politesse* and *humanité*, came to undermine the traditional legitimizing discourses of penal policy and forced the reconfiguration of penology in England.[14] Furthermore, these changes in penal practice were intimately linked to the same broadly based cultural assumptions that provided the impetus for changes in class and gender norms.

The Spectacle of Terror Undermined
Hanging in public was the principal means of executing felons for most offences throughout the eighteenth century. In London before 1783, the procedure for public executions in the metropolis had developed into a

highly ritualized 'cultural' event. Following the regular sessions at the Old Bailey, men and women convicted of capital offences and sentenced to death were returned to Newgate Prison to await their execution. On the day of execution, the condemned were placed in a cart and trundled along a regular, three-mile route through the streets of London to the gallows at Tyburn, near present day Marble Arch. On the way, crowds would gather to cheer or chastise the convicts as they made their way towards their final destination. The procession was intended to shame the prisoners and terrorize the populace as they contemplated the awful fate that awaited all such convicts. In 1783, however, the procession was abolished when the Tyburn gallows were removed permanently. James Cockburn has suggested that the decision to end the Tyburn procession and move the gallows to Newgate was due to a 'concern for public order rather than a change in penal philosophy.' And, indeed, the disruption that the procession caused to street traffic, to business, and to the work day is the usual reason put forward for the Tyburn procession being ended. But it was not simply the anxiety over the carnivalesque crowd that prompted agitation for the procession to cease.[15]

As Simon Devereaux shows in this volume, the debate over the execution of criminals at Tyburn and later the cries to abolish public executions altogether were enmeshed in the debates over law and order, the search for a suitable secondary punishment in face of the American Revolution, and anxiety about the response public executions had elicited in the particularly bloody years of the 1780s. He rightly places the specific issue of concern over public hangings into the cultural milieu of the 1780s and 1790s, when public punishment generally was exposed to critique and modification, and the high numbers of those being subjected to capital punishment became an awkward issue for the Home Office. James Boswell recalled 'the shocking sight of fifteen men executed before Newgate' in June of 1784. And it was clear to the *Times,* too, that the large number of executions, especially of young offenders, was devoid of any deterrent value because spectators were overwhelmed by the carnage.[16] One correspondent argued, 'The necessity of cutting off criminals of tender years is a defect in our police, which is really shocking to humanity. The whole continent of Europe does not execute as many criminals in four years, as England and Ireland do in one.'[17] The experience of the early 1780s was clearly important to the way capital punishment was perceived, but as historian Randall McGowen argues, other critics of the 'Tyburn Fair' perceived the fundamental faults of the early modern execution well before its demise.

The terror of painful physical punishments had been the cornerstone of English penology from earliest times. But as the terror became dulled by the frequency of executions, the reformers argued, the issue of executions came to rest on the condemned body itself. The festivity and ribaldry of the gin-soaked London crowd, criticized most notably by Bernard de Mandeville in the 1720s and Henry Fielding a generation later, masked general ambivalence towards or disrespect for the punitive meaning intended by the authorities and popular disdain for the bloody judicial system. At the execution scene itself, McGowen argues, the crowd 'saw only a punishment inflicted upon an individual offered to a crowd of individuals.' The execution of men and women had been drained of its judicial terror and by the late eighteenth century, the gallows 'only produced a powerful emotional response that one either felt or was indifferent to. The execution had become an inarticulate shock; it had been reduced to the single dimension of pain.'[18]

Pain, however, was not the primary objective of these terrible spectacles. Some degree of pain was acceptable, even desirable, in order to grab the attention and touch the hearts of the spectators, but sheer terror as a deterrent force was the real object of the state's endeavours. The empathetic experience of pain alone signalled the wrong message because it failed to strike terror into the hearts of the men, women, and children who watched. Observers were almost always struck emotionally by the barbarity of the event; the fact that pain became the sensation most prominently associated with public execution was of great importance to the reformers who sought its abolition. Indeed pain, which produced suffering, would be the issue on which abolitionists and reformers would largely focus their campaign to end executions altogether.

This is a highly significant point. It reveals a change in emotional focus from the criminal as a sacrifice to the law and state order to the criminal as sufferer of a punishment repulsive in itself. The change in focus also provides evidence of a growing uneasiness with the place of violent behaviour within society generally. Thus whether it is possible, or even necessary, to fix one particular reason for the end of the Tyburn procession, the point is that its end marked a fundamental break with customary practice in judicial punishment, and this was an important step towards the removal of all punishment from the public sphere.[19]

The end of the Tyburn procession on London's hanging days marked a paradigm shift in the way public executions were managed – a shift due in large part to the unique experience of the metropolis. Eighteenth-century London was not only the hub of political administration and commerce, but also the cultural and social centre of English life. With its thriving commercial enterprises and a growing population, the London metropolis provided fertile ground for the evolution of class and gender norms. The demands of the market created opportunities for women to expand their public roles and for working men and women to establish new relationships within similarly emerging social and economic spheres. For women in particular, the augmentation of their public roles brought with it the pressure to project a self-disciplined and civil public face that mirrored respectable male standards of gentility, honour, and fair dealing. Thus as women were integrated into spheres of social life traditionally dominated by men and as they gained some acceptance in their new roles, structural features of society that formerly separated men and women in other areas of daily life also fell under critical gaze. This was made clear in the movement to abolish the punishment of burning for women convicted of treason. Men convicted of treason were hanged to the brink of death, cut down, disembowelled, and decapitated. Women found guilty of treason or petty treason, however, were burned at the stake although in practice they were strangled to death by the hangman before their bodies were consumed by the flames. Blackstone explained this as a mitigation of the punishment, 'as the natural modesty of the sex forbids the exposing and publicly mangling [of] their bodies.'[20] In practice, Blackstone noted, 'through the humanity of the English nation' the condemned woman was strangled to death before her body was burned, occasioning 'very few instances (and those accidental or by negligence) of any person being embowelled or burned till previously deprived of sensation by strangling.'[21] In the debate over the punishment of burning women, the experience of London moved a few members of Parliament to propose the repeal of that grisly practice.

Despite Blackstone's assurances, the barbarity of the punishment provoked the disgust of William Wilberforce, one of a few reform-minded MPs. In 1786, Wilberforce introduced a bill that would have discontinued the sentence of burning for women and saw it through the Commons. But the House of Lords found other parts of the bill, calling for the dissection of the bodies of criminals other than murderers, unacceptable and rejected it.[22] The issue was revived in May 1790 when Sir Benjamin Hammett, MP for Taunton, Somersetshire, and a former sheriff of London, moved to bring in another bill to abolish the sentence of burning for women. As one of the sheriffs in 1788, Hammett would have been aware of the execution by burning of the convicted coiner Margaret Sullivan and was likely responsible for seeing the execution of Christian Murphy carried out for the same offence in March 1789. Hammett was no doubt aware of the incongruity of this unusual punishment, given the climate of the times. As one correspondent to the *Times* remarked after the execution of Sullivan: 'Must not mankind laugh at our long speeches against African slavery, and our fine sentiments on Indian cruelties, when ... we roast a female fellow creature alive for putting a pennyworth of quicksilver on a halfpenny worth of brass.'[23] Clearly, public opinion had found a focal point. Hammett informed the house that it had been 'his official duty to attend on the melancholy occasion of seeing the dreadful sentence put in execution' and having consulted with several judges, asked for leave to bring in a bill to alter the law with respect to this punishment. The burning of women was, he maintained, 'the savage remains of Norman policy, and disgraced our statutes, as the practice did the common law.' Hammett was confident that his proposal reflected the spirit of the age and that the sentence would be repealed, 'for he had no doubt but the House would go with him in the cause of humanity.'[24] The swift passage of the bill was important because a woman convicted of coining was to be executed by burning on May 19. William Grenville informed George III that a bill was then before Parliament altering the sentence of death by burning to hanging, although there was a provision in the bill empowering the king to grant respite to anyone sentenced to the old punishment before the bill was passed. Grenville also mentioned a petition from local residents stating the 'great inconvenience and disorder which arise from the execution of the sentences for burning women ... such sentences being now executed almost in the centre of the town.'[25] The king responded quickly to this information by granting respite to the woman sentenced to be burned, but ordered that she be held to suffer the punishment of death by hanging after the bill had passed into law. The bill was passed in the Lords on 5 June 1790 and gained royal assent in the same session.[26]

In these cases of hangings and burnings, then, we can see that the unique experience of public punishment in the metropolis was elemental to modifications in the manner of executing felons. The impetus for reform, in these cases, arose from the personal experience of prominent Londoners. The public burning of women also touched on the relationship between decorum and public space, and reveals how the female body in particular, as an object of punishment, became a problematic issue for a society grappling with the competing demands of politeness and civility, and with the changing expectations for women entering new public roles. But as we shall see, London's encounter with these highly ritualized techniques of penal practice was not manifestly different in character from other forms of public punishment more frequently witnessed in daily life.

Physical Pain and Public Shame

For less serious crimes or as a mitigation of certain minor capital offences such as larceny and sodomy, the law had recourse to other corporal punishments. The pillory, for example, which John Beattie has suggested was a punishment paradigmatic of eighteenth-century penal practice, could lead to serious suffering. With their heads and hands locked through the holes of the device, the prisoners were rendered helpless in the face of missiles, taunts, and jeers from the crowd. The unchecked brutality of the pillory has not always been appreciated and its severity is often undermined by focusing on the relatively pleasant experiences of Daniel Defoe and John Williams at the beginning and middle of the century, respectively, or of the radical printer Daniel Isaac Eaton on the eve of its abolition.[27] The more common reality, however, was an hour of largely unqualified abuse and attack from the crowd. Clearly, the pillory was the ideal form of popular, retributive justice. The prisoner was literally left to the will of the people, and the representatives of society who happened (or planned) to pass by the prisoner were free to bestow their 'just deserts' upon the unfortunate person. As one contemporary observer commenting in 1764 on the punishment of thief-takers put it, 'Though the Law could not find a punishment adequate to the horrid nature of their crimes, yet they met with their deserts from the rage of the people.'[28]

The shame and dishonour associated with this punishment were universally recognized. Dr. Johnson argued to Boswell that 'People are not very willing to ask a man to their tables who has stood in the pillory.'[29] This was most certainly because the pillory was the usual punishment for offences that transgressed moral or social boundaries – offences not so much against liberty or property, but those that exposed moral failings, that evidenced a weak or diseased character, and whose commission dishonoured not just the amorphous state, but the particular streets and neighbourhoods of the parish. But punishments like the pillory increasingly worked at the edges of English conceptions of liberty and justice. The fact that those punishments relied on public vengeance and physical pain tarnished the image of the law as an impartial and equal arbiter of justice.

As well, the punishment underscored class divisions and thwarted the notion of equal punishment for equal crimes. Latent in Johnson's comment is horror at the prospect of any person of his social station being exposed and judged by the common mob surrounding the pillory. One of the champions of its abolition in the early nineteenth century, Michael Angelo Taylor, suggested the pillory tainted the higher-class offender with an unequal dose of ignominy. 'The punishment,' he insisted, 'was unequal: to a man in the higher walks of life, it was worse than death: it drove him from society, and would not suffer him to return to respectability; while, to a more hardened offender, it could not be an object of much terror, and it could not affect his family or his prospects in the same degree.'[30]

The pillory was often associated with crimes that betrayed trust, such as fraud or informing, or those of a dishonourable sexual nature. Peter Danneley, convicted in 1763 of 'assault with intent to ravish' was sentenced to three months' imprisonment in Clerkenwell Bridewell and to stand once in the pillory, but he appealed to have the pillory part of his sentence mitigated.[31] He probably knew that being set in the pillory would cause terrible damage to his reputation and would possibly cost him his life. The punishment of homosexuals in the pillory often excited even deeper moral opprobrium of the mob. Sodomy, which was difficult to prove, was a capital offence, but attempted sodomy was punished with the pillory (often twice) along with fines and imprisonment. The stand in the pillory for such men was rarely a civilized affair, and offenders so convicted often feared for their lives. In April 1780, when William Smith and Theodosius Read were sentenced to their hour in the pillory, it led to manslaughter. After reading the newspaper reports of how Smith was killed in the pillory, Edmund Burke brought the matter before the House of Commons. He raised the point in terms of the necessity for proportionality in punishment and remarked, 'The Punishment of the Pillory had always struck him as a punishment of shame rather than of personal severity. In the present instance [however] it had been rendered an instrument of death, and that of the worst kind, a death of torment.' The attorney-general, Alexander Wedderburn, complimented Burke for raising the matter, adding that he would initiate an inquiry into the incident but would reserve judgment on Burke's appeal for the abolition of the pillory until he had consulted more widely.[32]

James Cockburn has found that once the brutality of the pillory was brought to the attention of Parliament by Burke, the secretary of state was more willing to remit pillory sentences.[33] Indeed later that month, Burke received an appeal for clemency, apparently from a pair of men convicted of fraud who were ordered to stand an hour in the pillory. Burke wrote to Wedderburn asking that only their sentence to six months' imprisonment be enforced, fearing that 'if the men are once in the Pillory, and the Mob from wantonness or Malice, begin to be unruly,' they would surely suffer 'more than it is the intention of the Law to measure out to them.'[34] However, such discretion in mitigating the law was not to become automatic. No such leniency was shown when the 'mollies' of the 'Vere Street coterie' were set in the pillory in September 1810. As the six men convicted of attempted sodomy took their stand, the mob grew particularly vicious. The *Times* reported, 'No interference from the Sheriffs and Police officers could refrain the popular rage.' The fact that this kind of behaviour was routine and predicted by the authorities explains why the condemned men were taken to Haymarket by 'the Sheriffs, attended by the two City Marshals, with an immense number of constables.' The mob's reaction to these men was described in detail: 'Numerous escorts ... constantly supplied the party of attack, chiefly consisting of women, with tubs of blood, garbage, and ordare [sic] from their slaughter-houses, and with this ammunition, plentifully diversified with dead cats, turnips, potatoes, addled eggs, and other missiles, the criminals were incessantly pelted to the last moment.' After their hour 'they were completely encrusted with filth.' As the carriage proceeded back to Newgate, the mob followed 'and the caravan was so filled with mud and ordure as completely to cover them.'[35]

Louis Simond, a visitor to England in 1810, remarked on the punishment of these six men, which received detailed reportage in the newspapers. He deplored 'the public and cruel punishment o[f] the pillory' and questioned, 'What are we to think of a people, and women too, who can for hours indulge in the cowardly and ferocious amusement of bruising and maiming men tied to the stake, and perfectly defenceless!' The effects of this punishment were, in Simond's opinion, to debase and brutalize the populace further: 'Tame tigers must not taste blood; and once let loose, cannot easily be muzzled again at pleasure. What a singular anomaly in a government of laws are these mob executions!'[36] Many contemporaries argued that brutal punishments made for brutal people and that violent, physical punishments were out of place and unacceptable in a society that valued human life, shunned pain and suffering, and encouraged sympathetic feeling. Thomas Talfourd, one of the most eloquent critics of the pillory, saw the 'pain' and 'evil' of that particular punishment employed not to reform the offender, but only 'to render evil more abundant. Thus the Pillory is the preparation for the scaffold, though a stormy interval of rapine and crime frequently elapses between them.'[37]

Most disturbingly, though, Simond's comments reveal the more sinister impression that these punishments threatened to undermine social order because they were themselves lawless, disorderly, and anarchic. This was especially the case because, as both Simond and the *Times* noted, women were the leaders of the uncivilized mob at a time when refined writers were beginning to call upon women to civilize men's coarseness. Anxiety over disorderly women was a widespread concern by the late eighteenth century, with countless proscriptive writers concerning themselves with the ill effects of lewd, immoral women and their companions: thieves and murderers. Like the Tyburn executions, the pillory scenes created public sites in which class and gender norms were easily overturned and the legitimacy of state-sanctioned violence was openly criticized or in some cases undermined by the lowest class rabble and, worse, women.[38] We might wonder, then, whether some objections to the pillory and the Tyburn mob were not reflective of a class-specific way of protecting 'civility' or 'respectability' against the lower orders, who were always keen to participate in the most foul displays of disorder and rebellion.

Finally, following Elias, one might say that the removal of the pillory was an example of the increasing centralization of power and the monopolization of violence by removing retributive vengeance from the hands of the mob. This imposed another layer of conduct in social settings involving criminals, one that imposed greater self-restraint. Today it is deemed unacceptable to throw eggs at people or hurl other missiles at police vehicles carrying criminals to and from trial or prison; and witnesses at executions in the United States are kept behind a protective barrier. Clearly, the present relationship between the mob and the criminal has changed since the eighteenth century. The civil distance that has been created between an angry mob and a convicted felon is a product of cultural change and evidence of a fundamental shift in the roles of violence and vengeance in the realm of judicial punishment.

From a modern penological standpoint, the interesting thing about the pillory was that it confused deterrence and vengeance with retribution. Retribution, as Ernest van den Haag points out, 'is not inflicted to gratify or compensate anyone who suffered a loss or was harmed by the crime – even if it does so – but to enforce the law and to vindicate the legal order.' Furthermore, 'retribution is to restore an objective order rather than to satisfy a subjective craving for revenge.'[39] But the punishment of the pillory served a directly opposite purpose. By allowing free vent to the emotions of the populace, the pillory vindicated the unchecked fury of revenge and sanctioned arbitrariness and individual discretion by creating a public arena for the extra-judicial settlement of class, gender, and legal scores. Indeed, as one critic suggested in the case of the pillory, 'The judge vacates the august chair of justice to the mob,' by which act 'the intention of solemn decisions is wholly frustrated by the appeal to [the mob].'[40] He added, insidiously playing upon the anxious memories of a then recently defeated Napoleon, that the idea of continuing such episodes of popular justice, 'if clearly examined, is of the wildest republican cast; and would, if generally admitted into our system of jurisprudence, subvert its deepest and most sacred foundations.'[41]

It is also interesting to note that Michael Angelo Taylor, one of the principal proponents of the pillory abolition bill, stated that 'the first end of punishment was the reformation of the offender': and only in the most severe cases, 'when the crime committed was of so deep a die as not to admit of a hope of amendment,' was the severity of the punishment – that is, death – supposed to admit the additional force of deterrence. The punishment of the pillory 'was not attended with any good to the spectator, because it only gave rise to the assemblage of a tumultuous rabble, who either contravened the sentence of the Court by exalting the criminal, or violated the law by an outrageous attack upon him. It was therefore evidently a punishment of a very unequal nature.' To Taylor, the punishment of the pillory in the worst circumstances, as when men died in it, 'was a species of violence which ... ought to be avoided.' He later said that his principal reason for pushing for the abolition of the pillory 'was that it was a punishment which could not be measured or dealt out by a court of justice, but was apportioned solely by the caprice of the multitude.'[42] Thus, an even more persuasive reason to end the pillory than its brutality and uncertainty was the very real opportunity it afforded for the kind of proletarian usurpation of judicial authority that could occur when a ferocious mob nearly killed an offender for a non-capital crime. The escalation of punishment permitted by the use of the pillory, beyond what may have been intended by the authorities, was supposed to be the exclusive preserve of the king. Indeed, he showed his mercy, even his civility, by *not* punishing beyond the law and by granting frequent pardons. Thus to continue a judicial practice that allowed the lowest of mob hooligans to undermine the authority of the sovereign was, truly, a world turned upside down!

The class dimension of Taylor's argument was excited in many minds when, in 1814, a colourful radical MP for Westminster was implicated, along with two others, in a stock exchange fraud. Thomas Lord Cochrane was thus sentenced to twelve months' imprisonment along with a £1,000 fine and ordered to stand for an hour in the pillory. Cochrane's sentence became the subject of much debate, especially since it would see the pillorying of a gentleman, quite possibly by the same sort of unruly, female-led mob that pelted the 'mollies.' To make things worse, Sir Francis Burdett, Cochrane's fellow Westminster radical, threatened to stand in the pillory with him should he be forced to serve his sentence. The government therefore remitted the pillory part of his sentence fearing it would incite a riot.[43] The class inequality of the punishment was certainly on Thomas Talfourd's mind when he penned his tract calling for the abolition of the pillory. He clearly thought the punishment itself detestable for reasons already mentioned here, but he was also clear in his reasons for deploring the pillory as 'exceedingly unequal,' ironically because it was a radical and brutal form of social levelling. Certainly its severity was unpredictable, as examples like Defoe and Eaton and the Vere Street coterie had shown, but moreover, its shame was shouldered unequally by anyone from 'the respectable walks of life ... One who has any thing of public character, who has been accustomed to the applause of the insulting populace,' would surely suffer a punishment 'more terrible than a thousand deaths.'[44] Lord Cochrane was, of course in Talfourd's opinion, such a man. But not only did the upper class suffer more shame from such a punishment, it was suggested that they were even discriminated against because of their social station. Thus judges, cautious of upholding the myth of equality before the law, especially in notable cases, were likely to forgo the exercise of discretion and mercy and see the law carried out to its full rigour.

Samuel Romilly, the nineteenth-century champion of capital law reform, noted in his diary that Cochrane's case had sparked renewed calls for the abolition of the pillory and the next year saw the first attempt to pass such a bill, although it was thwarted by the House of Lords.[45] The lord chancellor, Lord Eldon, opposed the bill on the grounds that no substitute for the pillory had been proposed. And Lord Ellenborough then chief justice of the Court of King's Bench (who, incidentally, had tried and sentenced Lord Cochrane) made it clear that he found the pillory, in fact, an adequate and suitable punishment, particularly for fraud and perjury. In his view, the punishment had already been curtailed, since 'the practice was milder at present, from an attention to some peculiarities in the time, which judges applied in the exercise of a sound discretion.'[46] Taylor reintroduced the matter in the next session of Parliament and did not hide his disappointment with 'the indisposition of the noble lord on the woolsack [i.e., the lord chancellor].'[47] Sir Robert Heron expressed the view that although he supported the spirit of the bill, he believed that the government was turning soft on crime. He said, 'The improved and mild morality of the present times had been disadvantageous so far as it was too lenient to crimes, and had too much pity for former acquainteances and connexions. This sometimes paralyzed the arm of the law, and gave facilities for the escape of guilty persons.' Alluding chiefly to sodomy, he feared 'certain offenses had of late much increased ... owing too much to the prevailing mildness and indulgence.'[48] A compromise was reached, however. The pillory would be restricted only to cases of perjury and subornation of perjury, but in 1837 it was abolished altogether.[49]

'Till their backs be bloody': Public Whipping in England

By far the most common form of corporal punishment was whipping. Whipping, privately in prison or in public, was usually the punishment for petty larceny. The jury's or magistrate's deliberate undervaluing of the stolen goods at a nominal 10d. meant that offenders could escape a grand larceny charge and thereby dodge the gallows. Since misdemeanours and petty larceny accounted for the vast majority of prosecuted crime in the eighteenth century, judges at the Old Bailey and the more frequent quarter and petty sessions often imposed the sentence of whipping. Whippings could be performed at a public 'whipping post,' which was fixed at some prominent spot in the city, but often the publicity of the act was fully exploited by having offenders whipped through the streets of their neighbourhood, as the courts ordered, 'till their backs be bloody.' Thus both male and female offenders could be flogged, as it was said, 'at the cart's tail,' whereby they were tied to the back of a cart, stripped to the waist, and whipped as the cart travelled a particular route through the city, until their backs bled from the wounds.

Whipping, like a stint in the pillory, could serve as a punishment on its own or, as in William Cranner's case, as part of a combined sentence. Cranner was convicted in 1768 of assault with attempted rape and was sentenced to pay a twenty-pound fine, along with twelve months in prison, and to be 'publicly whipped from the one End of Great George Street to the other.'[50] This was a stiff sentence indeed, but was likely given by a judge who suspected but could not prove that he had been guilty of rape. Nevertheless, Cranner appealed to the 'great Compassion and Humanity' of the justices of the peace of the City and Liberty of Westminster, pleading with them to grant a reprieve from all three parts of his sentence. It appears from Cranner's petition that people who were publicly whipped were exposed to the wrath of the mob as much as those set in the pillory. Thus Cranner was concerned to secure some remission from his sentence 'not only with regard to him self (who is of a very weakly Constitution) but also for the great Scandall that will on his Honest and Creditable Relations and Friends that reside thereabout besides the Danger of his being Murdered by the popolace [*sic*]. The Ignominy whereof may never be wiped off.'[51]

Like the pillory, the public flogging drew much of its punitive force from the shame and personal ignominy that it heaped on both the offender and his or her family and friends.[52] For example, in October 1760 Elanor Steed was sentenced to be 'whipped publickly in Holbourn from the end of Grays Inn Lane to the end of Red Lion Street and Comitted to the house of Correction for one month' for larceny.[53] Her son, George, wrote to the magistrates to petition for clemency in her punishment, especially to have the whipping replaced with some other punishment. As a master brick-layer, he feared he would lose business and local respect should the sentence on his mother be carried out. Thus George wrote, in his own phonetic style, on behalf of his mother for some mitigation to her sentence. He feared that since she was to be publicly whipped, 'in the Nabourhood Ware you Humble Pertisinor Gitts His Bread,' the stain upon his reputation would be irredeemable. Moreover, he 'Implys Men & Cheaply in that Nabourwood Wool'd to God Pray all Your Humble Pertisenior Beggs of the Cort is to Grant Him the favor of Having Hir Sentence altered to Be Punished any Way the Cort Shall think Proper But Publickly Wipt itt Being Shuch a Grate Scandell to Me in My Business & Wood Go Nere to Be My Ruing iff the Clemancy of the Cort Dont Consider the above afare.'[54]

We learn from cases such as this that reputation and standing were vital personal qualities for men and women of all social stations, and the modi-fication of punishments to prevent jeopardizing one's character was an issue without exclusive class or gender boundaries.

Whippings were also employed instead of transportation for first offences and for servants who stole from their masters. Cockburn has found that there were signs that the judiciary sought to rationalize corpo-ral punishments so that 'the severity of the whipping was carefully propor-tioned to the circumstances of the offense.'[55] But the records of the central government expose a more widespread and popular dissatisfaction with the use of corporal punishments. The Home Office was flooded with appeals from all over the country to have the whipping and pillorying part of sentences respited, many of which were granted.[56] There was some sense even at mid-century that the public, physical punishment of certain persons, especially elderly women, was simply unacceptable. Again, George

Steed had a clear idea of the severity of the punishment and feared his mother's life would be endangered should the sentence be executed: 'The Unhappy Woman Age is 62 Years & Very Much Giveing to the Goute & frequently at this time of the Yeare Wich iff Shee Should Be forst to Go through the Doue Sentence It is Thought Woold Be hir Death Wich Woold Be Ever a Sting a Pon Me & My fameley.'[57]

Obviously, the legitimacy of publicly whipping a sixty-two-year-old woman is questioned in her son's appeal for clemency. And his words indicate that perhaps some moral threshold was about to be transgressed if this punishment were carried out. Regardless of her guilt, for a mix of reasons ranging from selfish pride to humanitarian concern, George could not bear to see his mother punished in this particular way for her offence. His appeal, then, touches on the central concern of this article: that is, to expose the depth to which punishments are culturally embedded within a distinct context and the difficulty of modifying punishments for any particular reason.

A generation after Mrs. Steed's unhappy experience, legislation was passed that explicitly reapportioned the punishment of whipping along gender lines. By an Act of 1792, a female convicted of being 'loose and disorderly,' a 'rogue and vagabond,' or an 'incorrigible rogue' (the three categories of vagrancy) were explicitly exempt from the punishment of whipping, while the same Act ordered men to be either publicly whipped or sent to the house of correction for a minimum of seven days.[58] In 1814, corporal punishment was prohibited in poor houses, and an 1820 Act abolished all corporal punishment for women everywhere.[59] As Beattie has shown for the counties of Surrey and Sussex, and as the records of London's Old Bailey Court also reveal, this legislation *followed* rather than *dictated* judicial practice, since by the end of the eighteenth century, there had been a marked decrease in the number of women sentenced both to public and to private whippings in the jails and houses of correction.[60] However, men, including juveniles, continued to be subject to public and private whipping in the houses of correction and, in the nineteenth century, in the factories and the new prisons until the Criminal Justice Act of 1948 did away with the penalty altogether.

Public opposition to the whipping of males received its foremost attention in the military context. The early part of the nineteenth century witnessed a campaign, led by Sir Francis Burdett, to restrict flogging in the army. Military flogging was vastly more severe, with soldiers and sailors being sentenced to up to 1,000 lashes, and little mercy being shown by the officials who administered the punishments. Charles Napier, who campaigned for an end to military flogging in the nineteenth century, related how some young army recruits often fainted upon witnessing the brutal punishments the first time. According to Lord Brougham, there was a growing opinion that 'the punishment of flogging, to which our troops alone of all the European soldiery are subject, was cruel in its nature, hurtful to the military character in its effects, and ill calculated to attain the great ends of all penal infliction – the reformation of the offender, and the prevention of other offenses by the force of example.' Brougham's implication that the English could be worse than their Continental neighbours was a conscious attempt to construct a familiar image of British civility against the oppressed Catholic other and was, no doubt, calculated to strike at the arrogant patriotism that had helped define Englishness throughout the eighteenth century.[61]

Corporal punishments were not only excessive abuses upon the body of the offender, but they also 'g[a]ve offense to every decent inhabitant' who witnessed them.[62] Historian Martin Wiener argues that the deepest objections to violent punishments were due not to the suffering of the individual offender, 'but rather to the effects on those inflicting and watching the punishment.'[63] Thus the punishments themselves were sapped of any power to correct or reform the offender or deter potential offenders. Indeed, the physical punishments employed by the English state, in the opinion of William Henry Smith, observing in 1845, failed entirely in their opportunity to offer correction. He wrote: 'The very word correction has the double meaning of penalty and amendment ... You punish a child, and a short while after you receive the little penitent back into your love; ... But if you withdrew your love – if, after punishment inflicted, you still kept an averted countenance – if no reconcilement were sought and fostered, there would be no reformation in your chastisement. Between society and the adult culprit, this is exactly the case.'[64]

The shame and stigma attached to such punishments as the pillory and public whipping were sound examples of this kind of punishment, which criminologist John Braithwaite has labelled 'disintegrative shaming' or 'stigmatizing' punishment. Braithwaite argues that 'for all types of crime, shaming runs the risk of counterproductivity when it shades into stigmatization.'[65] Thus, such punishments are in the end ineffectual if the punished offender is not provided with an opportunity to become reintegrated within the shaming community. Thomas Talfourd, one of the pillory's sharpest critics, realized this in 1814, too. He conceded that 'shame, to a certain extent, is a feeling which should be excited by the penalty for every transgression; but it is very dubious whether it is politic so far to arouse it as to make it the sole object of fear.'[66] Shaming punishment, Braithwaite argues, 'is more deterring when administered by persons who continue to be of importance to us.'[67] But stigmatizing punishments, administered by an unknown, hired official, which labelled an offender and served to forever castigate him or her as a social other, had little hope of truly correcting the individual and improving society generally. Again,

Smith would have agreed: 'In drawing the picture of the helpless condition of the convicted and punished criminal, how often and how justly does he allude to the circumstance, that the reputation of the man is so damaged that honest people are loath to employ him – that his return to an untainted life is almost impossible – and that out of self-defence he is compelled to resort again to the same criminal enterprises for which he has already suffered.'[68]

Stigmatizing punishments like the pillory ensured that the offender would be 'set apart for ever as something polluted and debased,' even if he or she was vindicated eventually. As Johnson's earlier quip succinctly showed, the person set in the pillory was automatically ostracized from polite company and, as Talfourd mused, from 'those social ties which form the charm of existence ... those kindly affections, those heart-softening charities, which purify and elevate the soul.'[69]

Public Space and Public Punishment, or from Mean Streets to Clean Streets

I return briefly to William Grenville's point regarding the impropriety of executions in the centre of town. His comment seems to allude to a whole constellation of changes that formed the very real and important social and cultural background to all the modifications to penal policy discussed here. The changes involve the relationship between industrialization and social change and the effects of commercialization on the City of London. It is worth recalling that from medieval times, the execution sites were situated in unpopulated areas, usually on the outskirts of town. Thus in London, public hangings were once held in the area of Smithfield Market, west of the City, but were moved to Tyburn in the early fifteenth century because of the growth of the areas around the market. By the eighteenth century, as Dorothy George argues, London 'was growing more rapidly in brick and mortar than in population' and as surrounding areas, notably Middlesex, expanded rapidly and London's West End grew into a fashionable neighbourhood, the stage was set for a number of clashes between building speculators and city officials.[70] Metropolitan London was simply outgrowing its traditional geographical boundaries, and at the same time it was over-stretching its administrative capacity to maintain its ancient penal methods. Grenville's comment offers a clear example of how this problem was associated similarly with the public burnings.

The growth of London's retail trade from the sixteenth century through the eighteenth century is well documented. Much of that growth was due to the concentration of population in the urban metropolis, itself a result of the massive industrial, social, and economic changes of the period. The technological innovation and industrial organization of the 1750s and 1760s made possible the concentration of industrial activity in certain parts of the country and the wide-scale growth of commercial activity. The growing demand for goods was certainly noticeable in London, whose population grew from around 675,000 in 1750 to over 900,000 in 1801. London was the transportation hub for the rest of the country and for the colonies. The distribution of such a large volume of goods required a transportation system that could operate year-round; and that meant, at first, improved roads and a network of canals.[71] Small, public streets had long been the scene of both commercial and social activity; workers, journeymen, smiths, coopers, peddlers, and hawkers would ply their trades in the street since many did not have the luxury of shops or stalls. The larger roads and squares were often crowded with travellers and pedestrians.

But the character of street culture would completely change over the course of the eighteenth century. Roads were improved through better paving and lighting, for speed and efficiency, as well as cleanliness and safety. London's shopkeepers demanded a city that was attractive to its citizens of quality and unthreatening to potential customers. Fleet Street and Holburn were terribly congested and, at the end of the 1750s, this prompted the building of the 'New Road,' running north of the developed parts of the city. In 1760, the City obtained an Act of Parliament granting it special authority to improve the streets. The following year, all but one of the old gates were demolished – a move that opened up the City proper to a regular and growing stream of pedestrian and vehicular traffic. Already, businessmen, lawyers, and others of greater means were commuting from the more refined areas of the metropolis, like Mayfair, St. James's, and Bloomsbury, into the city on a regular basis. Londoners such as Horace Walpole quickly became accustomed to the growing ease and speed of travel and complained when their journey was delayed by traffic congestion: 'The town cannot hold all its inhabitants ... I have twice been going to stop my coach in Piccadilly, thinking there was a mob; and it was only nymphs and swains sauntering or trudging ... T'other morning ... I went to see Mrs Garrick and Miss Hannah More at the Adelphi, and was stopped five times ... for the tides of coaches, chariots, curricles, phaetons, &c. are endless.'[72]

By the 1780s, residents and local officials were voicing greater concern about the condition of the streets and the many hindrances to the steady flow of traffic. In their regular reports to the Middlesex Grand Jury, the parish constables would draw the court's attention to the various nuisances and disturbances that upset the peaceful and orderly operation of daily commercial intercourse. For example, the inhabitants of King Street in John Taylor's ward of Saint Margaret Westminster complained that 'the servants are Always a Cleaning the horses upon the pavement that the passingers Cannt pass By for them and are Very a Buisef to people if they speak to them.'[73] Such reports reveal how concerns about street traffic and the need for the smooth flow of pedestrian and vehicular traffic were prey-ing upon the minds of the constables. Of course, they were also concerned about other disruptions of city life. Boisterous ale houses and the drunken brawls that spilled out of them were constant problems. As well, consta-bles such as Wright Turnell of St. John Clerkenwell repeated regular fears that some publicans, such as Francis Palmer of the Roebuck Alehouse on Turnmill Street, kept an 'ill governed house to the terror of the King's subjects at large, and disturbance and terror of the neighbours in particular by harbouring a number of dangerous thieves, prostitutes and vagrants.' The maintenance of order and the regulation of morality that went hand in hand with this kind of surveillance were all part of a growing desire to cultivate what has been called a 'polite and commercial' society.[74]

The noise and disorder created by the crowds at the Tyburn executions have been mentioned as a threat to the symbolic power of the event. But residents of 'Quality and Distinction who Inhabit[ed] the Great Squares & Streets' in the increasingly fashionable area of Paddington had complained from the late 1750s about 'the Great inconveniences of the Situation of the Gallows' and that the regular flow of traffic along Acton and Edgeware roads and the Paddington New Road was 'very much incommoded by the great Concourse of Idle & Disorderly Persons who usually attend all Executions [thereby defeating] the Chief use of [the New Road] as designed by Parliament for a safe and easy Communication between the great Eastern, Western, and Northern Roads, and the different Parts of the Cities of London and Westminster and County of Middlesex.'[75]

The relocation of the gallows to the Newgate site had its critics too. In November 1787, a Mr. Edward Worsley who lived on the west side of the Old Bailey made a personal representation to a subcommittee of the City Lands Committee to complain of 'the inconveniences attending the present Method of fixing and removing the Scaffold' for executions in front of Newgate.[76] For at least two reasons, the gallows scaffold was erected under the cover of night, the evening before execution day. First, its construction was a fairly labour-intensive project, requiring at least twenty men, which would have caused considerable disruption to the street traffic during the day. Second, we might also surmise that the scaffold was not a permanent fixture because it was regarded with a certain degree of deri-sion, even superstition, as the primary symbol of the law's brutal power, and was thus susceptible to tampering or vandalism.[77] By December 1787, the Court of Common Council had resolved to adopt a plan for a new 'machine' for the execution of criminals that would reduce 'the expence [sic] noise and inconvenience of the numerous works necessary to be performed in the erection and taken [sic] down of the Scaffold now used.'[78]

So, as the street became more of an arena for commercial activity and as public life was reconstructed by both physical alterations to communal spaces and social changes in the modes of commercial interaction, the street itself lost some of its former neighbourliness. And its role as a cultural venue began to disintegrate. The streets became safer and more orderly and organized, with vehicles in the street and pedestrians, hawkers, and criers on the sidewalk. But concurrent with this 'civilizing' trend was, perhaps, the following realization: using the streets as a public space and particularly as a venue for the application of punishments that manipulated, coerced, and exploited that publicity had became more unseemly, more of a nuisance and a hindrance to the regular flow of commercial traffic, and out of step with the emerging roles of the new public man and woman.

Finally, the demise of public corporal punishments was also linked to certain practical or administrative factors worth mentioning. Such punishments were certainly a costly burden and an administrative nuisance for the City authorities. Aside from the fees to the common hangman himself, who often carried out many of the other punishments, there were costs for erecting and dismantling scaffolds, pillories, and stakes, and for the cleaning and repair of the streets after the terrible event. The City Lands Committee, one of the key administrative bodies for London, was perpetually concerned about the mounting costs of punishment in the City. The mayhem of the Gordon Riots in June 1780 saw the destruction both of Newgate Prison and of the stage and post in front of the prison, which had formerly served as the site for public whippings. Yet six years later, the City sheriffs were still complaining to the City Lands Committee that since the riots 'there has been no proper whipping Post or Scaffold erected' and feared, moreover, that 'the want of a similar Stage or Scaffold prevents the proper Execution of the Sentence, and defeats the Intention of the Judges, that the Punishment should be publick [*sic*], and attended with Shame to the Culprit.'[79]

Only a year after the executions had been moved from Tyburn to Newgate the Common Council was enquiring into the 'Expence of the Platform and Bell used at the public Execution of Criminals in this City,'[80] and through much of the next year the committee responsible for repairing Newgate Prison dithered over who should pay the bill of over £309 for constructing the temporary gallows and the 9 guineas that would have to be paid each time to have the gallows re-erected and removed.[81] By November 1786, the matter had still not been resolved and the subcommittee struck to resolve the issue reported to the Grand Committee of City Lands that it was 'of [the] Opinion that those expences ought not to be paid by the Corporation.'[82] Then in December, after being presented with the bill for 'raising and fixing the Pillory in Mark Lane' the City Lands Committee resolved that 'no charges for preparing or fixing the pillory ought to be paid by the Corporation.'[83] Of course, these petty administrative concerns were not enough to effect the wholesale reform of the penal order. The point, though, is to weave these everyday concerns into the larger picture to indicate the complexity of the forces acting on the minds of legislators and reformers. Like so many of the other criminal law reforms, both legislative and administrative, the reasons for such changes were manifold.

Conclusion

Imprisonment and fining, the two most widespread punishments in our day, came of age in the late eighteenth and early nineteenth centuries as acceptable alternatives to violent, physical forms of punishment. With these non-corporal punishments becoming more palatable and easier to administer, especially after the construction of penitentiaries, and with judges willing – with remarkable frequency after the mid-1770s – to sentence offenders to terms of imprisonment, there was an opportunity for reflection upon the morality and efficacy of punishing men and women physically. In the eighteenth century, imprisonment lacked the severity and terror that served the immediate deterrent aims of punishment. However, it suited a nineteenth-century penal philosophy, which embraced a rationale of 'disciplinary moralization' and sought to reform and rehabilitate the offender.[84] Corporal punishments were suited to an age when shame and pain encouraged, or were believed to encourage, self-restraint and moral edification. These punishments were effective only as long as the offender and the spectator shared some common understanding of the acceptability of pain and violence as corrective tools. Whipping and the pillory relied on such tools to fulfil their penological aims. Yet a growing number of critics began to argue that violent punishments to the physical body had lost their cultural significance and appeared increasingly out of step with the cultural and social forces of the day. To continue their application, one observer asserted, served only to reverse the benign intentions of the law – that is, to 'humanize society' and temper justice with mercy, and tended instead 'to bring us back to our state of original barbarism.'[85] They failed in their chief penological purpose to deter and to correct because their spectacular ability to publicly shame and degrade was seen more and more as a nuisance, and a stain and a blot on the character of the society as a whole. By 1826, Robert Peel was convinced that even transportation lacked the kind of 'salutary terror' that had formerly been expected from punishments, yet he was stymied in finding a suitable secondary punishment. And other alternatives, as he declared to Sydney Smith, such as 'public exposure by labour on the highways, with badges of disgrace, and chains, and all the necessary precautions against escape, would revolt, and very naturally I think, public opinion in this country. It is the punishment adopted in some countries, but we could not bear it here.'[86] Clearly, the age for punishments that highlighted publicity and shaming in an indecorous assault upon the human body was over. The emotional bias against physical punishments and the administrative impracticality of their widespread application in the old customary ways forced officials to redirect offenders into a new penal regime dominated by the prison and the fine. Imprisonment, including the greater use of bridewells and houses of correction and, as the option of transportation became more complicated, the committing of prisoners to the prison hulks and hard labour along the Thames all provided suitable alternatives – both in terms of their feasibility and public acceptability – to the violent, physical punishments that preceded them.

By the 1840s, most corporal and capital punishments had been abolished or had disappeared from public view, and the few that remained – the public whipping of men and the execution of felons – had been severely circumscribed. We have seen how these legislative and administrative changes were intimately linked to a wide, even disparate, range of cultural, social, and economic forces. Concerns over public order and public morality shaped how public spaces were reconceptualized and physically modified for changing purposes. The class inequality inherent in the manner in which physical punishment was meted out upon the individual was highlighted in a handful of early nineteenth-century cases. Changing gender norms and the transformation of notions concerning the female body, the treatment of women generally, and the degree of decorum increasingly expected of them all reveal their place in this complex story too. If we are to come any closer to explaining the swift and extensive reforms to the English criminal law and to penal practice specifically in the roughly eighty-year period after 1760, we must begin to explore the deep cultural tensions of this period revealed by such changes and try to work out more fully what the normative functions of those punishments were.

As we approach the end of the twentieth century, the theoretical or philosophical continuity that once seemed to unite reformers, parliamentarians, and social critics in the name of progress and improvement in the eighteenth and nineteenth centuries appears to have become fractured, rechannelled, and compartmentalized. Issues such as the conditions of prison life; the treatment of the poor, the mentally ill, or drug addicted; and the 'rights' of animals have found their own separate agendas, their own martyrs, and their own legitimizing discourses. The devolution of these issues into separate and developed forms has led historians to reconsider the assumptions and motivations that led earlier writers on these subjects to see them all as somehow connected and indicative of an 'age of improvement.' Rather than reformers and social critics trumpeting a general ethos of moral civility and progress, we are more accustomed to the apparent contradictions in the civilizing process such as those which produce persons who oppose abortion on demand but support the death penalty. Again, as the Fay case revealed, we accept or reject certain sanctions in our society for various culturally bounded reasons, and when the external circumstances that either justify or condemn those sanctions are challenged or strained, we discover that many of our deepest beliefs and convictions are themselves inherently susceptible to corruption, erosion, or revolution.

In considering the historical situation of corporal punishments, we might want to bear in mind the similarities between contemporary law reform campaigns and other causes whose supporters posit their superior civility or emotional sophistication. The most shocking evidence of this in our own times are the crowds of college students holding barbecues outside penitentiaries on execution days, or women standing and chanting death threats at accused murderers while clutching their young children. Furthermore, the animal rights activists in Europe who throw themselves in front of trucks transporting veal, the saboteurs who disrupt fox hunts, or the direct action groups who blow up research laboratories out of concern for the animals often proclaim a moral or ethical necessity for their actions. The willingness of these activists to resort to violence to promote so-called civilized or humanitarian causes suggests that strong reservations about our own claims to modernity and civility are not without legitimacy and that the ebb and flow of what Norbert Elias called 'the civilizing process' is a more striking and permanent feature of the cultural and social life of modern societies than its steady progressive growth.

As I have argued in this essay, the phenomenon of judicial punishment cannot be divorced from these other cultural concerns since they share many of the same deep foundations. We have seen that the specific forms of punishments are variable and change with the attitudes, sensibilities, and political and social objectives of the day. The experience of the late eighteenth and early nineteenth centuries has shown that even when the state had recourse to a very wide range of sanctions spanning the whole range of severity, there was no clear idea that any punishments in particular, or in combination, 'worked' in the sense that they satisfied short-sighted ideological objectives. Debates over punishment ultimately confront the fact that despite our best efforts to cultivate civility, humans will always act beyond the limits of the law. Thus it may be instructive to reconsider the experiences of past penal regimes before we launch into a superficial critique of the shortcomings of our own penal institutions. The study of the history of penal reform reminds us that if we want to untangle the complex skein of social forces that winds together the attitudes, presumptions, and philosophies that give punishment its legitimacy, its design, and its purpose, we must be prepared to deal with the complexity of that relationship. We must also commit ourselves to seeking a clearer understanding of how our own cultural tensions have constrained or undermined the penological purchase of our own modern corrective strategies.

Acknowledgments

I would like to thank the other contributors for their helpful suggestions and particularly Carolyn Strange for her criticism and encouragement. Funding for research was provided by the Social Sciences and Humanities Research Council of Canada, the Government of Ontario, the Associates of the University of Toronto, and the London Goodenough Association of Canada.

Notes

1 Brian Hogan, 'Crime and the Criminal Law,' in *Then and Now 1799-1974. Commemorating 175 Years of Law Bookselling and Publishing,* 109-17 (London: Sweet & Maxwell 1974), 116.

2 On the end of public executions in England, see David D. Cooper, *Lessons of the Scaffold* (Athens, OH: Ohio University Press 1974); V.A.C. Gatrell, *The Hanging Tree: Execution and the English People 1770-1868* (Oxford: Oxford University Press 1994).

3 David Garland, *Punishment and Modern Society: A Study in Social Theory* (Chicago: University of Chicago Press 1990), 19.

4 The interplay between forms of aggression and bourgeois culture in the nineteenth century are explored in Peter Gay, *The Bourgeois Experience: Victoria to Freud.* Vol. 3, *The Cultivation of Hatred* (London: HarperCollins 1994).

5 G. Rushe and O. Kirchheimer, *Punishment and Social Structure* (New York: Columbia University Press 1939); Michael Ignatieff, *A Just Measure of Pain: The Penitentiary in the Industrial Revolution* (New York: Pantheon Books 1978); G.J. Barker-Benfield, *The Culture of Sensibility: Sex and Society in Eighteenth-Century Britain* (Chicago: University of Chicago Press 1992).

6 Norbert Elias, *The Civilizing Process,* vol. 1: *The History of Manners,* vol. 2: *State Formation and Civilization,* trans. Edmund Jephcott (1939; reprint, Oxford: Blackwell 1994), vol. 1, 99.

7 Caning is a standard sentence in Singapore for those older than sixteen years for such misdemeanours as vandalism. It was introduced by the British colonials in the nineteenth century. *Newsweek,* 18 April 1994, 18-23. The quote is from Jim deMelo, *Winnipeg Free Press,* 26 May 1994, C11. In February 1996, the Reform party of Canada's justice critic Art Hanger visited Singapore to observe corporal punishment techniques.

8 Editorial, 'Time to Assert American Values,' *New York Times,* 13 April 1994, A20; Editorial, '"Justice" in Singapore,' *Washington Post,* 11 April 1994, A18.

9 Ellen Goodman, 'Spare the Rod,' *Washington Post,* 16 April 1994.

10 For a similar approach to criminal policy in the Victorian and Edwardian periods, see Martin J. Wiener, *Reconstructing the Criminal: Culture, Law and Policy in England, 1830-1914,* (New York: Cambridge University Press 1990).

11 The quote is from 'Philanthropos' in *Thoughts on Capital Punishments. In a Series of Letters;* that is, letters to the editor of the *London Magazine,* 36 (June 1767):307.

12 Michel Foucault, *Discipline and Punish: The Birth of the Prison,* trans. Alan Sheridan (New York: Vintage Books 1977).

13 The best example of an historian employing Elias's theoretical model is Pieter Spierenburg, *The Spectacle of Suffering. Executions and the Evolution of Repression: From a Preindustrial Metropolis to the European Experience* (Cambridge: Cambridge University Press 1984). For a discussion and critique of Elias and Spierenburg, see Garland, *Punishment and Modern Society,* ch. 10.

14 Elias, *The History of Manners,* 84.

15 J.S. Cockburn, 'Punishment and Brutalization in the English Enlightenment,' *Law and History Review* 12, 1 (Spring 1994):173, 155-79; Thomas Laqueur, 'Crowds, Carnival and the State in English Executions, 1604-1868,' in *The First Modern Society: Essays in English History in Honour of Lawrence Stone,* ed. A.L. Beier, David Cannadine, and James M. Rosenheim, 305-56 (Cambridge: Cambridge University Press 1989).

16 James Boswell, *The Journals of James Boswell 1762-1795,* Selected and Introduced by John Wain (London: Mandarin 1991), 325.

17 *Times,* 20 September 1785, 2h, quoted in A.H. Manchester, *Sources of English Legal History 1750-1950* (London: Butterworths 1984), 274-5.

18 Randall McGowen, 'The Body and Punishment in Eighteenth-Century England,' *Journal of Modern History* 59 (December 1987):672, 673, 651-79.

19 Peter Linebaugh, 'The Tyburn Riot against the Surgeons,' in *Albion's Fatal Tree: Crime and Society in Eighteenth-Century England,* ed. Douglas Hay, Peter Linebaugh, John G. Rule, E.P. Thompson, and Cal Winslow, 65-118 (London: Methuen 1975), 67.

20 William Blackstone, *Commentaries on the Laws of England,* 4 volumes (London 1765-9), vol. 4, 93. See also Ruth Campbell, 'Sentence of Death by Burning for Women,' *Journal of Legal History* (May 1984):44-59; Shelley A.M. Gavigan, 'Petit Treason in Eighteenth Century England: Women's Inequality before the Law,' *Canadian Journal of Women and the Law,* 3 (1989-90):335-74.

21 Blackstone, *Commentaries,* 4:370.

22 *The Parliamentary History of England* (London 1816), vol. 36: 1786-88, cols. 195-202; Sir Leon Radzinowicz, *A History of English Criminal Law and Its Administration since 1750,* vol. 1: *The Movement for Reform* (London: Stevens and Sons 1948), 209-13, 476-7.

23 *Times,* 24 June 1788, quoted in Cockburn, 'Punishment and Brutalization,' 156.

24 *Parliamentary History,* vol. 28: 8 May 1789-15 March 1791, cols. 782-4; *Journals of the House of Commons,* vol. 45, 454.

25 W.W. Grenville to George III, *The Manuscripts of J. B. Fortescue Preserved at Dropmore,* vol. 1 (London 1892), 586.

26 30 Geo. III, c. 48. The Act of 9 Geo. IV, c. 31, s. 2 abolished petty treason itself.

27 J.M. Beattie, 'Violence and Society in Early-Modern England,' in *Perspectives in Criminal Law,* ed. Anthony N. Doob and Edward L. Greenspan, 36-60 (Aurora, ON: Canada Law Book 1985), 39. For more on the brutality of the pillory see J.M. Beattie, *Crime and the Courts in England, 1660-1800* (Princeton, NJ: Princeton University Press 1986), 464-8, 614-16.

28 *Select Trials ... in the Old-Bailey* (1764), 3:153, quoted in Cockburn, 'Punishment and Brutalization,' 172-3.

29 James Boswell, *Life of Johnson* (Oxford: Oxford University Press 1980), 965.

30 *Parliamentary Debates* [hereinafter *PD*] 1st ser., vol. 30 (1815), col. 355.

31 Cited in Joseph Redington, ed., *Calendar of Home Office Papers of the Reign of George III,* vol. 1, (Nendeln, Liechtenstein: Kraus Reprint 1967), 351, 354.

32 The details of the incident were reported in the *London Courant and Westminster Chronicle,* 11 April 1780, 3; Edmund Burke, *The Speeches of the Right Honourable Edmund Burke, in The House of Commons and in Westminster-Hall,* 4 volumes (London 1816), 2:157; *Parliamentary History,* vol. 21 (1780), cols. 390-1.

33 Cockburn, 'Punishment and Brutalization,' 173.

34 Burke to Alexander Wedderburn (16 April 1780) in *The Correspondence of Edmund Burke,* ed. Thomas W. Copeland, 10 volumes (Cambridge: Cambridge University Press 1958-78), 4:230-1.

35 *Times,* 28 September 1810, 3. The context of this case is detailed in Rictor Norton, *Mother Clap's Molly House: The Gay Subculture in England 1700-1830* (London: GMP Publishers 1992), ch. 12.

36 Louis Simond, *Journal of a Tour and Residence in Great Britain during the Years 1810 and 1811, by a French Traveler with Remarks on the Country, Its Arts, Literature, and Politics, and on the Manners and Customs of Its Inhabitants,* 2 volumes (Edinburgh 1815), 1:355-6.

37 Thomas Noon Talfourd, 'Brief Observations on the Punishment of the Pillory,' *The Pamphleteer* 4, 8 (1814):538.

38 On female misrule, see Natalie Zemon Davis, 'Women on Top,' in *Society and Culture in Early Modern France: Eight Essays by Natalie Zemon Davis,* 124-51 (Stanford, CA: Stanford

University Press 1965). Class-encoded gender norms are discussed in Leonore Davidoff and Catherine Hall, *Family Fortunes. Men and Women of the English Middle Class, 1780-1850* (Chicago: University of Chicago Press 1987), ch. 9.

39   Ernest van den Haag, *Punishing Criminals* (New York: Basic Books 1975), 11.
40   Talfourd, 'Brief Observations,' 542, 544.
41   Ibid., 544.
42   *PD*, 1st ser., vol. 30 (6 April 1815), cols. 354, 355; vol. 32 (22 February 1816), col. 804.
43   *Dictionary of National Biography*, s.v. 'Cochrane, Thomas'; Henry Hunt, *Memoirs*, 3 volumes (London 1820-2), 3:298.
44   Talfourd, 'Brief Observations,' 538, 539.
45   Sir Samuel Romilly, *Memoirs of the Life of Sir Samuel Romilly, with a Selection from His Correspondence*, 3 volumes (Shannon, Ireland: Irish University Press 1971), 3:144.
46   *PD*, 1st ser., vol. 31 (5 July 1815), cols. 1125-6.
47   Ibid., vol. 32 (22 February 1816), col. 803.
48   Ibid., cols. 804-5.
49   56 Geo. III, c. 138 (1816); 1 Vict., c. 23 (1837).
50   Greater London Record Office [hereinafter GLRO], WSP/1768/OCT/35.
51   GLRO, WSP/1768/OCT/35.
52   The public whipping of people through the streets of London was a well-established feature of English penal culture. In 1524, vagabonds 'mighty of body' were ordered 'tayed at a cart's tayle [and] beaten by the Sheriff's offycers with whippes in dyuers places of the Citie.' Repertories of the Court of Aldermen, vol. 4, f. 215, quoted in E.M. Leonard, *The Early History of English Poor Relief* (Cambridge: Cambridge University Press 1900), 25.
53   GLRO, MJ/SBB/1165, f. 64. Her crime was stealing a piece of pork, MJ/SR/3105.
54   GLRO, MJ/SP/OCT 1760.
55   Cockburn, 'Punishment and Brutalization,' 172.
56   For examples, see the criminal entry books in Public Record Office [hereinafter PRO], HO/13.
57   GLRO, WSP/1768/OCT/35.
58   32 Geo. III, c. 45, s. 3.
59   54 Geo. III, c. 170, s. 7; 1 Geo. IV, c. 57.
60   Beattie, *Crime and the Courts*, 539-48, 596-616. See esp. Table 10.14, 612.
61   'Speeches in Trials for Libels Connected with Military Flogging,' in *Works of Henry, Lord Brougham*, 11 volumes (London: Griffin, Bohn and Company 1856-62), 9:3. For a fuller discussion, see J.R. Dinwiddy, 'The Early Nineteenth-Century Campaign against Flogging in the Army,' *English Historical Review* 97, 283 (April 1982):308-31. On British patriotism, see Linda Colley, *Britons: Forging the Nation 1707-1837* (London: Yale University Press 1992), 30-7.
62   G.O. Paul, *Address to the Justices of Gloucester*, (1789), v-vi, quoted in Ignatieff, *Just Measure of Pain*, 90.
63   Wiener, *Reconstructing the Criminal*, 93.
64   William Henry Smith, 'On Punishment,' *Blackwood's Edinburgh Magazine*, 58 (August 1845):130, 129-40.
65   John Braithwaite, *Crime, Shame and Reintegration* (Cambridge: Cambridge University Press 1989), 55.
66   Talfourd, 'Brief Observations,' 536.
67   Braithwaite, *Crime, Shame and Reintegration*, 55.
68   Smith, 'On Punishment,' 130.
69   Talfourd, 'Brief Observations,' 536, 538.
70   M. Dorothy George, *London Life in the Eighteenth Century* (Penguin 1965), 15.
71   Roy Porter, *London: A Social History* (Cambridge, MA: Harvard University Press 1995), ch. 6; Rick Szostak, *The Role of Transportation in the Industrial Revolution* (Montreal & Kingston: McGill-Queen's University Press 1991), 10-20.
72   Horace Walpole, quoted in Porter, *London: A Social History*, 99.
73   PRO, KB 32/14, 1786.

74 PRO, KB 32/14, 1790; Paul Langford, *A Polite and Commercial People: England 1727-1783* (Oxford: Oxford University Press 1989).

75 The New Road is today Marylebone Road and Oxford Street. V.A.C. Gatrell also mentions the concerns of respectable residents and cites this petition from ca. 1768 in which 105 estate proprietors petitioned against the 'great Tumults Disturbances Riots and Nuisances' caused by the execution crowd, and complained how 'the Public Roads leading from London to Oxford and Paddington are for several hourse so Thronged that neither Horseman nor Carriages can Pass or repass without the greatest difficulty and danger.' Corporation of London Record Office [hereinafter CLRO], Misc. Ms 21.31, cited in Gatrell, *Hanging Tree*, 602-3.

76 CLRO, City Lands Committee, Journals, vol. 79 (1787-8), 208.

77 That constructing the scaffold was a labour-intensive project is clear from the bill submitted by Mr. Banners, City carpenter, in December, 1786. CLRO, City Lands Committee, Journals, vol. 78 (1786-7), 316b-17. As George Dance reported to the City Lands Committee, 'Two more Men were to have been there [to erect the scaffold] but did not attend, and it appears evidently, that these Men perform this business very reluctantly, and I understand several have left Mr. Banners Service because they would not be subject to be called out upon this Business.' CLRO, City Lands Committee, Journals, vol. 78 (1786-7), 317.

78 CLRO, Journals of the Court of Common Council, vol. 71 (1787), 14-14b.

79 CLRO, City Lands Committee, Journals, vol. 78 (1786-7), 201b-2.

80 CLRO, Misc. Mss 185.8, Committees: Newgate Papers, 1783-5.

81 CLRO, Journals of the Court of Common Council, vol. 69 (1785), 218-19; CLRO, City Lands Committee, Journals, vol. 78 (1786-7), 261b-2.

82 CLRO, Journals of the Court of Common Council, vol. 70 (16 November 1786), 91.

83 CLRO, City Lands Committee, Journals, vol. 78 (1786-7), 314.

84 Wiener, *Reconstructing the Criminal*, 379.

85 Talfourd, 'Brief Observations,' 546.

86 *Sir Robert Peel from His Private Papers,* ed. Charles Stuart Parker, 3 volumes (London: John Murray 1891-9), 1:401-2.

2
In Place of Death: Transportation, Penal Practices, and the English State, 1770-1830

Simon Devereaux

Movements to turn back the clock on penal change have become increasingly vocal in recent years. A principal conviction underlying this trend seems to be that imprisonment is too merciful a punishment for the most serious criminal offenders and that we require a return to the more severe punishments of the past, most obviously capital punishment. The terms of reference around which this debate rages are not always clear. Advocates of severe punishment appear to take for granted that imprisonment is a 'soft' option whose only purpose is the reformation of offenders. They maintain not only that the reform of certain types of offenders is impossible, but that in many instances, it would be wrong even to attempt to do so. In short, a clear tendency exists among commentators on criminal justice to associate particular modes of punishment (execution versus imprisonment) with particular penal purposes (social retribution and/or general deterrence versus reform) in a mutually exclusive fashion. Such a perspective does not do justice to the complex mix of ambitions that both officials and the public bring to bear upon the penal order at any given time. The need to find and employ penal sanctions that span these disparate aims has been identified as a major component of penal culture during the late twentieth century.[1]

This administrative conundrum is by no means a recent development. All modern societies have at some time, from place to place and from person to person, displayed conflicting opinions on the ideal purpose or purposes behind the punishment of particular offenders for particular offences. This was certainly true of England in the late eighteenth and early nineteenth centuries. Traditional histories of penal change in England describe this as an era of progressive reform, characterized by a broad shift from a penal order centred on capital punishment to a more merciful, reformative system of imprisonment, which prevails today. Such a shift in the specific *modes* of punishment did take place. But I want to focus on how, after 1787, the specific punishment of transportation to Australia mediated this shift with respect to the purposes underlying punishments as a whole.

The place of transportation in English penal practices was not as straight-forward as it was once thought to be. Traditional histories have viewed it as a barbarity second only to death, and even as morally indistinct from it. More recent scholarship has drawn attention to its critical role in providing an alternative to capital punishment. To the extent that this latter was indeed the case, we might be tempted to view transportation as primarily a merciful practice. But context is everything. It is striking that in 1808, when the first substantial debate about the purposes of transportation to Australia appeared in the parliamentary record, no consensus seems to have existed about either the specific penal purposes underlying it or whether those purposes were being achieved. One MP asserted that trans-portation's uniformly harsh character obviated any capacity to distinguish the severity of offences. Another felt that transportation for only seven years lacked sufficient terror to deter other, potential criminals from simi-lar offences. Still others believed that it failed to secure the reform of offenders since it isolated them in the company of unregenerate offenders under life sentences. Transportation's leading parliamentary critic, Sir Samuel Romilly, observed in 1812 that transportation 'had been proceeded in for 25 years, without any proof of the beneficial effects of it having been at any time submitted to the House.'[2]

This failure to define transportation's specific penal purposes sustained a loosely centralized state structure – one that required a range of penal options at a time when the principal mode of punishing serious crimes, execution, was losing credibility in the eyes of many official and public observers. Authorities throughout England differed over what constituted the most appropriate response to particular offences and offenders. Officials in metropolitan London relied disproportionately on the practice of trans-portation. Elsewhere, other local officials accorded penitentiary ideas a greater role in their penal regimens. Yet both London and provincial offi-cials found transportation necessary to their overall penal purposes, in part because it muted their differences, sometimes extensive and sometimes subtle, over what the principal aim of punishments ought to be – severity, deterrence, or reform – as well as which modes of punishment most effec-tively achieved those ends.

The Purposes of Punishment

Between 1770 and 1840, the broad orientation of English penal practice shifted from execution to imprisonment. However, the essential purposes of punishment – retributive severity, deterrence, and reform – remained constant. Modern penologists contend that each of these goals deals with different but fundamentally related concerns. Retribution reflects the basic conviction that the harm done by the offence self-evidently warrants a severe response that, in some abstract fashion, restores a balance to the relationship between the individual offender and the social order that has been upset by his or her action. The principle of deterrence concerns the intention of authority to ensure future compliance by the experience of the punishment. In contrast to general deterrence, which directly addresses the wider society, reform focuses on the redemption of the individual offender. It should be self-evident that attention to the individual, society, and the appropriate relationship between the two – a concern that under-lies all conceptions of criminal justice (and indeed, all political relation-ships) – forms a clear link between these three purposes.

The expressed need for punishments simultaneously to fulfil these three aims can be found throughout the period examined here. In 1776 one anonymous advocate of punishing by hard labour noted that the profits generated thereby would act 'as a compensation for disturbing the peace and order of Society' and that 'a certain term of laborious confinement ... is all that ... ought to require[d] by way of example ... [In addition,] this manner of punishing common crimes seems to have a manifest aptitude to reclaim the criminal himself.'[3] Seventy years later, William Gladstone recalled a conversation with the Prince Consort in which the latter 'enumerated very clearly the several theories of State punishments: either as an image of divine justice: an instrument for the reformation of offend-ers: or a warning and terror to keep men from crime.'[4]

My concern here is not to tease out the various cultural and social imper-atives underlying transformations in the character of punishments during these years – themes that have been developed in the work of Randall McGowen,[5] as well as in the contributions of Greg T. Smith, Tina Loo, and Carolyn Strange to this volume. Rather, I want to emphasize the persis-tence of *all three* ambitions as justifications for different modes of punish-ment and of the particular adaptability of transportation to these disparate aims during these years. Not everyone viewed all three objectives as neces-sary or even desirable. A few observers felt that retributive severity was sufficient justification in itself for punishment. In 1781, one observer sarcastically described what he believed to be a lamentable decline in the general will to punish: 'It is the sweetest, best-humoured, & most compas-sionate age that we live in! There are now no crimes – they are all frailties, misfortunes ... Forging a note, & raising a sedition are unlucky accidents to which every man is liable, just as he may fall down & break his leg. [T]he present age has left itself but one virtue, humanity; & *that,* it has turned into a vice by its abuse of it.'[6]

More sophisticated advocates of severe punishments usually conjoined the obvious retributive aim with a concern for general deterrence, although

Robert Southey thought the connection to be mere cant: 'It is the fashion among the English to assert that prevention is the end of punishment, and to disclaim any principle of vengeance, though vengeance is the foundation of all penal law, divine and human.'[7]

By contrast, deterrence was often invoked as sufficient justification in itself for severe punishments. In 1800, the home secretary observed that 'the great object of punishment is example' and that some offences, in this instance, theft by a servant, must be 'marked and branded with the most rigorous hand of the Law as a warning and terror to misdeeds of a similar tendency.'[8] Even as late as 1836, the Duke of Wellington observed that 'he would have capital punishment inflicted whenever the crime was to a certain extent mischievous to society and could be prevented in no other way ... He condemned the modern maxim that the object of punishment was rather to reform the criminal than to give an example to society.'[9] So the notion that punishment ought to deter certainly did not simply fade away with the general decline in capital punishment.

Wellington's observations also indicate, however, that the notion that punishment ought primarily to reform the offender had acquired wide currency by the 1830s. This belief had a particularly strong hold upon the minds of evangelicals, who stressed the obligation of all individuals to manifest their moral worth and the miracle of God's redemptive love in their everyday lives, rather than passively to take for granted a final judgment after death. Such sentiments were expressed by James Mackintosh, Romilly's successor as leader of the parliamentary campaign against capital punishment, who advocated 'the mild doctrine, which desires not the death of a sinner, but rather that he should turn from his wickedness and live.' Yet Mackintosh also recognized a role for severity and deterrence in punishment, observing that punishments that would command respect must meet two fundamental conditions. The first was proportionality – the idea that a punishment ought to involve only 'as much and no more pain than what is necessary to deter men from the crime.' The other, a refined principle of retribution, was 'that the punishments be such as are generally felt to be due to the crime. On the sympathy of mankind with the punishment its whole example depends. Where it is generally felt to be excessive, it excites the feelings against the law, and consequently defeats the purpose of example.'[10] Mackintosh, who was an uncharacteristically thoughtful person with respect to such matters, recognized all three requirements that the criminal law must fulfil if all people, both those who used it to exercise authority and those who witnessed its processes and ends, were to believe that their particular ideas of the purposes of punishment were addressed and achieved.

Indeed, difficult as it may be for a modern sensibility to accept, there had been a time when even capital punishment could be read as possessing a reformative character. The state claimed the right to punish the body of the condemned person for purposes of retribution and deterrence, but the minister's presence at the execution served to remind the spectators that the final disposition of the condemned's immortal soul rested solely in the hands of God. Thus the *Annual Register,* describing the execution of a notorious murderer in 1767, abhorred the cries from some onlookers that the minister should 'pray for her damnation,' observing that 'to preclude the mercy of the Almighty was certainly cruel, and the best of mankind have no ground of hope but the gracious promise that extends to the worst.'[11] Randall McGowen has argued that the years after 1770 show a marked shift away from a willingness to subordinate the individual's body to the requirements of the state, and a shift towards an emphasis on the pre-eminent claims of the individual offender's physical and moral state – claims that the state could not override without compelling cause. The state might still impose suffering on an offender, but such suffering ought to be finite and, in most instances, hold forth the promise of redemption in the corporeal rather than the afterlife.[12] These growing concerns introduced a disequilibrium in the triad of penal intentions, giving the issue of reformation an unprecedented urgency and autonomy. Nowhere did this imbalance become more apparent than in London during the 1780s.

The Logic of Capital Punishment Undermined

In retrospect, the 1780s were a watershed in the history of capital punishment in England, and particularly in London. For at least a decade before this time, authorities and commentators had grown anxious about the rising number of prosecutions at the Old Bailey, the trial venue for capital offences committed in both the City of London and the county of Middlesex. The outbreak of the American Revolution in 1775 ended the transportation of convicts to America, at once closing off the principal secondary punishment deployed in the metropolis. The substitution of sentences to hard labour on board hulks was widely deemed a failure within only a few years of its implementation.[13] The Penitentiary Act of 1779 proposed a highly detailed penal labour regime, but it seems likely that the acknowledged failure of the hulks had already turned the minds of many metropolitan officials back towards more openly severe and deterrent penal practices. Confronted by an even steeper rise in prosecutions at the Old Bailey following the war's conclusion in 1781, they immediately began to canvass the central government for the reinstitution of transportation.

The most compelling indication of the anxiety of London officials to reassert the authority of the law was the abolition of the traditional procession of the condemned to Tyburn. This move was primarily an attempt to establish the kind of solemn, ceremonial order by which public execution could best achieve its intended effects. Metropolitan authorities intended to reassert order and control by consciously pushing the principles of severity and deterrence to their limits. In September 1782 the home secretary informed City officials that pardons would no longer be granted in any case of robbery attended with aggravating circumstances, a policy that City officials had been leaning towards a year before.[14] But the very nature of the Tyburn ritual may have hindered its implementation. It might not have been physically possible to hang as many people at once from 'the Triple Tree' as was now desired without increasing the number of execution days following each session, a development that would have pressed concerns about the procession's order and 'respectability' (as described by Greg Smith) beyond their limits. Whereas the fifty people hanged in 1780 constituted slightly more than half of all those condemned to death, the fifty-three hanged in 1783 were less than one-third. It is also striking that in the year following the removal of executions to Newgate in November 1783, the proportion of robbers and burglars executed – those offenders specifically targeted by the home secretary – leapt from 53 per cent to 79 per cent, falling only slightly to 76 per cent in 1785.[15]

This effort to maximize the number of executions in the metropolis during the 1780s was to form the backdrop to the astonishingly rapid rolling back of capital punishment forty years later. Indeed, the immediate reaction of contemporaries suggested not an enhanced respect for the law, but rather dumbfounded revulsion at the spectacle of ten and sometimes more than twenty people executed at once. Contemporary periodicals used words such as 'shocking,' 'horrid,' and 'terrible' to describe the scene at Newgate during the mid-1780s.[16] By the end of the decade, when King George III was recovering from his first attack of porphyria, the home secretary advised him to pardon the many convicts presently under sentence of death in London because 'the number of them, and the interruption which such a spectacle gives to the general joy and happiness of the present time' might prove to be counter-productive.[17]

This was the same home secretary of whom one correspondent had previously said that 'nothing can be more unjust than any outcry against you for not hanging people enough!'[18] So it must be emphasized that the revulsion aroused by the numbers executed outside Newgate did not necessarily signify tender-hearted objections to principles of severity and deterrence. Many of these observers pointed precisely to the failure of the new execution ritual to achieve those ends. Both the *Times* and the *Gentleman's Magazine* recommended the implementation of hard labour regimes precisely because of their greater deterrent value.[19] Indeed, although I have stressed the distaste that Newgate executions clearly aroused in some contemporaries, I must equally point out the silence on the matter during 1787, a year second only to 1785 in terms of the absolute number of people executed in London. The ends of punishment had not changed, but large-scale executions were no longer certain to achieve them. Such displays stupefied but did not impress.

In fact, the absolute number of executions in London dropped immediately after 1787; by the early nineteenth century, the proportion of capital convicts executed had also steeply declined. Beginning in 1820, the absolute number of executions again increased sharply and suddenly, but this increase was abandoned after 1822, probably because the renewed experience of large-scale executions revived issues and impressions that had fallen dormant in the minds of officialdom after 1787.[20] The most impressive and important of concessionary voices in the early 1820s was that of Lord Chancellor Eldon, who had the longest and most influential experience of the capital code in the metropolis. Save for a break of only fourteen months, he had been lord chancellor since 1801, a position that gave him the decisive voice in determining who among the London condemned would actually die on the gallows.[21] Late in 1822, the last year of high execution levels in the metropolis, Eldon bluntly informed the new home secretary, Robert Peel, 'Times are gone by when so many Persons can be executed at once as were so dealt with twenty years ago.'[22] The rollback in the number of London executions followed almost immediately. As we will see, Peel was no sympathizer with the idea of penal reformation, but he quickly developed a shrewd grasp of the limits under which the law's most severe sanction had now to operate – in a context in which public sentiment and scrutiny were ever more vigilant and to be taken account of. By 1828 he had to defend his determination to hang a forger on the grounds that 'it would be very difficult hereafter to enforce the capital sentence of the law in any case of forgery, if mercy be extended in this case.'[23]

Twenty years earlier, there could have been no question of the legitimacy of a particular offence being so jeopardized by a single execution. Eldon and Peel had apparently tested and quickly learned the limits of mass-executions as an effective punishment. The final retreat from capital punishment was rapid and, within a decade, virtually complete. No one at all was executed in London for more than three years after 1833, although the decisive reduction in the actual number of capital statutes was not made until 1837.[24] The principal facilitator of this retreat was the same as that of the late 1780s. In 1787, the last year in which convicts were executed in large numbers in London, the First Fleet left England for Botany Bay. In 1823, Peel reorganized the practice that that fleet had inaugurated, transportation to Australia.

The Universal Appeal of Transportation

Recent studies by scholars such as John Beattie and Margaret DeLacy have demonstrated that imprisonment played a far more substantial role in late-eighteenth-century penal practice than historians have traditionally thought. Many offenders who might otherwise have been subject to capital punishment or transportation were either sentenced to imprisonment or pardoned on condition of it. At the same time, a number of jail regimes were established and run by local officials with reformative aims in mind.[25] But Beattie and DeLacy studied counties (respectively, Surrey and Lancashire) whose social-economic experience was changing in advance of many other areas of the country, and their conclusions need to be viewed within a larger context. The timing with which 'reformed' jails appeared varied widely, as did the effectiveness with which reformative regimes were implemented in them, if indeed at all.[26] It was not until well into the nineteenth century that a uniform set of prison conditions was defined for all of England.

I will return to the crucial issue of variable penal regimes in the next section of this article. My focus for the moment is to stress the concerns of those who objected to imprisonment as a penal practice, thereby reinforcing the impulse to resume an effective system of transportation during the 1780s. This was an era of prison reconstruction in many areas of the country. Prison-building was driven mainly by the sheer pressure of numbers on a physical infrastructure that could no longer bear their weight, no matter what officials might intend should actually take place within the new prisons. In some places, it was also driven by a commitment among local officials to establish reformative regimes of the sort advocated by John Howard during the 1770s and 1780s.[27] John Byng, William Cobbett, and other contemporaries often remarked disapprovingly on these striking new edifices, partly because they connoted social and political repression during an era in which large numbers of radicals were confined in them, and partly because they believed that prisons provided convicted felons with a better standard of living than honest but impoverished rural labourers.[28]

The principal objections to imprisonment, however, were that it was neither sufficiently severe to constitute a just retribution on truly serious offenders, nor sufficiently visible to serve as a deterrent to others. Such objections had been voiced by Samuel Johnson as early as 1759: 'In a prison the awe of the publick eye is lost, and the power of the law is spent; there are few fears, there are no blushes.'[29] But two decades later, when the outer limits of public execution as a deterrent were first emerging, concerns for effective severity and deterrence became urgent. Transportation offered the best prospect of a punishment that was truly inclusive on all three counts.

Of course, we must not underestimate transportation's essential appeal: simply ridding British society altogether of serious offenders without actually killing them outright. The removal of convicts to the opposite end of the earth seemed to guarantee that none of them could ever return to renew their depredations.[30] But punishments reinforce authority in a community only when they can be interpreted as doing so in accordance with broadly acceptable ideas of the ends to be obtained by that punishment.[31] Axiomatically, they must also hold out some credible promise of achieving those ends or at least not transparently fail to do so. The failure of this promise in the eyes of some critics had undermined their faith in transportation to America as an effective penal option even before the American Revolution closed it off altogether.

As early as the 1750s, some detractors believed that conditions in America had progressed to the point where passage thereto may have seemed more a favour than a punishment. At any rate, the trade routes to North America were now so well-established that it was believed to be too easy for convicts to return home before their sentence expired.[32] However, one prominent London magistrate still lauded it in 1773 as the 'most humane and effectual punishment we have' because it 'immediately removes the evil, separates the individual from his abandoned connexions, and gives him a fresh opportunity of being a useful member of society, thereby answering the great ends of punishment, viz., example, humanity, and reformation.'[33] So transportation to America had served all the principal purposes of punishment but, according to some sceptics, these were now critically compromised by the enhanced possibility of return to England.

This last problem was not expected to apply to the far more remote Australia when the First Fleet departed England in 1787. Given the minimal prospect of returns, observers could easily rationalize it in terms of both the best and the worst of conventional intentions behind punishment: either severity and deterrence, by people who deemed these to be the principal purpose of punishment, or reform, by the growing body of opinion that held that even serious criminal offenders were redeemable.

The notion that the experience of transportation could be the vehicle of an offender's reformation was also asserted from the outset, not least of all in the Great Seal of New South Wales itself, as described to the Privy Council in 1790: 'Convicts landed at Botany Bay – Their fetters taken off and received by industry sitting on a bale of goods with her attributes, the distaff, bee-hive, pick axe and spade, pointing to oxen ploughing – to rising habitations and a Church on a hill at a distance.'[34] In many minds, however, confidence in the reformative influence of transportation was directly proportional with the confidence that few if any transported offenders would ever actually return to England. This issue was forced on Parliament's attention early in the nineteenth century, when both the passage of time and improvements in the passage to New South Wales first raised the possibility that convicts sentenced to terms of seven and fourteen years might actually return home. On the one hand, those who placed a premium on the reformative component of punishment assailed transportation precisely because, for most convicts, any term of transportation was tantamount to a life sentence.[35] On the other hand, the home secretary, Lord Liverpool, spoke for many when he stated that sentences of transportation offered 'the only chance ... of [convicts] becoming good Settlers or good Men,' and he observed, 'Such of them as look to return in a few Years ... make no attempt to conquer their Established Vicious Habits.' He himself transported convicts in the hope and expectation that they were gone for life, noting, 'This principle has been acted upon to a greater Extent of late Years than is Commonly Supposed.'[36]

At any rate, it is clear that the appearance of some reformative influence in transportation was crucial to its perceived legitimacy. Both the centrality of this conception and its sham quality were nicely expressed by James Mackintosh, who noted that although 'the experiment of a reforming penal colony [was] perhaps the grandest ever tried in morals,' it was also one that was 'perfectly safe' from critical scrutiny given its distance.[37] In general, most ministers and MPs seem to have been more attracted to transportation's prospects of severity and deterrence rather than its promises of reformation.

One of the most striking aspects of transportation to Australia is how often authorities, in invoking and characterizing it, explicitly used the language of deterrence rather than mercy and reformation. Local officials often requested that the central government uphold sentences of transportation in cases wherein they wanted an 'example' to be made for a particularly prevalent offence of the moment.[38] It may seem difficult to imagine how the removal of offenders from a jail might constitute even a striking, much less a terrifying, spectacle of the sort that execution traditionally provided. Two examples may serve to suggest how horrifying the promise of separation from loved ones could be, both to those going and to those they left behind. One is the crudely literate plea of a nephew to his aunt in 1791 to use what influence she could on his behalf: 'Their is no time to be lost but let me intreate you to exert your self & save your Unfortunate Nepthew from Bannishment from his Whif & Famely And all his relations that his Dear to him.'[39] Another example comes from the radical Samuel Bamford, thirty years later, recounting a leave-taking he witnessed while being held prisoner in Lincoln Gaol:

Her son soon made his appearance, dragging his chain. He extended his arms towards her, and she rushed into the gloomy passage, and to his bosom – uttered his name – and fainted ... At length they motioned him to return, but he broke away, and kneeling, caught his mother in his arms, and pouring tears fast on her face, he reverently kissed her wan forehead and her cheeks, and resigning her to the attendants, he said, 'Now let me go! I've killed my poor mother! – I've broken her heart!' – and they led him away. They then carried her out, for air, and when, after some time, her senses returned, she cast a look around, and peered down the passage. 'He is gone,' said one of the bye-standers, on which she sighed, and departed slowly out at the castle-gate, weeping.[40]

Bamford undoubtedly employed much melodramatic licence in describing this scene, but there seems no reason to doubt the essential authenticity of the emotions portrayed.

In fact, some officials even felt that the severity and sheer terror of transportation to New South Wales was such that it ought to be applied as sparingly as possible. One observed in 1793, 'Transportation to New South Wales from its distance, its infamy and the nature of the place can not be so regularly or immediately effected, nor ought it perhaps to be so general [as in the American case].'[41] A more indirect sense of the sort of terror that Botany Bay was meant to inspire is captured in Robert Southey's 'Botany Bay Eclogues.' A series of literal and internal dialogues among a number of transportees over the course of a single day, the poems are dominated by the loneliness and misery of exile from the familiar trappings of home.[42] Botany Bay had a lasting fascination for Southey. It is mentioned several times in his correspondence, and in ways that indicate that his assumptions about the intentions behind transportation, like those of many others, varied from the strictly punitive, to the deterrent, to the reformative.[43]

Explicit language of deterrence was more consciously used in the case of Ireland where, during the two decades after the Rebellion of 1798, transportation became the sentence of choice for political offenders.[44] (It was used with equally striking effect against the convicted rebels in Upper Canada in the late 1830s, as Barry Wright describes in this volume.) In 1806, the home secretary emphasized the need for a speedy execution of sentences of transportation in Ireland because 'a prompt execution is more calculated to produce effect on the minds of people like the Irish than any thing else.' Even the mere appearance of carrying out the transportation of convicts to Australia could be considered sufficient to the deterrent end. Should Irish convicts have to be held on board English prison hulks, removing them thereto would still 'be calculated to produce a greater impression on the minds of their associates ... than their remaining in custody anywhere in Ireland.'[45] In the minds of some authorities, then, a close cognitive association could be forged between execution and transportation as modes of exemplary punishment.

These associations were more explicitly enunciated in the creation of offences for which transportation was either the principal punishment or the punishment of last resort. The economic and social unrest of the 1810s gave rise to at least two such instances in England. One was the Act that punished framebreaking, an act of resistance among traditional cloth-industry workers to the introduction of mechanical looms. It had initially been defined as a capital offence but the government, as compensation for making permanent what originally had been only an emergency measure, reduced the punishment to transportation for life.[46] The government and its supporters insisted on the need for severity, deterrence, and reform alike. And reform, Liverpool and others believed, could only be assured by transportation for life. Interestingly, this move was also presented as a gesture of deference to Romilly's opposition to any further expansion of the capital code.[47]

An even more controversial example was the Libel Banishment Act of 1819, one of the infamous 'Six Acts' intended to suppress radical agitation at home during the intense social dislocation that followed the Napoleonic Wars. That Act made a second conviction for publishing a blasphemous or seditious libel punishable by banishment 'from the United Kingdom, and all other Parts of His Majesty's Dominions, for such Term of Years as the Court ... shall order.' Any person so banished who was found at large anywhere in the king's dominions forty days after sentence became liable to transportation for fourteen years.[48] Lord Liverpool, by then prime minister, justified the Act to a senior colleague on the grounds that 'the state of the press ... is really the root of the evil' prevailing in the nation. He anticipated that 'the wholesome Terror which [the Act] will tend to create [will be] the means of putting some check upon the great Licentiousness of the Press as it has existed for some years.'[49]

The original version of the Act would have made transportation for seven years an alternative to banishment for a second offence and death the punishment of last resort. However, partly in response to pressure from booksellers such as Thomas Allan, who viewed transportation as 'more ignominious and degrading than [banishment],' the House of Commons altered the bill to make transportation the punishment of last resort only.[50] Even in this moderated form, the Act drew the vituperation of radical critics of government during the 1820s, even though it seems never to have actually been enforced.[51] At any rate, both the Libel Banishment Act and the Framebreaker's Act strongly suggest both the increasing value placed on transportation – not as a merciful alternative to capital punishment but rather as a suitably deterrent one – and a belief that it was actually seen as a deterrent by the public.

Transportation's deterrent value was of central concern to government officials by 1823 when, as described above, London officials were once again confronted with the distasteful alternative of executing large numbers of convicts. By this time the government had been subjected to more than a decade of attempts by Romilly and his followers to establish penitentiaries as the principal mode of secondary punishment in England. But advocates of the penitentiary usually based their arguments either on a primary concern for the reformation of offenders – an argument that did not yet command broad acceptance among the central political elite – or on the contention that it was cheaper than the prevailing system of transportation, a premise that seems more often to have been asserted than demonstrated.[52]

Robert Peel himself, despite his reputation as the great rationalizer and humanizer of English criminal law, did not believe that serious criminal offenders were reformable. In 1828, he confided to his closest friend and colleague, 'I am not enamoured of the Penitentiary system generally. The Penitents are, at best, generally speaking Idle Hypocrites.'[53] Peel sought a punishment that would prop up a collapsing capital code with respect to severity and deterrence without alienating the growing numbers who pressed for an enhanced emphasis on reform. Perhaps for this reason his revision of England's penal order began with the Gaols Act of 1823 (4 Geo. IV, c. 64). This measure, traditionally viewed as the humane starting point of national standards of incarceration in England, was in fact inherited by Peel from his predecessor at the Home Office, Viscount Sidmouth, who had failed to pass it in two sessions of Parliament. Peel himself had little enthusiasm for it and sought to ensure a central role in jail discipline for the treadwheel, an activity solely contrived to be punitive.[54]

Peel's main concern was to sharpen transportation's character as a severe and deterrent punishment. Even before the Gaols Act was passed, he informed the attorney-general of his intention 'to bring in a Bill empowering the Crown to send a Convict ship to any of the Foreign Settlements, and thus to unite Transportation, Hard Labour, and the Discipline of the Hulks.' He hoped that system 'would be considered a more severe Punishment next to Death, than any that is at present employed.' He was particularly concerned that the punishment serve as an effective deterrent, wondering if it would 'be desirable to give the Judges a Power to sentence a Prisoner to a Punishment of this Nature, and thus in the case of a heinous offence, cause it to be immediately and generally known that such would be the fate of the Convict.'[55]

In fact, since 1818 at least, members of the government had maintained that New South Wales, like America before it, had now reached such a degree of development that transportation thereto no longer constituted any sort of threat in the eyes of either the convicts or the public, and was perhaps even an inducement to crime.[56] Thus, when Peel told the Commons that his Transportation Act of 1824 (5 Geo. IV, c. 84) 'was intended to make transportation a much more severe mode of punishment that it had generally been hitherto,'[57] he was speaking to an already widely held conviction, now given heightened urgency by the pressures upon

central conceptions of reasonable standards of punishment. The first such Act, making framebreaking a capital offence, appears to have originated with the Nottinghamshire magistrates; the second, reducing the punishment to transportation for life, originated with the central government and was passed over the local magistrates' objections.[78] Yet transportation could as easily be used to enhance as reduce the severity of punishment. The determination of the magistrates of Kent to transport a man in 1822 for stealing a single sheep was a striking example of this. Their attitude seemed harsh even by the standards of the time, but their spokesman justified it with reference to the county's specific circumstances: 'I am fully persuaded that the Administration of the Criminal Law in the County of Kent, for some time past, has not tended to repress Crime or to give Security to his Majesty's Subjects ... Sheep Stealing ... is an offence of almost daily occurrence in this neighbourhood ... The Magistrates expect to be supported, the people have a right to be protected.'

The judge who had tried the case did not view the offence in so broad a context, observing that although he was 'one of those who think sheep stealing a great offence,' nevertheless he always made 'a great distinction between stealing sheep to *sell* – and *a single sheep to eat.*' Although the judge had been unaware that the convict had been a locally notorious sheep stealer for many years, he maintained that the convict's crime warranted only a year's imprisonment. In partial deference to the magistrates' anxiety that the prisoner not be allowed 'to return to the Scene of his long continued plunder and Depredations,' Robert Peel decided to split the difference, altering the punishment to transportation for fourteen years but specifically instructing that the prisoner should remain on the hulks for the full term of that sentence.[79]

There must also have been variations among local authorities within individual jurisdictions as to the most appropriate modes of punishing particular offences, with some magistrates preferring more explicitly severe and deterrent modes of punishment to consciously reformative ones. The diary of the Staffordshire magistrate William Dyott records his resistance to the institution of reformative jail practices during the late 1820s. He frequently urged on his fellow magistrates 'the preference of *prevention* to any *effort* to *cure*,' and resisted the efforts of the local Ladies' Prisons Association 'to introduce *cant* into the prison ... Experience has proven to my mind that nothing but the terror of human suffering can avail to prevent crime, and the fallacious idea of reformation through the medium of moral persuasion must fail.' Of the great increase in offences prosecuted, he believed that one-third 'were for offenses for which a good horse-whipping would have been infinitely more beneficial to the culprit, and saved an unusual expense to the county.'[80]

All these examples of both local and personal variation point towards the characteristic that historians have identified as the defining feature of eighteenth-century criminal justice: discretion. Local influence could make itself felt in the determination of punishment at various stages in the criminal process, from informal discussions with the circuit judges on their arrival in town for the assizes, to the decision of the jury, and finally in the petitioning procedure in the event that a mitigation of punishment through pardon was sought. Douglas Hay has argued that such discretion in the pardon process was so pervasive that it was in fact the essential mechanism of rule in English communities, the means by which the dynamics of paternalism and deference were repeatedly reinforced.[81] But we do not have to attribute so encompassing a role to judicial discretion to appreciate the attraction that such flexibility held for a society in which most governance continued to be local and personal in orientation. Such local authorities, who also dominated the backbenches of Parliament, distrusted a system of criminal law that would be predicated upon a certain scale of punishments – a scale to be determined by a notion of the offence's severity that was wholly abstracted from its local contexts – thereby restricting their options in administering justice and intruding on their established privileges. Even though they might appreciate the abstract justice of such reform proposals, functional flexibility always remained more attractive to their sensibilities.[82] Romilly, observed one defender of the discretionary system, 'gives us the *principe,* the whole *principe,* and nothing but the *principe.* This frightens country gentlemen unnecessarily, and makes them ready to oppose every proposal originating in him, however just or reasonable its own nature. He sets about things in a foreign, and (which terrifies the squire) philosophical way.'[83] Local authorities, like the Kent magistrates with their sheep stealer, preferred a system of criminal justice whose definitions remained wide enough not to tie their hands when it came to determining the fate of individual offenders.

Moreover, a fixed scale of capital and non-capital punishments was not attractive to a central government that, as yet, lacked both the resources and the will intensively to assert and supervise such a system. Indeed, the intellectual task of untangling England's massive capital code was a daunting enough prospect in itself, aggravated, as William Pitt suggested in 1787, by the absence of any widely agreed principles of punishment upon which to base an alternative – principles that 'ought to be again and again considered before they should be adopted.'[84] Such extended consideration was the last thing that Pitt and most other statesmen at the centre wanted to be drawn into. They too preferred a loosely defined system in which the final determinations as to punishment were made, case-by-case, by the judge who had presided at trial, in consultation with local officials and under the final supervision of the home secretary. It was only with the explosion in capital cases that followed the end of the Napoleonic Wars, coupled with an increased attention to rules of criminal procedure, that this system began to collapse under its own weight. These pressures reinforced the moral logic underlying a certain, fixed scale of punishments – a system that, it was believed, would minimize the need for any substantively personal intervention.

Widespread debates over principles of certainty and proportion in punishment appeared in the 1770s and began to intensify in the second decade of the nineteenth century. In the meantime, transportation retained a vital role in England's penal policy and practice. This was not only because it extended the range of available punishments but because it lent itself to the full variety of penal interpretations without necessitating the sort of detailed consideration of the principles underlying punishment that most statesmen, at both the nation's centre and its periphery, were loath to undertake. Transportation was indispensable to the discretionary system of justice that prevailed in a nation wherein state authority remained largely decentralized.

Conclusion
The role of transportation in English penal practices during the late eighteenth and early nineteenth centuries seems paradoxical and ambiguous. The total number of convicts sent to Australia between 1787 and the 1820s was much smaller than we might be led to expect by the attention paid to the practice by both contemporaries and historians. Ironically, the numbers sent there actually increased after the 1820s, at a time when doubts were growing about its ability to terrorize and deter. Such doubters included the home secretary himself, whose scepticism about the scale and effectiveness of prison regimes at home led him to believe that there was simply no other alternative, given a large increase in prosecuted criminality.[85]

Yet those paradoxes and ambiguities gave the state the flexibility that allowed it to manage the pressure of numbers upon the institutions administering criminal justice. They also help to explain the spasmodic and uneven acceptance of new emphases in the purposes underlying punishment. The use of imprisonment to punish and reform serious offenders was growing everywhere, but both the actual nature of prison regimes and their specific roles in local penal cultures varied from place to place. Until recently, historians have tended to discuss the history of penal practice and reform from an uncritically centralist or otherwise uniform perspective, often assuming that the narrative of shifting beliefs and practical change may be constructed from the debates and legislative measures of Parliament. The result is a highly abstracted notion of how penal reform actually proceeded. In fact, penal policy-making at the centre accommodated a variety of criminal justice cultures throughout the nation.

So transportation to Australia did not simply provide a merciful alternative to a capital code that, in removing all hope of human redemption, was increasingly deemed to be morally objectionable. Such a humanizing process was occurring in the minds of some authorities, so it was important that transportation should appear to fulfil such an expectation. But transportation also provided a retributive and deterrent punishment in the place of a capital code whose logic in these areas was collapsing under the pressure of numbers. The momentarily unique capacity of transportation to be seen as either a justly severe and credible deterrent or as merciful and reformative encouraged policy-makers to retain it during an era of growing debate over the purposes of punishment, how best to achieve them, and variation in both the means and the collective will to do so. Then, as now, the authority of the state to punish was critically dependent on its apparent ability at once to satisfy the most optimistic and most pessimistic visions of human potential. By simultaneously holding forth the terror of exile and the promise of redemption, transportation to Australia fulfilled this role for nearly four decades. It was only in the 1830s and after, as the development of the Australian colonies (as well as their own mounting objections to receiving Britain's outcasts) became more widely known, that the retributive and deterrent characteristics of transportation began to lose credibility. The result was the first sustained momentum to build a nationwide system of penitentiaries, a system that was ultimately contrived so as to embrace the full range of penal purposes – retributive severity, deterrent terror, and reform – in the way that transportation had for nearly a century.[86]

This functional reconfiguration of penal ambitions and expectations has now broken down in the eyes of those who assert a need to 'return' to principles of severity and deterrence in punishment. It remains to be seen what new patterns of penal options we may be able to devise that will allay the complex mix of hopes and fears that has always underpinned anxieties about how best to deal with criminal offenders.

Acknowledgments
I am grateful to the Social Sciences and Humanities Research Council of Canada, the government of Ontario, the London Goodenough Association of Canada, and the University of Toronto for their financial support of the research on which this article is based. I would also like to thank my fellow contributors for their many helpful comments and suggestions, and particularly Carolyn Strange for her care, attention, and encouragement.

Notes
1 R. Antony Duff and David Garland, 'Introduction: Thinking about Punishment,' in *A Reader on Punishment*, ed. Duff and Garland, 17-18 (Oxford: Oxford University Press 1994).
2 T.C. Hansard, *The Parliamentary Debates from the Year 1803 to the Present Time* [hereinafter

Hansard], 1st ser., 11 (1808):877-86; and 21 (1812):604. David Meredith notes a similar ambiguity about the purposes of transportation during the debates about it in the 1830s. See his 'Full Circle? Contemporary Views on Transportation,' in *Convict Workers: Reinterpreting Australia's Past,* ed. Stephen Nicholas, 14-27 (Melbourne: Cambridge University Press 1988).

3   *Gentleman's Magazine* 46 (1776):254-5.

4   John Brooke and Mary Sorensen, eds., *The Prime Ministers' Papers: W.E. Gladstone* (London: Her Majesty's Stationery Office 1971-81), 3:17.

5   Randall McGowen, 'A Powerful Sympathy: Terror, the Prison, and Humanitarian Reform in Early Nineteenth-Century Britain,' *Journal of British Studies* 25 (1986):312-34; McGowen, 'The Body and Punishment in Eighteenth-Century England,' *Journal of Modern History* 59 (December 1987):651-79; and McGowen, 'The Changing Face of God's Justice: The Debates over Divine and Human Punishment in Eighteenth-Century England,' *Criminal Justice History* 9 (1988):63-98.

6   Ralph S. Walker, ed., *A Selection of Thomas Twining's Letters, 1734-1804: The Record of a Tranquil Life* (Lewiston, NY: Edwin Mellen Press 1991), 1:192.

7   Robert Southey, *Letters from England, by Don Manuel Alvarez Espriella,* 3rd ed. (London: Longman 1814), 1:253.

8   Public Record Office [hereinafter PRO], HO 13/12 pp. 421-3 (Duke of Portland to the Rev. Dr. Drummond & C. Lofft).

9   Carola Oman, *The Gascoyne Heiress: The Life and Diaries of Frances Mary Gascoyne-Cecil, 1802-39* (London: Hodder and Stoughton 1968), 212.

10   Robert James Mackintosh, ed., *Memoirs of the Life of the Right Honourable Sir James Mackintosh* 2nd ed. (London: Edward Moxon 1836), 1:155-6; and 2:370n.

11   *Annual Register* 10 (Chron. 1767), 197.

12   McGowen, 'Body and Punishment,' esp. 665-6, 668-78; and McGowen, 'Changing Face of God's Justice,' 67-74, 80-91.

13   The difficulties and experiments with penal practice during these years are discussed in Eris O'Brien, *The Foundation of Australia (1786-1800): A Study in English Criminal Practice and Penal Colonization in the Eighteenth Century,* 2nd ed. (Sydney: Angus and Robertson 1950), 77-133; A.G.L. Shaw, *Convicts and the Colonies: A Study of Penal Transportation from Great Britain and Ireland to Australia and Other Parts of the British Empire* (London: Faber and Faber 1966), chs. 1-2; and J.M. Beattie, *Crime and the Courts in England, 1660-1800* (Princeton, NJ: Princeton University Press 1986), 560-618.

14   *Annual Register* 24 (Chron. 1781), 191; and 25 (Chron. 1782), 220. The home secretary's letter is unclear on the point, but I presume that his definition of aggravated 'robbery' included burglary and housebreaking.

15   The figures for executions in the metropolis between 1749 and 1817 are given in the House of Commons Sessional Papers [hereinafter PP(HC)] 1818.xvi.183-7.

16   See, for instance, *London Magazine* N.S. 4 (1785):144, 386; and *Gentleman's Magazine* 55 (1785):484; and 56 (1786):102-3, 990.

17   *The Later Correspondence of George III,* ed. A. Aspinall (Cambridge: Cambridge University Press 1962-70), 1:402.

18   Brotherton Collection (Leeds University), Sydney/Townshend Papers K22 (Duke of Richmond to Lord Sydney, 7 April 1786).

19   *Gentleman's Magazine* 54 (1784):955; and *Times* (20 September 1785), quoted in *Sources of English Legal History: Law, History and Society in England and Wales, 1750-1950,* ed. A.H. Manchester (London: Butterworths 1984), 274-5.

20   For metropolitan execution figures between 1785 and 1825, see PP(HC) 1819.xvii.295-9; 1826-7.xix.199-200; 1830-1.xii.508-9; 1835.xlv.34; 1842.xxxii.545; and 1846.xxxiv.770.

21   *Hansard,* 2nd ser., 10 (1824):417; and 3rd ser., 13 (1832):987.

22   British Library [hereinafter BL], Add MS 40315 ff. 63-4.

23   *The Letters of King George IV, 1812-1830,* ed. A. Aspinall (Cambridge: Cambridge University Press 1938), 3:449.

24   PP(HC) 1846.xxxiv.770.

25   Beattie, *Crime and the Courts,* 576-82, 601-10; and Margaret DeLacy, *Prison Reform in*

Lancashire, 1700-1850: A Study in Local Administration (Stanford, CA: Stanford University Press, 1986), ch. 3.

26 A survey of local changes is given in Richard Herrick Condon, 'The Reform of English Prisons, 1773-1816' (PhD thesis, Brown University 1962), 39-43, 96-124, 160-74. The gap between intentions and practices in Lancashire is described in DeLacy, *Prison Reform in Lancashire*, chs. 3-4.

27 Condon, 'Reform of English Prisons,' chs. 2, 5, 7; Robert Alan Cooper, 'Ideas and Their Execution: English Prison Reform,' *Eighteenth-Century Studies* 10 (1976-7):73-93; Robin Evans, *The Fabrication of Virtue: English Prison Architecture, 1750-1840* (Cambridge: Cambridge University Press 1982), chs. 2-4; and DeLacy, *Prison Reform in Lancashire*, chs. 2-3.

28 *The Torrington Diaries,* ed. C. Bruyn Andrews and John Beresford (London: Eyre & Spottiswoode 1934-8), 2:400; and 3:36, 234; and William Cobbett, *Rural Rides ... During the Years 1821 to 1832; with Economical and Political Observations,* ed. Pitt Cobbett (rev. ed.; London: Reeves and Turner 1893), 1:295, 390-1; and 2:7-19, 347-8. For the controversies surrounding the imprisonment of political offenders, see Michael Ignatieff, *A Just Measure of Pain: The Penitentiary in the Industrial Revolution, 1750-1850* (New York: Pantheon Books 1978), 120-42; and DeLacy, *Prison Reform in Lancashire,*132-52.

29 *The Idler,* no. 38, in *The Works of Samuel Johnson, LL.D.* (London: Nichols and Son 1816), 7:153.

30 In 1791, however, only three years after New South Wales was established, eight men, one woman, and two children succeeded in a dramatic escape by open boat. The plight of those who were returned to England aroused much sympathy in some circles. See *Boswell: The Great Biographer,* ed. Marlies K. Danziger and Frank Brady (New York: McGraw-Hill 1989), 156-8, 216-9, 241-2, 226-9, 271. But such escapes were extremely rare, and the sympathy that they aroused reflected the conviction that transportation was, and ought to be, a severe measure.

31 Susan Dwyer Amussen, 'Punishment, Discipline, and Power: The Social Meanings of Violence in Early Modern England,' *Journal of British Studies* 34 (1995):2-12, 32-4.

32 Beattie, *Crime and the Courts,* 538-48; and A. Roger Ekirch, *Bound for America: The Transportation of British Convicts to the Colonies, 1718-1775* (Oxford: Clarendon Press 1987), 226-9.

33 *Calendar of Home Office Papers of the Reign of George III, 1760-1775,* ed. Joseph Redington and Richard Arthur Roberts (London: Her Majesty's Stationery Office 1878-99), 4:11.

34 PRO, HO 31/1 (4 August 1790).

35 *Hansard,* 1st ser., 11 (1808):886; 16 (1810):945-6; 17 (1810):327, 334; and 36 (1817):1305.

36 BL, Add MS 38323 ff. 22-3 (Liverpool to W. Wilberforce, 5 January 1810).

37 'The settlement never can be worse than it is now,' he continued, 'when no attempt towards reformation is dreamt of, and when it is governed on principles of political economy more barbarous than those which prevailed under Queen Bess' (*Life of Mackintosh,* 2:343).

38 PRO, HO 42/3 f. 116 (8 September 1783) & f. 142 (9 October 1783); HO 42/18 f. 140 (9 February 1791); HO 42/21 ff. 16-7 (2 July 1792); and HO 42/22 f. 506 (25 November 1792).

39 Buckinghamshire Record Office, D/SB/OE 6/22.

40 Samuel Bamford, *Passages in the Life of a Radical* (1844; reprint, London: Macgibbon & Kee, 1967), 349-50.

41 National Library of Scotland, MS 1051 ff. 86-7 (? to H. Dundas, 24 December 1793).

42 Four of the poems appear in *The Poetical Works of Robert Southey,* new ed. (London: Longman, Brown, Green, and Longmans 1847), 103-7. A fifth, omitted from the collected works, originally appeared in the *Monthly Magazine and British Register* 5 (January-June 1798):41-2.

43 *The Life and Correspondence of the Late Robert Southey,* ed. Charles Cuthbert Southey (London: Longman, Brown, Green and Longmans 1849-50), 4:109; and *Selections from the Letters of Robert Southey,* ed. John Wood Warter (London: Longman, Brown, Green, and Longmans 1856), 1:162; and 2:274.

44 George Rudé, *Protest and Punishment: The Story of the Social and Political Protesters*

Transported to Australia, 1788-1868 (Oxford: Clarendon Press 1978), 27-41; Con Costello, 'The Convicts: Transportation from Ireland,' in *Australia and Ireland, 1788-1988: Bicentenary Essays,* ed. Colm Kiernan (Dublin: Gill and Macmillan 1986), 114-16, 119-21; and Bob Reece, 'Irish Convicts and Australian Historians,' in *Irish Convicts: The Origins of Convicts Transported to Australia,* ed. Bob Reece (Dublin: University College 1989), 2-4, 21.

45 BL, Althorp Papers G270 (Earl Spencer to W. Elliot, 16 December 1806; and Spencer to the Lord Lieutenant, 20 December 1806).

46 52 Geo. III, c. 16 (1812); and 54 Geo. III, c. 42 (1813).

47 *Hansard,* 1st ser., 27 (1813):238-40, 246-52.

48 60 Geo. III and 1 Geo. IV, c. 8 (1819), ss. 4, 6.

49 Charles Duke Young, *The Life and Administration of Robert Banks, Second Earl of Liverpool* (London: Macmillan 1868), 2:434; and BL, Add MS 58936 ff. 124-5 (Liverpool to Lord Grenville, 27 November 1819).

50 BL, Add MS 38281 ff. 344-5 (17 December 1819). The text of the bill before and after its alteration by the Commons can be found in the House of Lords Sessional Papers CXIV (1819-20 and 1820), 17-32 (esp. 19, 28).

51 Cobbett, *Rural Rides,* 1:188-9; [John Wade], *The Black Book; or, Corruption Unmasked!* new ed. (London: John Fairburn 1828), 54n, 333-5; and *Recollections of a Long Life, by Lord Broughton (John Cam Hobhouse) with Additional Extracts from His Private Diaries,* ed. Lady Dorchester (London: John Murray 1910-11), 4:38.

52 *Hansard,* 1st ser., 16 (1810):944-9; 17 (1810):322-52; 19 (1811):186-8; 22 (1812):101-4; and 33 (1816):987-92.

53 Surrey Record Office, Acc 319 (Goulburn Papers), Box 39 (Peel to H. Goulburn, 1828).

54 BL, Add MS 40315 ff 85-6 (R. Peel to Lord Eldon, 16 January 1822).

55 PRO, HO 44/13 no. 14 (R. Peel to Attorney General, 10 February 1823).

56 *Hansard,* 1st ser., 38 (1818):1191-2; and 39 (1819):750-1, 1434; and *Hansard,* 2nd ser., 2 (1820):526-7; and 5 (1821):1000.

57 *Hansard,* 2nd ser., 11 (1824):1092.

58 *Sir Robert Peel from His Private Papers,* ed. Charles Stuart Parker, 3 volumes (London: John Murray 1891-9), 1:401-2.

59 For two contemporary descriptions, see Joseph W. Reed and Frederick A. Pottle, eds., *Boswell, Laird of Auchinleck, 1778-1782* (New York: McGraw-Hill 1977), 4-7; Jean Marchand, ed., *A Frenchman in England, 1784: Being the Mélanges sur l'Angleterre of François de la Rochefoucauld,* trans. S.C. Roberts (Cambridge: Cambridge University Press 1933), 137.

60 *Calendar of Home Office Papers,* 1:599 (emphasis in original); and 2:188 (emphases added).

61 Pat Thane, 'Government and Society in England and Wales, 1750-1914,' in *The Cambridge Social History of Britain, 1750-1950,* ed. F.M.L. Thompson, 3:1-61 (Cambridge: Cambridge University Press 1990); and Carolyn Conley, *The Unwritten Law: Criminal Justice in Victorian Kent* (New York: Oxford University Press 1991).

62 Based on my count of the lists recorded in PRO, PC 2/130-205.

63 Wilfrid Oldham, *Britain's Convicts to the Colonies,* ed. W. Hugh Oldham (Sydney: Library of Australian History 1990), 53-108; Mollie Gillen, 'The Botany Bay Decision, 1786: Convicts, Not Empire,' *English Historical Review* 97 (1982):745-50, 754; A. Roger Ekirch, 'Great Britain's Secret Convict Trade to America, 1783-1784,' *American Historical Review* 89 (1984):1285-91; and Ekirch, *Bound for America,* 233-7.

64 William L. Clements Library [hereinafter WLCL] (Ann Arbor: University of Michigan), Shelburne Papers 152/39-40 (J. Buller to the Earl of Shelburne, 2 April and 1 July 1782).

65 WLCL, Shelburne Papers 163 (Treasury minute, 28 December 1782); and a copy at BL, Add MS 42275 ff. 178-9.

66 William Cobbett, *The Parliamentary History of Great Britain, from the Earliest Period to the Year 1803* [hereinafter *Parliamentary History*], 25 (1785-6):903, 908.

67 *Gentleman's Magazine* 56 (1786):264.

68 A list of the occupants of Newgate from 1795 to 1801 indicates that no prisoners held there were technically serving sentences of imprisonment. Excluding debtors, about half the population was made up of those sentenced to transportation (Corporation of London

Records Office, Misc MS 235.5, Committee for Rebuilding Newgate: Rough Minutes & Papers 1783-1831).

69   *Hansard,* 1st ser., 17 (1810):324; and Condon, 'Reform of English Prisons,' 189-98.
70   Esther Moir, 'Sir George Onesiphorus Paul,' in *Gloucestershire Studies,* ed. H.P.R. Finberg, 195-224 (Leicester: Leicester University Press 1957); J.R.S. Whiting, *Prison Reform in Gloucestershire, 1776-1820: A Study of the Work of Sir George Onesiphorus Paul, Bart.* (London: Phillimore 1975); Sean McConville, *A History of English Prison Administration* (London: Routledge & Kegan Paul 1981), 1:88-104; and David Eastwood, *Governing Rural England: Tradition and Transformation in Local Government, 1780-1840* (Oxford: Clarendon Press 1994), 242-51. See also the references at note 27 above.
71   PRO, HO 42/9 f. 163v (G. Paul to Lord Sydney? 12 October 1786) and HO 13/4 pp. 254-6 (E. Nepean to G. Paul, 14 October 1786); HO 13/7 p. 343 (W.W. Grenville to C. Willoughby, 15 December 1789) and HO 13/10 p. 78 (Duke of Portland to C. Willoughby, 5 September 1794); and HO 13/7 p. 433 (W.W. Grenville to T.B. Bayley, 13 April 1790).
72   BL, Althorp Papers, G259 (G.O. Paul to the Earl Spencer, 31 August 1806; emphases in original). For letters expressing similar convictions, though not at such length or in such detail, see PRO, HO 42/9 f. 32 (Marquis of Buckingham to Lord Sydney? 15 October 1786); and HO 42/11 f. 71v (C. Willoughby to E. Nepean? 30 January 1787).
73   PRO, HO 42/66 ff. 309-10 (W.M. Pitt to G. Shee, 23 September 1802).
74   PRO, HO 42/6 ff. 2v and 39v (T.B. Bayley to Lord Sydney, 1 and 26 January 1785; emphases in original).
75   See for instance PRO, HO 42/6 ff. 39-41 (T.B. Bayley to Lord Sydney, 26 January 1785); and HO 42/15 ff. 431-2 (J. Higgins to W.W. Grenville, 27 December 1789).
76   BL, Add MS 33107 ff. 476-7 (W.M. Pitt to Lord Pelham, 13 September 1801).
77   Condon, 'Reform of English Prisons,' 200-2; Beattie, *Crime and the Courts,* 582; DeLacy, *Prison Reform in Lancashire,* 150-2, 220; and Eastwood, *Governing Rural England,* 250-60.
78   Malcolm I. Thomis, ed., *Luddism in Nottinghamshire* (London: Phillimore 1972), 44, 80-1.
79   PRO, PC 1/70 (E. Knatchbull to R. Peel, 5 September 1822; J. Park to Peel, 9 September 1822; and E. Knatchbull to Peel, 23 September 1823).
80   *Dyott's Diary, 1781-1845: A Selection from the Journal of William Dyott,* ed. Reginald W. Jeffery (London: Archibald Constable 1907), 2:15, 26, 40, 101 (emphases in original).
81   Douglas Hay, 'Property, Authority and the Criminal Law,' in *Albion's Fatal Tree: Crime and Society in Eighteenth-Century England,* ed. Douglas Hay, Peter Linebaugh, John G. Rule, E.P. Thompson, and Cal Winslow, 17-63 (London: Allen Lane 1975).
82   Randall McGowen, 'The Image of Justice and Reform of the Criminal Law in Early Nineteenth-Century England,' *Buffalo Law Review* 32 (1983):96-117, 123-5.
83   S.H. Romilly, *Letters to 'Ivy' from the First Earl of Dudley* (London: Longmans, Green 1905), 192.
84   *Parliamentary History* 26 (1786-8):1059. Similarly, a year beforehand, an anonymous writer observed that it was 'politically impossible to adjust the exact proportion of punishment to the magnitude of the offence.' (*Gentleman's Magazine* 56 [1786]:102).
85   BL, Add MS 40380 ff. 83-4 (R. Peel to the colonial secretary, 13 July 1825). This lack of alternatives clearly formed the backdrop to Peel's decision during the following year to implement preventive policing.
86   For these developments, see U.R.Q. Henriques, 'The Rise and Decline of the Separate System of Prison Discipline,' *Past and Present* 54 (1972):61-93; M. Heather Tomlinson, 'Penal Servitude, 1846-1865: A System in Evolution,' in *Policing and Punishment in Nineteenth-Century Britain,* ed. Victor Bailey, 126-49 (London: Croom Helm 1981); and David Smith, 'The Demise of Transportation: Mid-Victorian Penal Policy,' *Criminal Justice History* 3 (1982):21-45.

3

'Harshness and Forbearance': The Politics of Pardons and the Upper Canada Rebellion

Barry Wright

The exercise of discretion in the administration of criminal law is formally discouraged under the modern premises of the rule of law and utilitarian governance. Yet, the ideals of certainty and consistency are constantly undermined in practice, from enforcement, prosecution, and pleas through to sentencing and punishment. The exercise of such discretion is often a necessity, usually unacknowledged and sometimes consciously disguised. The eighteenth and early nineteenth centuries stood in stark contrast to this current philosophy. The prevailing ideology in those earlier times maintained that justice was to be tempered by mercy; discretionary authority was celebrated and prominently displayed, most notably in the granting of pardons.

A number of historians point out that the ideology of the rule of law had popular resonance, its formal claims sometimes drawn upon to effectively contest or question the legitimacy of arbitrary authority.[1] Mercy had similar popular resonance where the rigours or harsh applications of the law were perceived to cause injustice.[2] Although the pardon plays a small role in modern criminal law, and discretionary mercy has been displaced to more hidden areas of the law's administration, the pardon seems to have a popular life of its own. The pardon looms large in historical memory, as evidenced by the quest for posthumous pardons, especially in cases with overt political overtones. Descendants of convicts from the rebellions in the Canadas still periodically pursue posthumous pardons with the Department of Justice over a century and a half after the events. The issue of a posthumous pardon rages around Louis Riel and other politically charged executions, such as the Chilcotin Chiefs hanged in British Columbia in 1864.[3]

This essay explores the role of the pardon in the political turbulence of early-nineteenth-century Upper Canada, misleadingly described by some as a 'peaceable kingdom,' although certainly idealized as such by the governing elite of the time. The exercise of the pardon was a colonial translation of the royal prerogative and must be situated in a particular stage of state formation. Capital punishment and the pardon had come under sustained attack from reformers in the 'mother country' during this period. British utilitarians pointed out that discretionary pardons frustrated the deterrence objective of punishment, one that demanded rational proportionality and certainty, not severity, of penalties. Moral reformers fostered the growth of the rehabilitative ideal whereby new institutions and procedures tailored to the needs of each offender would displace arbitrary punishment and its suspension. In the new American and French republics, where such arguments were also influential, the very existence of the pardon was called into question. Because the pardon was one of the prerogatives relating to offences against the king, the question arose: Should a new executive prerogative be developed where there is no monarch and offences are against the people? Alexander Hamilton dismissed challengers to the pardon in republican democracies and prevailed in setting it out as a presidential power in the US Constitution, arguing, 'In seasons of insurrection or rebellion, there are often critical moments, when a well-timed offer of pardon to the insurgents or rebels may restore the tranquillity of the commonwealth.'[4] Royal prerogatives continued to be exercised widely in loyal British North America, and it was precisely the situation described by Hamilton that faced the government in Upper Canada in 1838 in the aftermath of the rebellion and in the midst of 'Patriot' raids from the American border.

An historical examination of the context of pardons reveals their *symbolic* and *administrative* dimensions, arguably not only of political cases but also of the more routine capital ones. Just as the request for a pardon is instrumental, so too is its granting. We see that its exercise is intended to bolster the state's power and legitimacy. The 'political pardon' clearly poses one of the central rationales of all pardons: an expression of an authority wishing to appear to be secure in the exercise of its power, where, to borrow Douglas Hay's terminology, the 'justice' dictated by the rule of law can be tempered by 'mercy' on the part of confident and beneficent governors.[5] The secure but benevolent exercise of power is, as Hamilton implied, symbolically important in reinforcing the legitimacy of authority.

Historians with access to records of government deliberations, which are hidden from contemporary public view, tend to find that pardons are not granted simply out of compassion but according to political and tactical considerations, agendas that often have little to do with the circumstances of an individual case. During the Upper Canada Rebellion, a conscious decision was made to deal with democratic ferment and disaffection as much as possible through legal means rather than through unregulated state violence. This lent greater legitimacy to repression and stigmatized the insurrectionists as criminals. The pardoning that took place was an outgrowth of this strategy – to subject as many rebels as possible to the legal process on capital charges, with no intention of resorting to mass hangings.

The political uses of the law and the role of pardons during the rebellion crisis are the focus of the main portion of this essay. The official administrative standpoint is richly documented; we see how the government's consideration of pardons encompassed all stages of the criminal law process, affecting everything from the scope of numbers charged to the final disposition of cases. Legislation to facilitate conditional pardons usurped the constitutional exercise of the royal prerogative and was premised on the availability of a substantial secondary punishment in the form of transportation. In combination with the pressures brought to bear on those charged with capital offences to plead guilty, the means were created to 'process' rebels quickly during the fast-breaking events and far in excess of the numbers the provincial courts could normally handle. The pardon therefore played a key role in enabling the government to extend its repressive reach while maintaining the appearances of legality.

The government's actual success in legitimating its repressive actions was a mixed one. The response of imperial administrators in London is well-illustrated by the records, but popular attitudes and responses are more difficult to discern. Although the rebellion was suppressed, the tide of reform could not be turned back.

Where does the 'political pardon' fit into in the variety of modifications of punishment that exist? Are the circumstances of political trials and the status of political convicts unique or can they be compared to the more routine business of the criminal courts and convicted felons? This essay sheds indirect light on these questions. It begins by situating the pardon within the administration of criminal law in the early nineteenth century and concludes by briefly looking at the provincial legacy of the pardon after the rebellion – its relative decline in the face of contemporary utilitarian law reform. While there is no attempt here to examine the record of pardons for non-political offences over the roughly fifty years of Upper Canada's existence,[6] the context framing the 1838 pardons suggests that the political pardon is not a species apart. Rather, it is one particularly dramatic form in which mercy was dispensed by those with powers of life and death.

Pardons before the 'Great Reforms'

Criminal law in Upper Canada was received and administered at a time of great upheaval in the English institutions of criminal justice. Ostensibly utilitarian and humanitarian reforms extended from law enforcement (Peel's professional police) to the dramatic reduction of capital offences, to procedural changes, and to punishment (the rise of the penitentiary). As examined elsewhere in this volume, the pardon played a prominent role before these sweeping reforms were introduced and during a time when the administration of criminal law had to deal with wide-ranging capital offences and limited penal options. Although the pardon survived the early-nineteenth-century reforms, its role was much reduced.

Eighteenth-century English criminal law had been based on the notion that terrifying exemplary punishment would prevent crime, with worthy convicted felons reprieved of the automatic penalty upon the recommendation of juries and discretion of judges. The Crown, exercising the royal prerogative of mercy, decided who would receive pardons and who would be hanged. The different stages of the administration of criminal law were closely connected under this regime, with the availability of penal options and pardoning having significant implications at earlier stages of the process.[7] The development of transportation as a viable secondary or adjunct punishment paved the way for the extensive use of *conditional* pardons. It brought a discretionary flexibility to the automatic capital sentence upon a felony conviction and allowed the introduction of still more capital offences (a fourfold increase over the century, passed at the behest of new economic interests or in response to perceived crises).[8] Although the system became overburdened with convictions as the century progressed, calls for reform were resisted because, as Douglas Hay convincingly argues, the exercise of discretion in the administration of criminal law had ideological implications that helped to legitimate and sustain the authority of the ruling class.[9]

As Greg T. Smith's essay indicates, Tory opposition to reforms continued as late as the 1830s. By then, however, what McGowen has described as 'the Whig image of justice' had prevailed.[10] The reforms dealt with what had become an overburdened system in crisis and with the intellectual irrationality of the contradiction between the law's terrifying claims and its increasingly lenient practice. The reforms allowed the criminal law to reach and deal with far greater numbers.[11] Exemplary bloody example and the openly discretionary exercise of mercy had become features of an increasingly obsolete concept of authority.

Those who dominated Upper Canadian government attempted to replicate the hierarchical social purposes of eighteenth-century English criminal law (in McGowen's phrase, the 'Tory image of justice') in the unpromising environment of colonial Canada. A modified colonial version of the eighteenth-century English system prevailed. English criminal law of the 1790s, which contained around two hundred capital offences, formed the core of the province's criminal law, with a provincial Act passed in 1800 declaring the applicability of the largely unreformed English laws that were in effect until 1792. The Act went on (as its stated purpose suggests, 'for the more effectual punishment of certain offenders') to modify English punishments in accordance with local conditions.[12] Banishment from the province was an alternative punishment for a number of offences that were punishable by transportation or where transportation was imposed as a condition of pardon.[13] Transportation as a penalty or secondary punishment came to be confined largely to military cases and the cheaper, less administratively troublesome alternative of banishment (usually to the United States with return constituting a capital offence) resorted to as the main condition for pardons in more routine serious cases.

Until the 1830s, the provincial government largely resisted the reforms sweeping English criminal law, although sustained pressure for reform began in the 1820s. In Upper Canada, the crime problem was much less serious than in England, which had long experienced the consequences of the Industrial Revolution. Influenced by utilitarian and humanitarian thinking in Britain and the United States, the political reform movement nonetheless embraced 'the Whig image of justice' and called for a more modern administration of criminal law. Egregious cases, such as women facing infanticide charges, placed the harshness of capital punishment and the uncertainties of the pardon in stark relief.[14] Administrative reform proposals followed, including calls for professional policing, the reduction of executive influence and partisanship in the administration of criminal law (affecting prosecutions, jury selection, and judges), and the construction of a penitentiary.[15]

The governing elite, which became known as the Family Compact, was initially reluctant to change a highly discretionary system that complemented its hierarchical social pretensions. Judge John Walpole Willis, who had arrived in the province in 1827, commented on a case, held at the Home District assize, of a boy prosecuted, convicted, and sentenced to death for killing a cow:

> This, according to Mr. Secretary Peel's Amendment of the Criminal Law of England, is now only a transportable Offence ... I took occasion, shortly after this occurred, to give Mr. Peel's Acts, which I brought from England with me, to Mr. Attorney General Robinson, and suggested him the Propriety of assimilating the Criminal Law of Upper Canada altogether to that of England, or at least giving the Province the Benefits of Mr. Secretary Peel's improvements ... I at length discovered that any proposition that did not originate with himself was not generally attended with his Approbation.[16]

John Beverly Robinson, who was to preside over the 1838 treason trials as chief justice, was a leading figure in the Family Compact. Appointed to the bench following Willis's removal, he addressed the grand jury by celebrating the province as a 'peaceable kingdom,' an assertion more a product of wishful thinking than fact.

By 1833, Robinson had actively promoted the necessity of criminal law reforms and may well have intellectually embraced it earlier.[17] A legislative committee that reported in 1831 stated in clear terms the practical problems caused by the lack of penal options:

> The necessity of a penitentiary in this country must be obvious to everyone who has ever attended a court of justice in this province, whether the penal code as at present exists is too severe or not, it is not necessary to enquire, the fact is enough for us that even when juries find a verdict of guilty, and the judges pronounce sentence of death in any case of less atrocity than murder, the person administering the government will not allow the law to be carried into execution, and if he did, it is very probable that in such cases juries would cease to convict, and the judges to sentence, so that the law as practised at present amounts very nearly to an act of indemnity for all minor offences.[18]

Indeed Robinson, in his grand jury addresses of the same year, appears to have become a convert to the ideas of Jeremy Bentham and John Howard: 'The prevalence of good example, the effect of moral and religious instruction, and the *CERTAINTY* rather than the *SEVERITY* of punishment (through the prompt and vigilant administration of justice) may so far repress outrages and disorder.'[19]

The political context was undoubtedly important. The compact was increasingly anxious about social disorder (arising from increased immigration of Irish and British labouring poor) and political difficulties arising from an increasingly powerful political reform movement.[20] Bold new measures were required to shore up authority and fend off community breakdown.

Given this consensus, a package of sweeping reforms passed in 1833 dramatically reduced capital offences from an uncertain two hundred felonies to a certain twelve specified capital offences.[21] Imprisonment and transportation were set out as primary punishments for offences that were previously capital ones. By 1835, the Kingston penitentiary replaced the jails for long internments and although transportation played a smaller role in punishment, it was important enough for Attorney-General Jameson to expressly declare that transportation was indeed restored.[22] Where the pardon was exercised, banishment continued to be favoured over transportation until the rebellion.

The old system of ideological modulation of terror and mercy was, however, largely displaced by a new system of governance involving 'total institutions.' As Taylor suggests, 'Planned far in excess of any conceivable needs for the incarceration of prisoners, [the Kingston penitentiary] was ... a visible panacea for many of Upper Canada's real or imagined ills.'[23]

The reforms reduced the scope of the pardon in the routine administration of criminal justice. Simply put, fewer condemned meant fewer candidates for pardons. Wide-ranging capital offences had been the raison d'être of the conditional pardon and their reduction meant a diminished role for royal mercy.[24] But when the governing elite's embrace of such reforms failed to stave off the difficulties that led to the rebellion, the pardon regained, in dramatic fashion, its pre-reform prominence. Once again, the governing elite seized upon the pardon in an attempt to influence the climate of popular thought.

The Rebellion and the Administration of Justice and Mercy in 1838

Overview

The rebellions in Upper Canada and Lower Canada were unsuccessful but they ultimately transformed the nature of British colonial government. Insurrection in Upper Canada was sparked by political ferment and disaffection arising out of economic difficulties and long-standing grievances over the policies of a largely unaccountable, executive-dominated provincial government. The target was a colonial governing clique rather than British imperialism. The ultimately loyalist convictions of most provincial inhabitants appear to have been demonstrated after the failure of the initial insurrection, when the rebels regrouped in the United States and failed to make significant inroads, despite the support of American 'Patriots.'

In the whiggish historiography, some stress is put on the severity of the official responses to the rebellions. Certainly this was the case in Lower Canada. The 1838 political trials in Upper Canada reflect a government comparatively more repressive than the one that contended with traitors from the War of 1812 against the United States, when the numbers of those charged were much lower and no civilians were tried by courts martial.[25] There was nevertheless an awareness in 1838, as in the earlier conflict, that official actions would have greater legitimacy if criminal trials, rather than military repression, were resorted to. More important for our purposes here, the exercise of mercy figured prominently in 1838, and the numbers pardoned were much higher than those hanged. This form of mercy nonetheless had decidedly repressive implications; the stigma of capital charges extended widely, the granting of pardons remained uncertain, and their conditions, particularly the secondary punishment of transportation, were harsh.

Offenders convicted of treason received an automatic sentence of death. Whether a pardon was granted depended entirely upon executive discretion. Such discretion was not based on executive whim – public opinion was certainly a consideration in the exercise of this discretion, gauged most directly through jury and judicial recommendations and popular petitions. But the provincial Executive Council faced other pressing considerations. Its decisions largely reflected an attempt to deal with the obvious political challenges to its authority and with an array of difficult legal issues. As we shall see, in dealing with the rebellion crisis through legal means, the government had to consider not only popular expectations from 'below,' but also imperial concerns from 'above.'

In cases involving political charges, the royal prerogative of mercy remained in the hands of the Crown in Britain. Emergency legislation was passed to circumvent this impediment to the speedy resolution of cases.[26] The provincial government assumed the prerogative and this enhanced the government's ability to manipulate other more preliminary aspects of the criminal law process. The ready availability of pardons – for those convicts given reprieves and for those who pleaded guilty, induced to do so by what appears to have been the expectation of a conditional pardon – served important strategic purposes. It opened up the possibility of charging a far larger number of rebels with political offences. Encouraging guilty pleas avoided bogging the courts down with trials. Ready pardons might also reduce the risk (to the Crown) of jury acquittals for those who stood trial.

Such remarkable objectives obviously required close coordination between the judiciary, prosecution, and executive. This proved to be of little difficulty in a colonial setting where the separation of powers was virtually non-existent, despite ongoing provincial controversies about the Executive Council's partisan influences on prosecutions and the judiciary.

Another practical consideration was the availability of a reliable and substantial secondary punishment. Here we see the importance of transportation, which as Simon Devereaux's essay shows, had been used for over a century in Britain. Two factors ensured the prominence of transportation in the Executive Council's considerations. The first was the legal opinion confirming transportation as a colonial penal option in 1835.[27] The second was the influence of the head of the provincial council, the lieutenant governor, Sir George Arthur, who presided over the executive decisions on punishment and clemency. He had had much experience in the administration of transportation and had served as lieutenant governor of Van Diemen's Land from 1823 to 1836. He actively encouraged the provincial government to embrace transportation as a secondary punishment for the conditionally pardoned and as a primary punishment for those convicted by court martial. Transportation would permanently rid the province of the convicted offenders without the security risks entailed by imprisonment or mere banishment to the United States. With these main points in mind, let us now turn to the events and proceedings that followed.

Charging and Dispositions: The Pivotal Role of Pardons
Over 800 people were arrested in the aftermath of the rebellion in late 1837 and during the Patriot border raids the next year.[28] Many were held on capital charges whereas others were held under no charges at all. The jails of the Home, Niagara, and London Districts remained full to the end of March 1838, and minor offenders were kept confined in London until well into June. Many of those charged were placed on bail, but others were imprisoned under suspension of habeas corpus with no idea of the details of their warrants or when they would face proceedings. As Lieutenant Governor Arthur put it, the government faced 'the difficulty of proceeding to extremes where so large a number of persons were concerned; and much consideration was given to framing some plan for classifying the offenders, among whom were many shades of moral guilt, although all were alike amenable to the legal penalties of High Treason.'[29] Clearly, Arthur continued in his report to Lord Glenelg, the secretary of state, it had become necessary to exercise discretion: 'In order to relieve the country from the perplexity of dealing with the great body of persons daily apprehended on the charge of high treason, my predecessor appointed certain commissioners ... for the purpose of inquiry and taking the dispositions of witnesses, and the commissioners, very properly I think though perhaps not quite constitutionally, took upon themselves the responsibility, in certain cases, to suffer the accused to be at large in bail.'[30]

The numbers problem and its solutions were rooted in Loyalist zeal and emergency legislation passed in January and March 1838. The Acts broadened the definitions of treason and created procedural expedients. The most important of these, for our purposes, was the pardoning legislation. This, perhaps more than any other measure, made it possible to deal with the 'perplexity' of numbers in an expedient and politically effective manner.

All provincial legislation was subject to imperial review, but in the fast-breaking first months of the insurrection the government had a relatively free hand. The first wave of legislation passed in January and approved by Arthur's predecessor, Sir Francis Bond Head, expanded the scope of treasonable practices and suspended habeas corpus (1 Vict., c. 1), created further procedural expedients by allowing for the selection of juries and trials out of district (1 Vict., c. 2), and dealt with the Patriot disruptions involving foreigners by creating a new capital political offence, 'alien lawless aggression' (1 Vict., c. 3).[31] Arthur arrived in late March with instructions calling for restraint, underscored by a strong letter from Lord Glenelg: 'Representations have reached this department from various quarters that during the present Session of the Legislature measures of unusual severity and of extensive application have been proposed against those who may have been in any way implicated in the insurrection in the province.'[32] Arthur was nonetheless unwilling to decline assent to further legislation passed in March. Printed copies of all the emergency legislation were not sent to England until early May.[33]

The March legislation contained the Act that most concerns us here – 1 Vict., c. 10 – which was to exceed all others in controversy. This Act, entitled 'An act to enable the government of this province to extend a conditional pardon in certain cases to persons who have been concerned in the late insurrection,' was designed for proceedings against the immense numbers charged with capital political offences.[34] It provided that persons charged with high treason could petition the lieutenant governor for a pardon before arraignment, which, if granted, would be conditional upon transportation or banishment. Chief Justice Robinson, who, as a *de facto* member of the executive appears to have had a direct hand in drafting the legislation as well as in its administration, drew parallels with measures during the Irish rebellion in 1798 and stressed that the Act was both expedient and humanitarian:

> When this Act was passed, there were probably not less than three hundred or four hundred persons in close custody, charged with High Treason. If they were tried and convicted, the Lieutenant Governor had not, by his commission, the power to pardon them, because he is expressly restrained in cases of treason. Thus an immense number of trials would probably be followed by the necessity of keeping the great body of prisoners in gaol during the next summer, until reference could be made to England, occasioning a vast inconvenience and expense in guarding them, continuing in great measure and uneasy state of excitement produced by the insurrection, and subjecting them to the danger of disease and death, and the certainty of much suffering, many unhappy persons whom the Government would doubtlessly consent to pardon.[35]

The jurisdiction of the lieutenant governor to exercise the prerogative was implicit in the Act. Aware of probable objections, Robinson went on to justify the local assumption of the prerogative by drawing parallels with the local discretion exercised in the Crown's decision to prosecute and suggesting that the results would be similar. The chief justice was being less than forthright and would later be closely questioned by the British government for the assumption of the pardoning prerogative and its consequences.

Discretionary power over pardons provided political advantages not available from mere prosecutorial discretion. Refraining from prosecution risked embarrassing the government politically. Dropping charges created a perception of weakness and the appearance that the government was faltering in the determined resort to the criminal law. These problems could be avoided with discretionary power over pardons and, moreover, substantial conditional penalties could be imposed. While Robinson's remarks stressed the administrative need for such legislated power, the strategic political requirements were implicit but obvious.

It is less clear whether the legislation actually encouraged offenders to plead guilty in exchange for the expectation of a conditional pardon upon a petition. While I have found no direct evidence of promises to that effect, Robinson did observe, 'The Act has proved most beneficial in its consequences; a great majority of the prisoners ... have freely confessed their guilt, and thrown themselves upon the mercy of the Government, and these can now be spared on such terms as may be thought proper. A small number have been left for trial.'[36]

Trials began in late March 1838 with a selected twelve associated with William Lyon Mackenzie tried for treason out of 134 charged. Lount and Matthews were convicted and hanged; two pleaded guilty and under the special legislation were sentenced to transportation; and four were convicted, given respites on the automatic sentence, and considered for mercy. Two sets of trials were held in the Gore and London Districts to deal with the uprising led by Charles Duncombe – twenty-six were tried in Gore District and ten were found guilty and reprieved. In the London District, fifteen were tried and five were found guilty and reprieved. The Patriot raids followed – the Short Hills skirmish in the Niagara District in June 1838 led to the indictment of twenty-four subjects and five Americans. One of the convicted, James Morreau, was hanged and more could well have followed (Jacob Beamer, Samuel Chandler, and Benjamin Wait) had the new governor general, Lord Durham, not intervened. Seven of those convicted were reprieved and conditionally pardoned, twelve pleaded guilty and were sentenced to transportation. Battles in Prescott in November and Windsor in December led to summary executions and courts martial against civilians in London and Kingston (seventeen hanged after trial and seventy-seven conditionally pardoned), although a number were pardoned outright and the large numbers indicated for transportation were reduced on the intervention of the lieutenant governor, despite the opposition of his council.[37] A number of acquittals, some of which were dramatic, are not mentioned here because they do not directly relate to issues of pardon (Table 3.1).

The disposition of convicted political offenders proved contentious. The final numbers reflected the balance between the local policy of satisfying Loyalist demands for vengeance and deterring Patriot raids, on the one hand, and respecting British signals for leniency and, later, more direct intervention, on the other. Such intervention resulted in the sparing and transportation of three condemned men who did not receive local pardons. In the end, ninety-two were transported to Van Diemen's Land, although

Table 3.1

Disposition of treason convicts, 1838-9*

	Prisoners pleading not guilty			Prisoners pleading guilty
	Convicted	Hanged	Conditionally pardoned	Conditionally pardoned
Home	6	2	4	2
Gore	10		10	
London	5		5	
Niagara	8	1	7	12

*Acquittals (including those in the Midland District) not listed. For sources and fuller description, see note 29 and E. Guillet, *The Lives and Times of the Patriots* (Toronto: University of Toronto Press 1968).

the numbers would have been much greater had the British government not intervened.[38] Twenty of those convicted of treason and originally destined for transportation were simply banished to the United States, and another thirteen destined for Australia were added to the twelve who received penitentiary terms. There were twenty-seven in the first group of transportees to Australia;[39] fourteen of these escaped en route, including a dramatic break out of the Quebec Citadel. The remaining thirteen in custody were conveyed to England and confined in prison hulks until British administrators sent them to Hobart in Van Diemen's Land in 1839 and 1840. A larger group of seventy-eight Upper Canadian convicts later embarked from Quebec with Lower Canadian political prisoners and sailed directly to Australia on the HMS Buffalo; the journey lasted 137 days.[40] After Lord Durham and Lord Glenelg intervened in the conditions set on pardons, 600 rebels were dismissed outright from custody.

The provincial government's disposition policies were facilitated by the emergency measures, which enhanced the government's administrative ability to process offenders. It was free to cast the net widely on charges, to intern or release on bail, and then to focus on the orderly disposition of cases unhindered by the usual procedural protections such as habeas corpus. The legislation allowed for the orderly release of those who had been charged, while allowing the government to continue arresting insurrectionists who, for legal and logistical reasons, would not otherwise be charged – thereby reinforcing the impression that the government was acting with resolute firmness.

The pardoning legislation was a particularly important measure in achieving these objectives. The enormous numbers were broken down into minor cases in which bail was to be granted and the more serious cases in which inducements appear to have been offered for guilty pleas, thereby avoiding the delay and backlog of trials – and suggestive of modern plea bargaining. In the remaining serious cases where the accused held out some hope of acquittal and decided to risk a trial, the local exercise of pardoning power expedited the resolution of the cases. Those who were convicted and condemned could receive more rapid decisions on their reprieves. The speedy execution of Lount and Matthews underscored the determination of the government and conveyed a sense of terror, which further induced offenders to plead guilty and take advantage of the opportunity to petition for a conditional pardon. The execution of a relative few highlighted the pardons as merciful even though they were part of a larger process that was repressive and designed to legitimate the government's rule.

Punitive Mercy and the Transportation Solution
Lieutenant Governor Arthur was called upon to make the difficult decisions about punishment and commuting the sentences soon after his arrival. He endorsed the chief justice's view of the need to proceed quickly on the more serious charges and the utility of the pardoning legislation. Although, as mentioned above, locally exercising the prerogative expeditiously resolved a large number of cases,[41] full pardons were little better than prosecutorial restraint, and conditional pardons resulting in imprisonment or banishment to the United States entailed security risks. An effective, practical, and substantial secondary punishment was required.

Shortly after approving the executions of Lount and Matthews, Arthur convinced the Executive Council that convicted offenders and those who had pleaded guilty should be physically removed from the province without expectation or opportunity to return. The best means to achieve this was transportation to Australia for life.[42] As lieutenant governor of Van Diemen's Land he had dealt with a rapidly growing convict population and complaints that transportation had declining deterrent value by establishing a 'panopticon without walls,' an elaborate penal bureaucracy of classification, reward, and punishment.[43] Between his recall from Van Diemen's Land and appointment to Upper Canada, Arthur gave evidence to a select committee of the House of Commons where he called transportation 'the most effective, as well as the most humane punishment that the wit of man ever devised.'[44] The penal option of transportation was supported by Jameson's 1835 legal opinion on its availability. Arthur justified his decision to Glenelg: 'Confinement to the Province would only provoke attempts at rescue, and would not in the end rid society of them. Simple banishment ... would be worse than useless; to extend the punishment of death much further was to be avoided – in short after much consideration it was determined that the only way left effectively to rid the country of these men was by commuting their punishment into transportation to one of Her Majesty's penal colonies.'[45]

Given the limits on the capacity and vulnerability of the Kingston penitentiary, and that banishment might simply strengthen the Patriot raids, transportation appeared to be the sensible condition for the local administration of pardons. Although Arthur had characterized it as humane punishment, as Simon Devereaux's essay indicates, it was an unknown and terrifying prospect for most convicts.

Armed with the pardoning legislation and the transportation solution, Arthur and his executive then engaged in a complex balancing of exemplary terror, mercy, and administrative expediency that gave rise to the original disposition of cases. On 14 April 1838, he wrote to London about the offenders who had pleaded guilty and large numbers of others who had made full confessions of guilt, questioning whether their petitions under the legislation could spare them all the penalties for a high treason conviction, including forfeiture of property.[46] The British government responded with concerns about much larger issues. It was highly critical, on constitutional and financial grounds, of the local assumption of pardoning powers and resort to the condition of transportation. The secondary punishment was imposed on many who should not have been proceeded against in the first place.

Imperial Controversy and the Bureaucratic Politics of Pardons

The tensions between the provincial and imperial governments over the pardons and transportation are well illuminated by the records. Slow communications due to distance made imperial supervision difficult in times of peace, let alone rebellion.[47] Provincial laws, policies, and measures were reviewed well after their implementation during the fast-breaking crisis. The British government found the alien lawless aggressors offence, which was bound to create international difficulties with the United States, alarming enough. The local assumption of pardoning power caused even greater concern.[48]

The large numbers selected for transportation saddled the British government with enormous costs and administrative nuisance. Convicts would have to be shipped and located in penal colonies at Britain's expense. Moreover, there were serious constitutional concerns. Undersecretary James Stephen of the Colonial Office was unimpressed by Chief Justice Robinson's arguments on the province's assumption of the Crown prerogative, which, as noted above, drew a parallel between the devolution of pardoning and the attorney-general's discretion on prosecutions. The political sensitivities raised by pardons and their conditions in political cases meant they were a matter to be handled solely by the secretary of state.[49] In addition to usurping the prerogative, an important object of the pardoning legislation was constitutionally suspect. To plead guilty to high treason was not strictly illegal, but it was constitutionally questionable. It was contrary to the spirit of the procedural safeguards enacted in 1696 under the shadow of the Bloody Assize of 1685, when Judge Jeffreys, facing more than 1,300 cases, had duped prisoners into pleading guilty in order to dispose of them expeditiously.[50]

Little could be done about the commencement of proceedings but it was possible to intervene with local authorities in their decisions on penalties, including the extravagant resort to transportation. Lord Glenelg had warned at an early point, 'Great circumspection will, I think, also be requisite in carrying into effect any capital sentences which may be passed on persons convicted of political offences.'[51] He said later, 'In the present instance the good of society will be best consulted by subjecting as few to such penalties as may mark the sense entertained by the Government of the heinousness of the offence, and by mercy and complete indemnity towards all others.'[52] Upon hearing word of Arthur's decision not to grant pardons to Lount and Matthews, the British government warned against further executions, noting, 'No further advantage could be gained by inflicting the extreme penalty of the law on many of their [Lount's and Matthews's] associates.'[53] Fearing from these signals that the imperial authorities might impose a full amnesty, the provincial Executive Council sifted through the various cases and decided that it was politic to reduce the numbers considered for transportation and make their pardons conditional on penitentiary terms and subsequent banishment instead. The Colonial Office caught up with matters when it came to proceedings arising out of the Patriot raids.

The delays involved in sending correspondence across the Atlantic meant that local actions and imperial instructions failed to come to the timely attention of decision-makers. Moreover, it had become apparent to the British government that the discretion of local authorities could not be relied upon. London soon recognized that the effective implementation of its preferred policies during rapidly unfolding events required some sort of delegation of pardoning power – for the very reasons the provincial government used to justify the 'conditional pardoning legislation' (1 Vict., c. 10). The solution was to send an official into the field with an explicit understanding of British policy and whose discretionary judgment imperial authorities could have confidence in. Lord Glenelg despatched notice to Arthur of Lord Durham's appointment as governor general with exceptional delegated prerogative and other unprecedented powers in his commission, including instructions to exercise a tight rein over provincial lieutenant governors.[54]

Durham demanded that all pardoning decisions be forwarded to him upon his arrival in July. Arthur's initial reaction to the Short Hills raid in June was to call for the execution of no less than four of the convicted offenders. Durham's intervention was too late to save Morreau but Beamer, Chandler, and Wait were saved at the last moment and given conditional pardons. Durham's appointment implicitly called Arthur's judgment into question and his rapid intervention pleased neither Arthur's council nor the chief justice:

> The Governor General ... desired that all the cases might be referred for his consideration and decision, and in consequence no further execution has taken place, and all prisoners have been respited. I have felt it my duty to submit to the Earl of Durham, that the course his Lordship has pursued in this matter is, as I am advised unconstitutional, and likely to lead to very painful results ... the lenity which has been shown to persons is not a popular course; very far from it.[55]

Raising the constitutional question appears to have originated with none other than Robinson, who, as noted earlier, had not only drafted the emergency legislation but advised the Executive Council on prosecutions and pardoning decisions. Arthur defended this: 'The high character and great experience of the Chief Justice led me to consider that his presence and assistance ... were likely to be eminently useful, both to the prisoners and to the Government, and I therefore made a point of requesting his attendance in Council.'[56]

Robinson's mixing of judicial and executive functions had caused conflict with James Stephen before the rebellion. When in 1838 Stephen demanded an explanation, Robinson avoided the constitutional issue and defended his measures and policy consultations on the grounds that slow communications would cause injustice to the prisoners and that reference to the judiciary in pardoning deliberations was common.[57]

The distance between Durham and the Upper Canadian executive widened when Durham made it clear that a general amnesty would be extended to all political prisoners. Arthur again complained to the Colonial Office, rejecting discretion when it smacked of lenience: 'The Governor General ... has acted from the best motives; but I think his Lordship has far exceeded his powers in thus interfering with the ordinary course of justice in this Province; and I differ, also entirely with the policy which his Lordship has pursued in this matter [general amnesty].'[58] Arthur nonetheless submitted amnesty proposals to Durham when requested to in October.

This resulted in the outright release of many connected to the rebellion and the Short Hills raid who had not received the executive's modified dispositions. The offenders from the Prescott and Windsor Patriot raids were tried by courts martial. Loyalist backlash to the amnesty encouraged Colonel John Prince to take the law into his own hands following the invasion of Windsor, a move that Arthur refused to condemn (not wishing to alienate the militia). Nonetheless, after the courts martial, Arthur released all those recommended for mercy and those under twenty-one years; and a large number of the condemned were spared with transportation. To Arthur's dismay, Durham's successor Charles Poulett Thomson (Lord Sydenham) had the same extended powers in his commission.

Justice, Mercy, and the Public Politics of Pardons

Most of the historical records on the rebellion are contained in official correspondence, so we have a clear picture of the bureaucratic politics. It is important to keep in mind, however, that for most of the period of the rebellion and Patriot raids, the provincial government's discretionary decisions were less hindered by imperial supervision from above than animated by concern for public opinion from below. The public politics of the pardon were indeed the politics that counted most during the crisis. We have seen how pardons were closely linked to the entire criminal process, including prosecution strategy. From an administrative standpoint, the government sought to extend the criminal law process over as many persons as possible while disposing of cases efficiently. The government recognized that refraining from prosecution was a sign of weakness in the public's perception, but alternatively, mass hangings could also backfire. Pardons thus played a pivotal role in the judicious balancing of justice and mercy. Exemplary terror could be visited on the public by carefully timed examples. Pardons for those reprieved after conviction and for those induced not to contest the Crown's charges – coupled in the more serious cases with effective punishment through transportation – demonstrated the confidence of authority.

The pardoning legislation's role in expanding the government's power to modulate the 'terror' of justice with mercy appears to support Kenneth McNaught's observation about the historical pattern in Canadian political trials – namely, initial firm rigour followed by longer-term lenience.[59] McNaught goes on to suggest this pattern reflects the confidence of constitutional authority and the positive characteristics of Canadian legal and political culture, one that emphasizes peace, order, and good government. I would suggest that the qualities of justice/rigour and mercy/lenience were not simply characteristically Canadian, but served political purposes similar to what Hay has observed about the 'majesty, justice and mercy' (and the central role of pardons) in the administration of eighteenth-century English criminal law. We also see in this collection, particularly in the essays by Strange and Loo, the political objectives of wider practices of mercy. I have explored these ideological dimensions of the provincial treason proceedings at some length elsewhere, but some of the main points bear revisiting to highlight the public politics of pardons.[60]

Insight into political purposes, and to some extent the public effect, of the criminal law process and the modulation of justice with mercy can be gleaned from official records, newspaper reports and diaries, and the texts themselves of petitions for mercy and pardons. The official records suggest an awareness that criminal trial proceedings would have more public credibility and would thus more powerfully legitimate the state's actions than arbitrary repressive actions. Once the decision was made to proceed by the rule of law, a conscious and calculated prosecution and sentencing strategy was designed to maximize political effect. Prosecution entailed the justice side of the political equation – namely, proceeding against as many offenders as possible by trial, avoiding the disastrous consequences of acquittals, and, above all, striking terror with the automatic sentence of death upon conviction, backed up by exemplary hangings in the most serious cases. The sentencing strategy entailed the mercy side of the equation – namely, moderating the rigours of the law through the judicious granting of pardons. It was this calculus of politics, designed to powerfully reinforce the government's authority in the eyes of the public, that informed the government's discretionary choices in administering the criminal law.

The need to be perceived to be acting resolutely – justice according to the rule of the law – is set out in clear terms by Chief Justice Robinson in a letter to Arthur:

> Punishment, on this occasion, should be carried so far as possible to produce a strong and lasting impression that treason is in fact, and not merely in the contemplation of the law, regarded as the most highly criminal and that it meets with no countenance or indulgence in general, from the Government or from the community, whatever forbearance may be shown to individuals upon considerations applying to their particular cases.[61]

Arthur and his council, of course, fully concurred, underscoring how the terror of the justice of the law of the land would have a powerful impact on the public credibility of authority: 'The Council are of the opinion that the cases in question are of great urgency; that severe public example is actually required in some instances ... believing that the execution of the sentence of the law with promptitude will do much towards its beneficial operation.'[62] Arthur, persuaded to agree with the quick executions of Lount and Matthews,[63] was anxious to assure the British government of the salutary social effects of these executions. They demonstrated that no weakness existed on the part of authorities and satisfied Loyalist demands for retribution. Yet they also promised to yield social peace and tranquillity.[64]

Arthur was also aware that the terrifying effects of justice must be balanced by mercy: 'Harshness and severity are distinguishing marks of weakness and apprehension. It is to [governments of] undoubted power and security alone that belong the magnanimity and serenity which accompany acts of forbearance and mercy.'[65] Governments that are confident in their exercise of authority have no need to continue to terrorize once they have asserted their resoluteness.

James Stephen, upon receiving Arthur's reports, applied a more modern utilitarian critique to the provincial executive's considerations: 'I am not clear that he [Arthur] would have done better had he refused to permit these executions ... My objection to what was done rests upon this, namely, that I do not find in all these papers a deliberate estimate of the probable effect of the executions on one hand, or of a more lenient course on the other, on the public mind.'[66] If carefully calculated deterrence was the objective, it was far from clear that mere 'lieutenants' such as Lount and Matthews should have been made examples of.[67]

While the ideological modulation of the harshness of justice and the forbearance of mercy are evident in these official considerations, the actual *public* impact of the proceedings is less clear. The difficulty with Hay's thesis is empirical demonstration of ideological effect. Did majesty, justice, and mercy really serve to disguise elite interests and legitimate the existing structure of authority to the extent that Hay suggests?[68]

Newspaper reports provide a glimpse of unofficial views and interpretations. Chief Justice Robinson's charge to the Grand Jury at the Home District trials was a widely published summation of the idealized peaceable kingdom, the Family Compact's view of the desirable social order and how it was undermined by offences that struck at its tranquillity.[69] The trials were widely reported, with the dramatic focus being the horrific sentence for those convicted of treason. The *Christian Guardian* reported on the case of Lount and Matthews: 'The unhappy men appeared to be deeply affected during the address which was listened to with almost breathless attention by an immense concourse of people.'[70] A report of the removal of the scaffold upon which Lount and Matthews were executed, one day before the other condemned men were to be hanged, provides a further indication of a segment of public opinion: 'The examples that have been made, we humbly apprehend, are sufficient to vindicate the majesty of the law, and it is to be hoped that they will produce the desired effect upon that portion of the community, who may have been led into the snare.'[71] Another paper reported, 'There may be more gained by clemency than by a too scrupulous adherence to the demands of justice, now that the majesty of the law had on one occasion been asserted, thereby proving that justice *dares* array herself in terrors when it is deemed necessary.'[72] It seems that non-official circles clearly perceived the need to modulate the majesty and justice of the law with mercy and clemency.

A final place in which ideological effect may be gleaned is in the analysis of petitions of mercy and pardons themselves.[73] The executive acknowledged an overwhelming number of petitions for mercy.[74] In his criticisms of Arthur, Durham declared that there had been a remarkable 30,000 petitions supporting clemency for Lount and Matthews (the real number was 4,567). Perhaps the most dramatic example of petitioning was the case of Benjamin Wait, whose wife Maria travelled to Quebec to plead for his life before Lord Durham. Wait's conditional pardon arrived just thirty minutes before the deadline set by the court.[75] An address by pardoned prisoners to Arthur reflects the expected discourse of those enjoying royal mercy: 'That your Excellency may ... long remain in this province, to guard the helpless offspring of our deluded fellow sufferers now in prison ... from artifice such as seduced us; to temper justice with mercy; and to secure at our hands, on behalf of a most gracious Queen, such proof of our gratitude and contrition as we ought to manifest, is our most anxious wish. By giving such demonstration of our sincerity, gratitude, and contrition ... attachment and fidelity awakened in us by the mercy that we have received.'[76]

It was obviously difficult to challenge authority while treason prosecutions were being pursued. Reform criticism, where it existed, tended to focus on the minutiae of procedural details in individual cases rather than the broader objectives of the government. Cynicism became evident when rebel leader Mackenzie took advantage of the general amnesty and returned from his fugitive exile in the United States in 1849, making it apparent that political expediency rather than individual justice underlay the repression.[77] Benjamin Wait, pardoned at the last minute and transported to Van Diemen's Land via Britain, clearly saw through the symbolism of mercy and identified the more expedient political and administrative considerations underlying it: 'To talk of clemency, as connected with the Queen, I knew to be hyperbolical; for very rarely did any communications, designedly made for her, ever meet the eyes of majesty, particularly when not agreeable to ministers through whose hands they must proceed. Ours, for instance, must be addressed to the Secretary of State for the Colonies, under whose arbitrary policy, explained to the Canadian governor, it was that we were suffering.'[78]

Nonetheless, during the crisis itself, political calculations of resolute resort to the law tempered by mercy appeared to have some ideological effect in strengthening authority and deference to it. This points to the centrality of the criminal law in managing the rebellion crisis. It was only in retrospect that some segments of the public, especially those most affected by the proceedings, may have come to a more complete understanding of the political calculations hidden under the majesty of the law.

The Broader Significance of the Rebellion Pardons

As demonstrated throughout this volume, mercy could be exercised at various stages of the criminal law process. In the case of the rebellion crisis, it was important that the exercise of mercy be open and dramatic to maximize the political effect of criminal proceedings on the public mind. This meant it had to take the form of a pardon. Although the provincial government had full discretion over prosecutions, it had to overcome restrictions on the local exercise of the royal prerogative of mercy in political cases if resort to legal process was to be politically effective. Dropping charges during the crisis would be a sign of weakness. The government wanted to appear resolute in resorting to criminal trials. But it also did not want to appear to be acting in too repressive a fashion for this too would betray weakness. The rigours of the law and the terrible effects of justice could be tempered by mercy at the last moment with a pardon, thereby displaying confident authority that could afford to be benevolent. The pardoning discretion enabled the provincial government to exploit the full ideological potential of the criminal law to influence the climate of popular thought in a manner that appears to have strengthened government authority. The legislated assumption of pardoning power caused controversy with the British government, and imperial intervention in the end resulted in more lenience than the provincial government intended, but in many cases the mercy that was exercised had decidedly punitive consequences, particularly for those who were transported.

The suppression of the rebellion and the Patriot raids was a Pyrrhic victory for the governing Family Compact. Lord Durham's famous report eventually paved the way for the union of the Canadas and responsible government. Arthur and the governing provincial elite could not effectively battle reform and British imperial policy sympathetic to it. Criminal convictions and pardons could not completely eradicate the political discontent that had inspired the rebels.

What light do these overtly political pardons cast on the more routine business of the Ontario criminal courts in the early nineteenth century? The rebellion arguably marked a watershed in the role of the pardon in Upper Canada. As we have seen, the pardon in the 1838-9 cases hinged on a readiness to charge and prosecute widely, facilitated by the pardoning legislation and the apparent availability of transportation, which was legally restored in the 1830s and brought forward by Arthur's keen advocacy of it. The eventual amnesty directed by the British government in the political cases was mirrored in more routine criminal cases in the 1840s – there were no executions in the province in that decade.[79] The government seems to have shrunk from its embrace of the terrors of justice.

The long-term decline in the prominence of the pardon was ultimately the result of changes in the state and new strategies of social control and punishment. The pardon did retain potent symbolic significance in later political trials, as demonstrated by Louis Riel's execution in 1885 in particular, and continues to do so as debates over posthumous pardons suggest. Of course, the pardon also remained important in cases involving the few capital offences still left. But as Carolyn Strange points out in her essay in this volume, where mercy was exercised in the disposition of capital cases, it became less an open expression of personalized royal authority than the bureaucratic processes of the Department of Justice acting on behalf of the Crown.[80] Generally, discretion in the modification of punishment was routinized in hidden processes such as ticket of leave (later parole) and plea bargaining.

Changes to the administration of criminal law were propelled by institutional transformation in the wake of the rebellion crisis, although as we saw, they were substantially prefigured in the 1833 reforms. The reduction of capital offences and the construction of the Kingston penitentiary marked the end of the routine, widespread use of the pardon. The prominence of the pardon during the rebellion thus reflected a temporary reversion to the 'Tory image of justice.' The crisis demanded that there be full engagement of the ideological potential of the law. The features of majesty, justice, and mercy, which Hay identifies as so prominent in the public face of criminal proceedings in the eighteenth century, were similarly fostered to bolster the authority of the governing elite in Upper Canada in 1838. By this period, however, the royal prerogative of mercy had become an increasingly anachronistic conception of authority, for routine criminal offences at least. Utilitarian institutional reform and ambitious new strategies of social administration, which historians have described in 'state formation' literature and which were spearheaded in Canada by Lord Sydenham, brought in new forms of authority.[81] The symbolic act of mercy central to the pardon, expressing the benevolent power of authority, gave way to a regularized institutional processing of convicts in the new 'total' institutions.

Notes

1 See Edward Thompson, *Whigs and Hunters: The Origins of the Black Acts* (New York: Pantheon 1975); 'The Moral Economy of the English Crowd in the Eighteenth Century,' *Past and Present* 50 (1970):74-136; Greg Marquis, 'Doing Justice to "British Justice": Law, Ideology, and Canadian Historiography,' in *Canadian Perspectives on Law and Society: Issues in Legal History*, ed. W. Wesley Pue and Barry Wright, 43-70 (Ottawa: Carleton University Press 1988).

2 Douglas Hay, 'Property, Authority and the Criminal Law,' in *Albion's Fatal Tree: Crime and Society in Eighteenth-Century England*, ed. Douglas Hay, Peter Linebaugh, John G. Rule, E.P. Thompson, and Cal Winslow, 17-63 (London: Allen Lane 1975); K. McNaught, 'Political Trials and the Canadian Political Tradition,' *University of Toronto Law Journal* 24 (1974):149-69.

3 See Tina Loo, 'The Road from Bute Inlet: Crime and Colonial Identity in British Columbia,' in *Essays in the History of Canadian Law*, vol. 5: *Crime and Criminal Justice*, ed. Jim Phillips, Tina Loo, and Susan Lewthwaite, 112-42 (Toronto: Osgoode Society 1994). Cariboo Chilcotin Justice Inquiry (see 'News release,' Ministry of the Attorney General, Province of British Columbia, 28 October 1993) has made this the most recent posthu-

mous pardon cause célèbre. Pardons are the responsibility of the National Parole Board and the federal minister of justice.

4   Quoted in K.D. Moore, *Pardons: Justice, Mercy and the Public Interest* (New York: Oxford University Press 1989), 26. Presidential pardoning power was created under article II, section 2 of the US Constitution and exercised by George Washington, who pardoned participants in the 1794 Whiskey Rebellion, as well as by John Adams (Fries Rebellion) and Thomas Jefferson (deserters from the Continental Army). Pardons conditional on military service were used to fill up the ranks in 1812 and during the Civil War. A more recent example includes Ford's pardon of Nixon and Carter's 1977 amnesty for Vietnam War draft evaders – see Francis MacDonnell, 'Reconstruction in the Wake of Viet Nam: The Pardon of Robert E. Lee and Jefferson Davis,' *Civil War History* 40 (1994):119. The pardon was abolished in France in 1789, only to be restored in 1802.

5   Hay, 'Property, Authority and the Criminal Law.'

6   Susan Lewthwaite and John Beattie have collected research on this in an ongoing project.

7   See J.M. Beattie, *Crime and the Courts in England, 1660-1800* (Princeton, NJ: Princeton University Press 1986).

8   Transportation became well organized by the early eighteenth century, allowing the pardon to displace the plea of 'benefit of clergy' as a means of mitigation while retaining a punitive element as the condition of the pardon.

9   See Hay, 'Property, Authority and the Criminal Law.'.

10 R. McGowen, 'The Image of Justice and Reform of the Criminal Law in Early Nineteenth Century England,' *Buffalo Law Review* 32 (1983):89-125.

11 On the reforms to this system in crisis see L. Radzinowicz, *A History of English Criminal Law and Its Administration*, 4 volumes (London: Stevens from 1948), C. Emsley, *Crime and Society in England, 1750-1900* (London: Longman 1987); M. Ignatieff, 'State, Society, and Total Institutions: A Critique of Recent Social Histories of Punishment,' *Crime and Justice: An Annual Review of Research* 3 (1981):153-91.

12 'An Act for the further introduction of the criminal law of England in this province, and for the more effectual punishment of certain offences, 40 Geo. III, c. 1 (1800, UC). The area that became Upper Canada went through the reception of English law at the time of the Quebec Act, but the establishment of a separate province in 1791 with a separate legal system resulted in confusion over the applicable corpus of English criminal law. The exact reception date was set at 17 September 1792 (the date of the provincial legislature's first meeting). On the adoption of English style criminal courts in 1794 and the impact of executively controlled local administration of justice, see Robert Fraser, '"All the Privileges Which Englishmen Possess": Order, Rights and Constitutionalism in Upper Canada,' in *Provincial Justice: Upper Canadian Legal Portraits from the Dictionary of Canadian Biography*, ed. Robert Fraser (Toronto: Osgoode Society 1992), xli-xlii.

13 The Act added that a fine or whipping could be substituted where legislation specified branding or branding was the result of a successful plea of benefit of clergy. Imprisonment in the local jails was not seen as a viable sentencing alternative.

14 See most notably the case of Angelique Pilotte, an Aboriginal woman who had returned to Upper Canada from France after becoming pregnant by a British officer. She abandoned the child in a field and was convicted of infanticide. Reprieved, she spent months in wretched conditions before receiving a pardon. See Constance Backhouse, *Petticoats and Prejudice: Women and Law in Nineteenth-Century Canada* (Toronto: Osgoode Society 1991), 112-124. Reformer Robert Gourlay and his supporters embraced the case as a cause célèbre in 1818 to underscore calls for the reduction of capital offences and the right to defence counsel.

15 See, for instance, the murder trial of printing assistant Charles French, which prompted reform-inclined editor Francis Collins to deplore the disorder of the provincial capital and call for professional policing along the lines of Sir Robert Peel's Metropolitan London Police. See R.L. Fraser, 'French, Charles,' *Dictionary of Canadian Biography* (Toronto: University of Toronto Press 1976), 4:265-6.

16 National Archives of Canada (NAC), Colonial Office Records, Series 42, vol. 386, p. 484 [hereinafter NAC, CO 42] John Walpole Willis, Narrative of Occurrences in Upper Canada, 5 December 1828; see also NAC, CO 42, vol. 386, p. 356, Robinson to Maitland, 20 May

1828 – both reproduced in British Parliamentary Papers, 'Papers Relating to the Removal of the Honourable John Walpole Willis from the office of one His Majesty's Judges of the Court of King's Bench' (London 1829), 273, 21.

17 Russell Smandych, 'Beware of the "Evil American Monster": Upper Canadian Views on the Need for a Penitentiary,' *Canadian Journal of Criminology* 3 (1991):125-47

18 Report of a Select Committee on the Expediency of Erecting a Penitentiary, *Journal of the House of Assembly* (1931) Appendix, 211-12, reproduced in J.M. Beattie (with the assistance of L.M. Distad), *Attitudes Towards Crime and Punishment in Upper Canada, 1830-1850: A Documentary Study* (Toronto: Centre of Criminology, University of Toronto, Working Papers 1977), 80.

19 Address of the chief justice to the Grand Jury of the Midland District, 1831 *Brockville Gazette*, 11 August 1831, reproduced in Beattie, *Attitudes*, 37 (emphasis added).

20 This was at odds with actual crime levels, which remained stable (Beattie, *Attitudes*, 1-2). However, the sudden influx of immigrants, many of whom worked as transient wage labourers on public works projects, led to increased disorder, economic distress, and overwhelmed the jails. See J.J. Bellomo, 'Upper Canadian Attitudes Towards Crime and Punishment, 1832-1851,' *Ontario History* 64 (1972):11, 16; Rainer Baehre, 'Origins of the Penitentiary System in Upper Canada,' *Ontario History* 69 (1977):188; J. Weaver, 'Crime, Public Order, and Repression: The Gore District in Upheaval, 1832-1851,' *Ontario History* 78 (1986):175, 176, 207; M. Cross, 'The Shiners' War: Social Violence in the Ottawa Valley in the 1830's,' *Canadian Historical Review* 54 (1973):1.

21 3 Wm IV, c. 3 (1833, UC): 'An Act to reduce the number of cases in which Capital Punishment may be inflicted; to provide other punishment for offences which shall no longer be Capital after the Passing of this Act; to abolish the privilege called benefit of clergy; and to make other alterations in certain criminal proceedings before and after Conviction.' Aside from the usual capital offences (murder, violent robbery, rape) the other retained ones reflected public order/security concerns. (The Riot Act, 1 Geo. 1, c. 5 [1717], was left in force, as were treasons and illegal correspondence with the enemy, with modification of the horrific traditional tortures for political convicts.) The plea of benefit of clergy was abolished and many of the previously capital offences had a new range of punishments, including transportation and banishment for seven years and imprisonment up to fourteen years. J.D. Blackwell, 'Crime in the London District, 1828-1837: A Case Study of the Effect of the 1833 Reform in Upper Canadian Penal Law,' *Queen's Law Journal* 6 (1981):540-1.

22 See opinion in NAC, RG 1, Executive Council Submissions E 3 vol. 63 P 15, p. 177-88, which contains a circular letter from the Earl of Aberdeen (2 March 1835) complaining of inconsistent practices in the colonies concerning transportation, including the Canadian practice of sending convicts (largely military) to Bermuda. In responses dated 10 June and 1 July 1835, provincial Attorney-General Robert Jameson declared that by the 1800 provincial statute (40 Geo. III, c. 1) transportation was discontinued and substituted by banishment; but by recent legislation (3 Wm IV, c. 35), all persons convicted of any offence previously punishable by death should be liable to banishment or transportation. A provincial proclamation reviving transportation was issued 1 July 1835.

23 C.J. Taylor, 'The Kingston, Ontario Penitentiary and Moral Architecture,' (1979) 24 *Histoire sociale/Social History* 24 (1979):385-406, reprinted in *Lawful Authority: Readings on the History of Criminal Justice in Canada*, ed. R.C. MacLeod, 223-45 (Toronto: Longman 1988), 242. He says, at 241, 'The idea of the penitentiary was much more than a system of dealing with transgression of the law; it became a projection of the world as it should be. The penitentiary represented a community ... where the old values of obedience by the lower orders to a higher power were implicit.'

24 The decline was gradual. Susan Lewthwaite has pointed out that the twelve remaining capital offences were the primary capital offences before 1833 and were therefore the focus of pardoning.

25 See P. Romney and B. Wright, 'Security Proceedings in Upper Canada During the War of

1812,' in *Canadian State Trials*, vol. 1: *Law, Politics, and Security Measures, 1608-1837*, ed. F.M. Greenwood and B. Wright, 379-405 (Toronto: Osgoode Society 1996).

26 1 Vict., c. 10 (1838, UC) (discussed at length below).

27 Attorney-General Jameson's opinion was retrieved. See also RG 1 Executive Council Submission E 3 vol. 3 A 6, p. 112 and A 9, p. 128 in reference to imperial statutes 5 Geo. IV, c. 4, s. 7; 1 Vict., c. 10; 1 Vict., c. 3, s. 1 and whether militia courts martial have authority to pass a sentence of transportation. This was resolved in the affirmative.

28 See E. Guillet, *The Lives and Times of the Patriots* (Toronto: University of Toronto Press 1968), which lists 825 arrested, by district, between December 1837 and November 1838.

29 Arthur to Glenelg, 14 April 1838, printed by order of the House of Commons in British Parliamentary Papers [hereinafter BPP], 'Affairs of Canada, Correspondence Relative to Upper Canada 1838-39' (much of the imperial correspondence, with enclosures of executive deliberations from CO 42, vols. 446, 447, and 450, may be found in these papers and in NAC, *Report for the Year 1944*). Rebellion records at the NAC are conveniently catalogued in NAC, *Report for the Year 1938*, recently supplemented by a useful finding aid (M. Corbett and P. Kennedy, F.A. 910).

30 Arthur to Glenelg, 14 April 1838, BPP.

31 While c. 1 and c. 2 had precedent in temporary legislation passed in Britain and in Upper Canada in 1814, c. 3 caused great anxiety for Glenelg, who urgently requested an official British legal opinion (Glenelg to the Queen's Advocate NAC, CO 42/446/118). Robinson defended the legislation to deter Americans citizens by putting them on the same footing as British subjects charged with treason. Admitting the measure was of 'questionable propriety,' he added that invaders could always be tried by courts martial. 'Remarks [Chief Justice Robinson] upon certain acts passed during the last session of the legislature of Upper Canada, in consequence of the insurrection,' enclosure 4 in Arthur to Glenelg, 23 April 1838, BPP. Irish Americans Sutherland and Theller had been convicted and condemned, but Arthur, concerned about the legalities, commuted sentence. Minutes of the Executive Council, enclosure in Arthur to Glenelg, 14 April 1838.

32 Glenelg to Arthur, 14 March 1838, BPP.

33 Arthur despatched the chief justice's remarks on the emergency legislation on 14 April but copies of the Acts were delayed to 5 May.

34 1 Vict., c. 9 substituted the unwieldy process of outlawry and was designed facilitate the capture of fugitives and rebels who continued to be involved with the Patriots.

35 'Remarks' [Robinson] enclosure 4 in Arthur to Glenelg, 23 April 1838, BPP.

36 Ibid.

37 Col. John Prince summarily executed five prisoners after the Patriot raid in the Windsor area.

38 See Guillet, *Patriots*; J.A. Gibson, 'Political Prisoners, Transportation for Life and Responsible Government,' *Ontario History* 67 (1975):191; *The Wait Letters*, ed. M. Brown and C. Cross (Erin, ON: Porcepic 1976). An anglophone Quebecker may have joined the Upper Canadian convicts, three of whom escaped from Hobart to America. Several died and others received full pardons at intervals until 1844. When the files were closed in 1847, four were known to be still on the island. On the fifty-eight French-speaking Lower Canadian political convicts transported to New South Wales, see *Land of a Thousand Sorrows: The Australian Prison Journal of the Exiled Canadien Patriote François-Maurice Lepailleur*, ed. F.M. Greenwood (Melbourne: Melbourne University Press 1980); B. Boissery, *A Deep Sense of Wrong: The Treason Trials and Transportation of Lower Canadian Rebels to New South Wales after the 1838 Rebellion* (Toronto: Osgoode Society/Dundurn 1995). More generally, see G. Rude, *Protest and Punishment: The Story of the Social and Political Protesters Transported to Australia, 1788-1868* (Oxford: Clarendon 1978).

39 Arthur to Glenelg, 10 September 1838, CO 42/450/17; 29 September 1838, CO 42/450/270.

40 See Guillet, *Patriots*, Gibson, 'Political Prisoners.'

41 Robinson explained to Arthur that he had been president of the Executive Council as well

as Speaker of the Legislative Council and despite his subsequent formal exclusion from the executive, he continued to offer his services to Arthur's predecessors as a valued adviser and would continue to be freely available. Archives of Ontario [hereinafter AO], Robinson Papers, Robinson to Arthur, 16 May 1838. On the delicacy of his executive advisory role, see note 48 below.

42 Arthur declared in council, 'Transportation should be resorted to, both as deterring punishment and as the means of effectively ridding the country of the worst and most dangerous traitors.' Minutes of Executive Council, 31 March. See also Minutes 2, 3, 9 April 1838 NAC, RG 1 E 1, extracted in Arthur to Glenelg, 14 April 1838. See also NAC, CO 42/447, 51-2 and Gibson, 'Political Prisoners,' 188.

43 Arthur's penal administration reflected a utilitarianism overlaid with Calvinist reformation. He alienated Australian free settlers and emancipated convicts alike by opposing the introduction of trial by jury and representative institutions, although he had reformist sentiments on abolition of slavery and capital punishment and sought to limit the exploitation of Aboriginal populations in both Tasmania and Upper Canada. See generally, Phillip Buckner, 'Arthur, Sir George,' *Dictionary of Canadian Biography* (Toronto: University of Toronto Press 1985), 8:26-31; A.G.L. Shaw, *Sir George Arthur* (Melbourne: Melbourne University Press 1980).

44 Quoted in Buckner, 26.

45 14 April 1838, CO 42/446/ 27 reprinted in part in BPP. The judges views are reflected in Robinson C.J. and Jones J., 'Report to Joseph (Arthur's secretary),' Toronto, 2 May 1838, NAC, RG 5 A 1 *Upper Canada Sundries*, vol. 193, 107309-11. In their view, 'such a sentence, if carried into effect without mitigation, is scarcely less rigorous than death, for in effect it is civil death.'

46 Arthur concluded that 1 Vict., c. 10 was not intended to pre-empt the Crown's final discretion on the conditions. Arthur to Glenelg, 14 April 1838, BPP. The prisoners petitioning for mercy under the legislation fell into several categories. Over fifty rebels (and eventually hundreds more) who were no longer regarded as a threat were simply released on bail and bound to keep the peace and maintain good behaviour. Banishment was thought expedient only for the American prisoners, since Canadians could cause trouble on the border. For most who had committed minor political offences and property offences, penitentiary terms were recommended. For the remainder of petitioners, transportation was recommended (the Executive Council's decisions on secondary punishments are summarized in Arthur to Glenelg, 30 May 1838, CO 42/447/30-38).

47 All provincial laws and local executive policy decisions were sent to the Colonial Office for review and the British government could disallow legislation within two years regardless of the lieutenant governor's assent. The lieutenant governor could, alternatively, reserve applicability of legislation until after imperial review. P. Knapland, *James Stephen and the British Colonial System 1813-47* (Madison: Wisconsin University Press 1953), 228-9.

48 Stephen to Grey, 25 May 1838, CO 42/446/47, 49.

49 Stephen exercised a tight reign over colonial legal affairs and the colonial judiciary. As a result the colonial judiciary held tenure according to royal pleasure (but with salaries independent of local executives). Some semblance of judicial independence was created by Stephen's insistence that judges not sit in Executive Council, a matter that placed him in conflict with Robinson earlier in the 1830s. See Knapland, 237-8. The matter of Robinson's executive activities was revisited in Stephen to Grey, 25 May 1838, CO 42/446/49; Robinson to Stephen, 7 and 10 January 1839, AO, Robinson Papers.

50 R. Clifton, *The Last Popular Rebellion* (London 1985), ch. 8; C.C. Trench, *The Western Rising: An Account of the Rebellion of James Scott, Duke of Monmouth* (London 1969), 247-8. See also J.M. Beattie, 'The Cabinet and the Management of Death at Tyburn after the Revolution of 1688-1689,' in *The Revolution of 1688-1689: Changing Perspectives*, ed. Lois G. Schwoerer, 218-33 (Cambridge: Cambridge University Press 1991).

51 Lord Glenelg to Colborne, 30 January 1838, BPP.

52 Glenelg to Arthur, 12 July 1838, CO 42/447/20.

53 Ibid., 30 May 1838, CO 42/446/59.

54 Ibid., 12 July 1838, CO 42/447/20.

55 Arthur to Glenelg, 10 September 1838, CO 42/450/17.

56 Ibid., 30 May 1838, CO 42/447/21, 29.

57 See note 48 above.

58 Arthur to Glenelg, 19 September 1838, CO 42/450/270.

59 McNaught, 'Political Trials and the Canadian Political Tradition.'

60 B. Wright, 'The Ideological Dimensions of Law in Upper Canada: The Treason Proceedings of 1838,' *Criminal Justice History: An International Annual* 10 (1989):131-78. I have attempted to address earlier errors in this essay.

61 Robinson C.J. and Jones J., 'Report to Joseph,' 107309-11.

62 Arthur to Glenelg on Minutes of the Executive Council, 2 April 1838, BPP. Justices Robinson and Jones observed, 'In the two instances in which the sentence of Death has been executed, we have no doubt that the propriety of suffering the law to take its course must have been generally, if not universally felt' (Robinson C.J. and Jones J., 'Report to Joseph,' 107310-11).

63 Arthur to Glenelg on Minutes of the Executive Council, 2 April 1838, BPP.

64 Arthur to Glenelg, 30 May 1838, CO 42/447/21, 21-2.

65 Executive Council Minutes, 31 March 1838. Arthur included the minutes and elaborated the point in Arthur to Glenelg, 14 April 1838, BPP.

66 Stephen to Grey, 25 May 1838, CO 42/446/47, 'Instructions to Publish Arthur's Despatch,' at 48-9.

67 Ibid., 48.

68 See Alan Hyde, 'Legitimation in the Sociology of Law,' *Wisconsin Law Review* (1983):379.

69 'Charge of the Hon. Chief Justice Robinson to the Grand Jury,' printed in *Toronto Patriot*, 13 March 1838.

70 *Christian Guardian*, 4 April 1838.

71 *British Colonist*, April 26, 1838.

72 *Niagara Reporter*, 8 May 1838, extracted in Beattie, *Attitudes*, 56.

73 For an exploration of the possibilities of textual analysis, see Natalie Zemon Davis, *Fiction in the Archives: Pardon Tales and Their Tellers in Sixteenth-Century France* (Stanford, CA: Polity Press 1987).

74 Extract from Minutes of the Executive Council, 9 April 1830, BPP.

75 See *The Wait Letters*, ed. Brown and Cross.

76 'Address of the Prisoners pardoned and lately liberated from Gaol to Lieutenant Governor Sir George Arthur,' July 1838, CO 42/447/173-74. The address and replies were widely published in the province's newspapers.

77 *British Colonist*, 20 May 1845, expressed opposition to the abolition of capital punishment in favour of rehabilitative ideals using the example of the amnesty: 'The Government of Great Britain has, in its lenity and forbearance, pardoned traitors; men who had been the instigators, if not the actual perpetrators, of many murders in working out their treasons; but we have seen no symptoms of their repentance.'

78 *Wait Letters*, 79

79 Claude Desaulniers, 'La Peine de Mort dans la législation Criminelle de 1760 a 1892,' *Revue Générale de Droite* 8, 2 (1977):141-84.

80 C. Strange, 'Discretionary Justice: Political Culture and the Death Penalty in New South Wales and Ontario, 1890-1920,' (in this collection). New South Wales perhaps continued to reflect the eighteenth century 'Tory image of justice' with wider ranging capital offences and more localized and personalized authority.

81 See P. Corrigan and D. Sayer, *The Great Arch: English State Formation as Cultural Revolution* (Oxford: Basil Blackwell 1985); Greer and Radforth, 'Introduction,' 3-16 and Radforth, 'Sydenham and Utilitarian Reform,' 64-102, in *Colonial Leviathan: State Formation in Mid Nineteenth Century Canada*, ed. A. Greer and I. Radforth (Toronto: University of Toronto Press 1992).

through the institutions and personnel of formal law such as we do now is actually a problem at least as old as the nation-state, and it is one that had particular resonance in the age of European imperialism. From the sixteenth century on, the expansion of Europe brought diverse cultures into contact and conflict. Given the demographic imbalances of colonization (in which Europeans were invariably outnumbered by indigenous peoples) as well as the economic pressures of expansion, which dictated that ruling be done as cheaply as possible to ensure the greatest profits, the need to find a way to deal with conflict in a cross-cultural context was all the more pressing.

The difficulties of governing diversity were acutely felt in distant dominions of the British Empire such as British Columbia over the nineteenth century. Here was a colony whose population was predominately Aboriginal until the turn of the century, and whose European inhabitants were, true to their Victorian origins, possessed of a heightened racial awareness that allowed them to see indigenous peoples as inherently savage. As a result, many Europeans felt justified in meting out a savage justice to Indians who broke the 'Queen's law' because savagery was the only thing savages could understand. Indeed, the predominant image of law in colonial British Columbia is that of the 'Hanging Judge,' Matthew Baillie Begbie. From 1860 to 1869, Begbie sentenced fifty people to hang. Twenty-seven of them were hanged, and of these, twenty-five (or 93 per cent) were Aboriginal (see Table 4.1).

As one historian observed, these numbers suggest that while Begbie might not have been the 'Hanging Judge' (as the biographer bent on restoring his reputation maintains), he surely could be called the 'Indian-Hanging Judge,' for despite their numerical predominance, Native peoples were over-represented among those who found themselves on the gallows.[8]

Table 4.1

Number of people sentenced to death and executed in British Columbia and Canada, 1860-99

	Number sentenced to death			Number executed		
	N[1]	BC[2]	CAN[3]	N	BC	CAN
1860-9	32	50	26[4]	25	27	12[4]
1870-9	11	13	114	2	4	33
1880-9	10	24	95	8	14	55
1890-9	8	20	80	2	10	46

Notes
1 Native peoples in British Columbia
2 British Columbia (including Native peoples)
3 Canada
4 1867-9 only
Source: Capital Case Files, NAC, RG 13

While these instances of what one contemporary called 'judicial murder' have captured the attention of most historians, their spectacular nature has also obscured the historical contingency and complexity associated with administering the law in a cross-cultural context by deflecting attention away from what happened in the period after 1871.[9] Though Native people continued to make up a large *proportion* of those sentenced to death and executed (Table 4.2), in the last three decades of the nineteenth century there was also a fall in the *number* of Native peoples sentenced to hang and the number of them actually executed. From a high of thirty-two in the colonial period (1860-9), the number of Native people sentenced to death declined to a quarter of that by the end of the nineteenth century. The decline in the number executed was even more precipitous, falling from twenty-five in the 1860s to two in the 1890s (Table 4.1). As the work of Foucault, Elias, and Spierenburg, as well as that of Greg T. Smith (in this volume), reminds us, however, the decline and disappearance of capital punishment should not be read as evidence for the rise of a humanitarian impulse that accompanied society's march towards modernity.[10] Though punishments aimed at the body were less evident after the eighteenth century, they were replaced by other modes of discipline aimed at 'governing the souls' of deviants rather than just their bodies.[11] Capital punishment was thus an historically specific form of state control that must be read in the context of other disciplinary regimes, which, in the case of the indigenous peoples of Canada, included reserves, residential schools, and the regulation of land use and fishing and hunting through licensing. As these were developed and economies of scale came into play, capital punishment became less central to the colonization of Native peoples, and other forms of control, including mercy – itself still an expression of power and an instrument of control – became more frequent.[12]

Table 4.2

Percentage of Native peoples sentenced to death and executed in British Columbia, 1860-99

	% Natives of total	% Natives of total sentenced to death	% Natives of total executed
1860-9	70.8[1]	64	93
1870-9	51.9[2]	85	50
1880-9	27.8[3]	42	57
1890-9	16.2[4]	40	20

Notes
1 1871
2 1881
3 1891
4 1901
Source: Population data taken from Jean Barman, *The West beyond the West: A History of British Columbia* (Toronto: University of Toronto Press 1991), 363.

Even during the colonial period, however, the application of the law was somewhat more complicated than Begbie's bloody record suggests. Though some European British Columbians had no compunction about stringing up any 'red devil' who had the temerity to break the 'Queen's law,' it is important to remember that this was also a British settler society that prided itself on its commitment to the rule of law. In fact, as I have argued elsewhere, extending the alleged benefits of the rule of law to Native peoples (despite their alleged savagery) was important to establishing their own identity as members of a community of civilized nations.[13] A commitment to the rule of law, however, precluded wanton bloodshed, or at least made it an ethical problem for European settlers. To make matters worse, a strict application of the rule of law would have required them to ignore the cultural differences they had drawn between themselves and the 'savages' that surrounded them, for it implied that such differences were irrelevant: all individuals were deemed equal and had to be treated as such. Their dilemma amounted to what is now termed 'cognitive dissonance': a lack of consistency between the knowledge, beliefs, and ideas held by an individual or group of individuals. British Columbia was a culturally diverse place in which the dominant minority perceived diversity in terms of race and a racial hierarchy. At the same time, however, that minority also defined itself by its adherence to a system of law that denied the relevance of racial differences in adjudicating cases.

In capital cases involving First Nations this dissonance was diminished to a certain extent by the possibility of *executive* mercy, which allowed differences to be taken into account. Unlike the juries who heard *Kimura* and *Ly*, nineteenth-century criminal trial juries could not formally give weight to cultural factors in reaching their verdicts; however, if they believed culture explained the behaviour of the accused, they could recommend him or her as deserving of executive mercy. Judges could acknowledge culture in the same way in their post-trial reports to the executive. Such recommendations of mercy – particularly those coming from judges – were influential in helping the executive decide whether the death sentence would be carried out or commuted to a term of imprisonment. But because mercy was dispensed by the executive rather than the judiciary, European British Columbians could continue to see their world in racial terms and acknowledge cultural differences without compromising their commitment to a system of law premised on denying the legal relevance of those differences.

The possibility of mercy not only diminished the dissonance created by diversity: it also reproduced the relations of power that were at the core of European colonization. Though Native culture was acknowledged by the courts, cultural outsiders – judges, the colonial governor and his council, and later the minister of justice – decided where in the legal process culture mattered and ultimately if it mattered enough to spare an individual from the gallows.

More significantly, the same cultural outsiders decided what Native culture was. In making their recommendations to the executive, British Columbia's judges relied on popularly held ideas about the Indian character. These ideas were part and parcel of a European ethnographic imagination that was itself given particular form by nineteenth-century colonialism and its intellectual spawn: the discipline of anthropology.[14] Colonial expansion created new knowledge about faraway peoples and places – knowledge that in the Victorian and Edwardian ages left the confines of the lecture hall and university library and was disseminated widely and popularized through newspapers, books, magazines, and juvenile literature as well as museums, exhibitions, and the more intellectually modest circuses and travelling shows. The savagery of the Indians during the Mutiny and the exploits of Stanley and Livingstone in 'darkest Africa,' for instance, could be followed almost as they happened from the comfort of armchairs throughout the empire. Later, long after the dust had settled (but before the sun had set), these images lived on in the fiction of Rudyard Kipling, Rider Haggard, and John Buchan, to name a few, whose tales of Mowgli, King Solomon's Mines, and Prester John influenced generations of youngsters who as adults continued to consume 'the primitive' in other forms, whether as art, furniture, clothing, or 'ethnic tourism.'[15] However, the availability of the strange and exotic in these multiple forms did nothing to make them familiar, and in fact worked to widen the gap between the civilized and the savage. Indeed, the knowledge of 'others' that came as a result of imperialism lent scientific credence to the notion of separate races of humans and the existence of a great chain of being – an evolutionary hierarchy whose pinnacle was the Victorian Briton. As such, anthropology served as a convenient justification for further colonialism, providing, perhaps, one of the clearest examples of the relationship between knowledge and geopolitical power. As Nicholas Thomas observed, 'the practice of governing [in the late-nineteenth century imperial world] ... entail[ed] an ethnographically specific knowledge of particular populations, enabled by various methods of documentation, accounts of disorder and backwardness, and conceptions of reform and advancement.'[16] The ethnographic imagination, it seemed, was very much part of the practice of conquest and colonization.[17]

Through the judges' post-trial reports, that ethnographic imagination was also implicated in the exercise of legal power – the power over life and death – for it was the judges' interpretation of Native culture that saved some First Nations people from the gallows and launched others into eternity. However, exercising mercy on the basis of that interpretation necessarily reinforced racial stereotypes, embedding them in the very practice of the law. The mercy dispensed to Native people was thus a savage mercy, premised as it was on a particular understanding of the ways of the 'savages.' Moreover, it was also one that was meant to be savage in its effects, for the mercy shown to Native peoples in British Columbia was not always motivated by compassion or benevolence but by the desire to terrify. If, as one European settler pointed out, man came closest to emulating God when he tempered justice with mercy, the God he had in mind must have been a wrathful rather than a forgiving one if the quality of the mercy shown to Native peoples is any measure.[18] In the final analysis, though the possibility of mercy allowed for the recognition of cultural diversity, the way mercy was dispensed and the rationale that underpinned it precluded any challenges to the hegemony of whiteness in British Columbia.

In what follows, I develop these themes by looking at a number of murder cases that resulted in capital convictions and that involved what we would now term 'cultural defences.' In all of them, the accused was a Native man. The victims were generally other Native men, but not always – as Amos 'Charley' Youmans discovered.

'The Indian Mind': the Cultural Construction of Provocation and Deterrence

It was December, and Charley had been dead for some months. Dead and buried; but not forgotten either at the Forks of the Skeena, where he had lived, or in distant Victoria. Indeed, at that moment, the events of the last months of his life were being recalled in solemn, if not loving, detail by a number of men in the provincial capital. Men, for instance, like miner John Bryant, who recalled saying, '"Charley, when you get to the Forks you'll have to make some compromise with the boys [meaning the Indians] up there."'[19] Charley apparently had agreed, having done so before when he found himself in a similar position. But for some reason, this time he never got around to it. His procrastination cost him his life, for, as others would attest, it led the middle-aged Indian sitting in the dock to cut Charley's throat.

Bryant was one of the witnesses for the defence in the trial of Ha-at, the Gitksan who stood accused of the murder of Charley, known to the court as Amos Youmans. In the summer of 1884, Ha-at approached trader Youmans in his store at the Forks of the Skeena River and, without a word and in the presence of several witnesses, plunged a knife into his neck. Youmans collapsed and was dead within half an hour. Ha-at offered no resistance during his arrest and was tried before Supreme Court Judge Henry Crease in December for murder. According to the Crown – represented by no less than the province's attorney-general – the case was a simple one: the killing was premeditated, there was no provocation, it took place in front of several eyewitnesses, and – if that were not enough to send the prisoner to the gallows – Ha-at himself admitted to the crime.

It was Ha-at's good fortune to have an able and imaginative lawyer in Montague Drake, his court-appointed counsel (and future Supreme Court justice). Drake disagreed with the Crown's reading of the facts, offering what we would now term a cultural defence. As many who lived along the Skeena knew, Ha-at's son, Billy Owens, had been killed in a spring canoe accident while he was working for Youmans. According to Drake, Gitksan law dictated that as an employer, Youmans was responsible for Billy Owens and should have gone to Ha-at immediately after the death, informed him of what had happened, and offered him some kind of compensation. Instead, Youmans chose to avoid Ha-at and his responsibilities. As the defence's witnesses testified, Youmans was fully aware of Gitksan law and the consequences that would befall anyone who violated it. According to Bryant, Youmans 'said he expected to make it all right by paying a small amount to the Indians' friends or people ... He knew what was customary to be done – he'd often done it before in disputes with Indians by paying a little to the offended parties.'[20] For whatever reason – perhaps fear – Youmans never sought out Ha-at.[21] So Ha-at found him.

Drake's defence was thus aimed at showing that Ha-at was pushed into taking Youmans's life and that his actions were prescribed by Gitksan law. The lawyer's strategy reflected one of the most common ways culture found its way into British Columbia's court rooms: in the discussion of provocation.[22] Both judges and defence counsel often made reference to the 'imaginary harms' and 'superstition' that 'impelled' Indians to act,[23] and to the need to consider how 'the Indian Mind' would perceive white actions.[24] Such value-laden language is enough to suggest that while these men were cultural pluralists they were still moral absolutists. Still, in their own way, judges and defence counsel recognized that 'wrongs' and 'harms' were culturally constructed. Acts that might not give offence to Europeans could inspire a lethal response from Native peoples. Thus, the courts could not, in all fairness, hold Natives to the same standard of behaviour expected of Europeans, for to do so would deny the cultural differences between the two groups.

Even in 1884, the degree of legitimacy given to cultural differences in Ha-at's case was not something new, evidence of the inevitable march of progress and enlightenment that accompanied British Columbia's transition to modernity. Since the fur trade period, European British Columbians had recognized that homicides perpetrated by Native peoples were often provoked by earlier killings that had gone unavenged or uncompensated. English traders, American mountainmen, and later the colony's judges even recognized these 'principles of vengeance' as 'law' – tribal or customary law, but law nonetheless.[25] David Cameron, Matthew Baillie Begbie, Joseph Needham, and Henry Pering Pellew Crease – British Columbia's first judges – were not so naïve as to assume that Native peoples discarded their laws with the change in European rule. These judges, in reporting on capital cases to the governor, acknowledged both the existence of Native laws and their legitimacy.[26]

For instance, in 1861 Vancouver Island Supreme Court Judge David Cameron recommended that Dick, an Aboriginal convicted of murdering a member of the Squamish Nation, have his sentence commuted, because, as the *British Colonist* reported, his 'father had been killed by Squamish Indians. He was a boy then, but his mother had brought him up to take vengeance on the tribe when he had an opportunity.'[27] Three years later, referring to how the executive had disposed of Dick's case, Cameron deemed Howamatcha a worthy recipient of the Queen's mercy, noting that a relative of his had been killed by a member of the victim's tribe. 'I believe the understood custom of the Indian tribes [in cases like this is] ... to avenge the death of a relative by the death of a member of the tribe which first inflicted the injury.'[28] As Ha-at's case suggests, judges continued to recognize that the dictates of Native law governed Native peoples' conduct into the late nineteenth century and the provincial period.

However, in arguing that Ha-at was provoked by a violation of Gitksan law and that the killing was prescribed by Gitksan culture, Drake – as did all the lawyers who had tried cultural defences before him – hoped only to secure a recommendation of mercy, not an acquittal, from the jury. In doing so, he could claim adherence to the broad principles of the rule of law while still acknowledging the importance of his client's cultural background. But for all his recognition of Gitksan custom, he considered it distinct from English law and of lesser standing: 'I do not put forward these considerations to blind you as to the *law* of the case,' he told them in his closing statement, 'that is clear & if it were a white man I should not think of it. But there are extraordinary circumstances which may well plead in the mitigation of the offence.'[29] Framed in this way, Drake's appeal to the jury for mercy did not challenge the racial order in British Columbia, but reinforced it, premised as it was on the notion that Native people were of diminished responsibility.

Judge Crease agreed with Drake's distinction, taking pains in his report on the case to distinguish judicial discretion – exercised by both the jury and himself – from the administrative discretion wielded by the executive. 'There is nothing *in the case itself* which called for the exercise of the mercy of the Crown,' he wrote, 'but there are considerations *external* to the case to which it is my duty to call attention as possibly influencing His Excellency's action in the matter.' Taking a rather peevish tone, the judge then outlined the circumstances leading to Youmans's death, attributing it to his miserly nature. 'If he had proclaimed the accident and offered any small reasonable compensation for the loss of the services of the lad ... everything would have passed off smoothly,' he told the secretary of state. 'Yet for the sake of saving a trifling compensation of a few blankets or $100 or overestimating his own influence, he deliberately chose to run the risk rather than pay; and paid the penalty of his meanness or rashness with his own life.'

However much Crease may have been annoyed by Youmans's negligence, he did not believe the cultural factors outlined by Drake were a matter for the jury to contemplate in coming to their decision, but went on to say that 'it would be very unwise for the pardoning power not to consider the matter.' While the final decision in the case lay with the executive, he felt that justice would be served if Ha-at's sentence were commuted to ten years' imprisonment – which it was.[30]

If the 'motives and springs of action by which the Indians [were] guided' were different from those that shaped the conduct of Europeans, so too were the punishments that deterred them.[31] Thus, in addition to taking account of culture in assessing motive, the executive was also called upon to consider the wider cultural impact of terror and mercy in rendering its decision on whether to carry out a capital sentence or commute it. Unlike Europeans, Native peoples were not necessarily terrorized by the spectre of the gallows. Given this cultural impediment to terror, hanging was not likely to deter would-be Native offenders.

In the wake of the execution of three Aboriginals for the murder of white settler Frederick Marks and his daughter Caroline Harvey in 1863, John Robson, editor of the *British Columbian,* wondered whether capital punishment should be applied to Indians, given the way they met death on the gallows. Though there was little doubt that capital punishment worked among Christians, 'in its application, however, to mankind in a pagan state, holding such a diversity of views as to a future state and the final destiny of man, there is still room for much argument.'[32] One need only look at 'their deportment on the scaffold,' he asserted, to doubt the efficacy of hanging. 'The stolid indifference with which the Indian listens to his sentence, the impatient eagerness with which he awaits the fatal hour, and the heroic calmness and fortitude with which he demeans himself upon the scaffold, even joyfully chanting his death song, all tend to show that he views the terrible ordeal ... with neither fear nor dislike. Indeed, it would appear from the manner in which both the victim and the relatives and people tend to regard an execution that they hold it to be a sort of honorable and heroic martyrdom.'[33] Until the Indians had assimilated Christian values sufficiently to view capital punishment with the awesome terror it deserved and thus to help the state make a 'good death,' it would be far better, Robson concluded, to devise a punishment that they would regard as degrading.[34]

Fifteen years of colonization, it seemed, did not diminish the cultural differences that made capital punishment ineffective, for in petitioning the minister of justice on behalf of Jacob, a Barclay Sound Aboriginal who had killed another in a drunken fight, eight white residents of the Sound argued that 'imprisonment will better serve the ends of justice inasmuch as by a native law the name of a person hanged is not permitted to be even mentioned by the members of the tribe to which he belonged.' Since no one could speak of the executed man or the deed that led to his downfall, *'the force of example would be materially weakened if the death sentence were carried out.'* [35] Given this, it would be wiser to impose a sentence of life imprisonment on Jacob. The executive agreed, commuting his sentence to ten years' imprisonment.

A similar case in 1884 illustrated that mercy, as well as terror, resonated differently across cultures. When Tattaguna was convicted of murdering another Native person while drunk, Judge Crease recommended showing mercy to the condemned man by allowing the execution to proceed. Why? Because it was his understanding that Native peoples considered imprisonment a crueller punishment. Echoing John Robson's sentiments two decades earlier, he noted, 'To an Indian especially of such a wild tribe incarceration for a term of years is slow torture far worse than death. It is a greater mercy to carry out the sentence.'[36]

While these examples show that European British Columbians believed that deterrence, like provocation, was culture-specific, the examples also suggest that exercising mercy could be motivated by a desire to punish better, not – as we tend to think – to punish less. In these cases, a sensitivity to cultural differences did not translate into the kind of compassion, forgiveness, and benevolence that we usually associate with the exercise of mercy. Instead, when mercy was dispensed to British Columbia's Native peoples it was done to make the white man's law more exemplary; to instil a terror greater than that wrought by the spectre of death by hanging. When it came to dealing with Aboriginal offenders, then, the distinctions between terror and mercy that Douglas Hay drew in his classic formulation of the ideological functions of the law disappear.[37] In a cross-cultural context, the words and acts of those who administer the law lose their meaning: terror becomes mercy and mercy terror. Thus, in assessing the ideological functions of the law, it is important to take the cultural, as well as the class, position of both rulers and ruled into account.

If a recognition of cultural differences shaped the exercise of administrative discretion – whether it was in understanding provocation or in weighing the impact of hanging or dispensing mercy – then it should come as no surprise that some British Columbians argued that the cultural differences between Indians and Europeans were so great as to exempt the former from the strict application of the 'Queen's law' all together. For instance, in his petition on behalf of Qutlnoh (whose case will be discussed later), former Hudson's Bay Company chief trader and surgeon William Fraser Tolmie asked Begbie and Crease whether it was not 'altogether premature[,] if not in the abstract unjust[,] that the rigors of modern English Law should be brought to bear in such cases as that of Qutlnoh.' This was especially the case, he continued, 'when it is remembered how many generations of the most civilized nations of Europe it took to get over this same superstitious belief in witchcraft of old [which] led to deeds that, whether sanctioned by law or winked at when performed, are now generally equally considered as wrong.'[38] According to Tolmie, justice required that the untutored be treated mercifully. Similarly, in making his case for Ha-at, defence counsel Drake argued that Indians relied on their tribal customs because of the negligence of the Dominion government. 'The Indians,' he told the jury, 'are in the care of the Dominion to teach them the law and the benefits of peace and order and to give them the instructions of civilization. Yet there has been no Indian Agent for the past 10 years or any representative of the law there.'[39] Given the government's neglect of its 'National children' it was only just that Ha-at's sentence be commuted.[40]

In the light of the paternalistic tone of remarks like these and the bloody record of British Columbia's judiciary over the nineteenth century, few people now would characterize British Columbia's judges as legal pluralists. While they certainly did not believe in the equality and legitimacy of all legal systems as modern pluralists do, the province's judges did recognize that the diverse peoples of British Columbia were governed in their behaviour by culturally prescribed rules of conduct. Moreover, they also believed that cultural diversity was something that should be taken into account in capital cases, particularly when it came to understanding motive and the deterrent value of punishment. The legal pluralism they practised, however, was of a very limited variety, for the power of culture to shape the disposition of a case was limited by how and where culture figured in the legal process. Culture could not transform guilt to innocence, though it was a mitigating factor that could divert someone from the gallows to the penitentiary. Nor was culture a matter of fact or law – that is, it was not a matter for juries or even judges to decide. Rather, it was a matter of executive discretion: the colonial governor and his Executive Council, or later, the governor general and the federal cabinet weighed culture behind closed doors and beyond the gaze of the public. Thus, while executive discretion alleviated the tension between the social need to acknowledge differences and the demands of the legal system to deny them – the tension, to use James Boyd White's characterization, between life and law – it also reinforced the structures of power by giving the executive, not the accused or members of his or her community, the power to determine where, when, and how culture would matter.[41]

Savage Mercy

Having looked at where Native culture entered into the legal process (in discussions of provocation and deterrence and as a factor in shaping the exercise of executive mercy), I now examine why cultural defences often worked to secure recommendations to mercy. I suggest that insofar as cultural defences worked, they worked as stories, and hence we need to pay attention to their qualities as narratives – to their 'poetic' qualities – and not just their forensic ones. As the writing on law and literature argues, the stories that persuade in the law are not simply informed by a thorough knowledge and artful manipulation of legal rules and procedures.[42] Forensic skill alone does not guarantee success; rather, the power to persuade in court – and outside it – depends on the degree to which the stories told incorporate the common-sense notions of the listeners regarding how the world works and how the people in it should behave. However, the plausibility of the stories also depended on who was doing the telling, on the tellers as well as their tales. It is to that I turn first.

Rendering culture visible to judges and jurors usually requires the intervention of experts who, by virtue of their professional training or membership in the culture in question, can provide the context that cultural outsiders need to understand the actions of the accused. In *Kimura*, for instance, the court heard testimony from two clinical psychiatrists who were familiar with Japanese culture; in *Ly*, the chairman of an association of Vietnamese refugees was called to explain the cultural significance of infidelity; and, leaving the sphere of the criminal court for a moment, in land claims cases in Canada, anthropologists loom large in explaining indigenous patterns of resource use and concepts of property and ownership.[43] The representations of these experts – both their testimony and the images of the culture they project – constitute culture in a powerful way, for it is largely on the basis of the specialized knowledge they convey that cultural defences succeed or fail.

No psychiatrists, anthropologists, or Native leaders found their way into the witness boxes of nineteenth-century courtrooms in British Columbia to explain the actions of Native people accused of murder; nor did those accused testify on their own behalf. However, while recognizable experts might have been lacking, expertise was not. In deciding whether or not to hang Qutlnoh, Begbie and the minister of justice heard from representatives of three different agents of colonization – missionaries, the Royal Navy, and the Hudson's Bay Company – each of whom commanded a certain status and respect in European society and each of whom had direct contact with the province's Native peoples. Qutlnoh was found guilty of murdering another Native man, Maulachah, at Fort Simpson in 1872.[44] As was the case with Ha-at, the killing appeared to be unprovoked, Qutlnoh shooting Maulachah in the back in full view of a number of witnesses. According to Qutlnoh himself, Maulachah had made him ill and caused his sisters to die by 'singing his medicine songs.'[45]

One of the principal witnesses for the defence was Anglican lay missionary William Duncan. Duncan had worked among the First Nations of the Northwest coast since 1859, establishing Metlakatla, the model Indian village located near Fort Simpson on the Alaska panhandle. Run according to Christian principles and a strict time-work discipline, the village stood as a monument to Duncan's missionizing and his belief that assimilation was the key to the survival of all indigenous peoples.[46] Duncan's experience among the Tsimshian made him a credible witness on both Native custom in general and the particular events under scrutiny. On the stand, Duncan testified that 'the general opinion among the Indians was that this man (Maulachah) had the power of life and death.'[47] Qutlnoh's actions were motivated by revenge and self-defence for harms inflicted by the supernatural powers – the 'ill wishing' as Duncan called it – of the medicine man.

Henry Wentworth Mist, who commanded H.M.S. *Sparrowhawk* and who had taken Qutlnoh into custody added his voice to Duncan's, recommending that the condemned man be shown mercy 'on the grounds that he was so impressed with the belief that Maulachah was the cause of his own illness ... he took the only alternative he believed in his power, and shot the man who had bewitched him.'[48] Mist's support was somewhat surprising, for unlike Duncan, he was not a man whose actions bespoke a particularly liberal attitude towards Natives. Mist's ship was regularly engaged in 'Indian patrol' on the coast, and just three years earlier, in 1869, he had sailed to the west coast of Vancouver Island and helped burn the houses and shell the canoes of the Hesquiat in an attempt to persuade them to turn over the murderers of the crew of the *John Bright*.[49] Nonetheless, Qutlnoh's case struck a chord with him – as it did with Hudson's Bay Company trader William Fraser Tolmie.

By the time of the Qutlnoh trial, Tolmie had been in the northwest for almost forty years and considered himself something of an expert on Indian affairs, having compiled a number of dictionaries of indigenous languages.[50] In his petition and accompanying letter, he confirmed that Native 'sorcerers' were often killed by relatives of their victims, as a way of securing both revenge and the status that would come from besting a powerful enemy. Indeed, 'as further proof of the Indian belief in such powers,' he noted, 'Thirty years ago two officers of the Hudson's Bay Company, one at Kamloops, and the other at McLeod's Lake in this province were assassinated by Indians on the supposition that they by sorcery had each caused the death of an Indian.'[51]

Though it might appear amateurish by modern standards, the expertise provided by the missionary and the officers of the Royal Navy and Hudson's Bay Company had a powerful effect, securing a commutation for Qutlnoh even though there was no groundswell of support for him, no petitions from his own people, and indeed, almost no discussion of his case in the popular press. The fact that the executive accepted their views on Native custom at face value, with nary a doubt raised, was in part a measure of the status these witnesses commanded. From the colony's beginnings on Vancouver Island, critics observed that political, economic, and social control was vested in a Hudson's Bay Company elite referred to as 'a squatocracy of skin traders,'[52] or somewhat more generously and accurately as the 'Family-Company-Compact,' a term that included members of the Royal Navy.[53] Although British Columbia shed its colonial status in 1871 when it joined Canada, Confederation did not diminish the power of this elite, who remained generally influential well into the late nineteenth century.[54] Though they never rivalled the HBC or the Royal Navy in terms of social status and economic power, the Christian missionaries who worked in British Columbia certainly had a degree of social standing because of their religious calling and were particularly influential in shaping public opinion and policy regarding Native peoples.[55]

Though the status of the witnesses for the defence certainly lent credence to Qutlnoh's cultural defence, cynics might argue that the commutation was possible because both the condemned man and his victim were Aboriginal. Since European British Columbians were not likely to care much about the victim or his killer, the executive could use the opportunity to look merciful without having to worry about enraging the sensibilities of a public bent on revenge. While the state was certainly concerned about the politics of death and managed capital punishment in that way, there was more to mercy than cynicism allows.[56] In any case, one could just as easily use the same set of facts to explain why the state might have hanged Qutlnoh. Here was an Indian who had killed another Indian: why not string him up as yet another example in a long series of examples? After all, few people would care – few people that 'mattered.' The point is that Qutlnoh was not hanged; nor was Ha-at, whose victim was white. Thus, while the status of the witnesses and the race of the condemned person and the victim were important in determining legal outcomes, these commutations suggest that other factors could and did influence the exercise of executive mercy.[57]

The juxtaposition of George Bell's case (which was tried at the same assizes) with Qutlnoh's suggests that the quality of the story told in court influenced the success or failure of a cultural defence and hence the exercise of mercy. More specifically, as W. Lance Bennett and Martha Feldman argue, the plausibility of specific stories told in court depended on the degree to which they corresponded to the 'implicit framework of social judgment that people bring into the courtroom from everyday life.'[58] This framework of judgment, or 'social knowledge,' is knowledge that is usually tacit, or unstated, about how the world works: it is what a society considers to be common sense and incorporates, among other things, assumptions about social roles and ideas about race, class, and gender.[59] Since that stock of social knowledge is itself organized in a narrative form, the plausibility of new stories is measured in terms of the degree to which they fit with the already existing ones that organize judges' and jurors' understanding of the world.[60] It is not that we have a huge inventory of detailed stories in our heads against which all subsequent stories are measured; instead, we possess the broad outlines, or as Bernard Jackson calls them, 'implicit structures,' of stories – a sense of how particular combinations of people, places, and actions should unfold.[61] Hence the degree to which the new stories fit is not measured in terms of specific details but rather in terms of their overall narrative coherence, a coherence defined by an internal consistency between the story's setting, its central action, and final resolution.[62] In assessing why cultural defences worked, then, we need to see where and how they corresponded with the social knowledge of judges and jurors, and what sort of internal coherence they possessed.

Both Lancashire-born George Bell and his victim, Thomas Datson, a 'half-breed,' worked in Robert Dunsmuir's coal mines outside Nanaimo and lived in neighbouring company cottages just twelve or thirteen yards apart. The physical proximity of the two cottages facilitated the intimate relations that developed between Datson and Bell's Native wife, Annie. According to the evidence produced at the trial, Bell, a much older man, had raised Annie from her infancy, and only recently had married her and fathered two children. When this extremely jealous man learned of what had taken place between Datson and his wife, he gave Datson twenty-four hours to leave Nanaimo. Though he quit his job and began making preparations to leave, Datson openly boasted of his deed in the company town, asserting he would do it again. This was too much for Bell, who armed himself with a double-barrelled shotgun and a knife and declared his intention to kill Datson 'so openly that people seemed not to believe him.'[63] They should have, for Bell was as good as his word.

Bell's supporters both inside and outside the courtroom emphasized the 'great'[64] and 'gross'[65] provocation that led him to kill his fellow miner. Bell was guided in his actions by male codes of honour that defined Datson's actions as insulting and a challenge to his masculinity and dictated that he respond as he did. Though the killing was premeditated, it could be excused. Indeed, in other jurisdictions similar cases had resulted in acquittals.

Nevertheless, the jury found Bell guilty and made no recommendation to mercy. Chief Justice Matthew Baillie Begbie, who presided over the Bell trial, agreed, and could see no reason why the condemned man's sentence should be commuted. In outlining his reasons, Begbie compared Bell's case with that of Qutlnoh. Though we might see both cases as involving cultural defences – a white, masculine, working-class one in the former case, and a Native, masculine culture in the latter – Begbie clearly did not. 'Qutlnoh's case really merits a more curious consideration,' Begbie told the secretary of state, 'based as his act was on a firm part of the *quasi*-religious belief of the Indians.'[66] Whereas 'culture' motivated Qutlnoh, George Bell's actions were not understood as being culturally driven. They appeared natural because, as a white man, Bell was a member of the hegemonic social group in the province. Hegemony erased culture; it made what was a set of culturally specific behaviours look universal.

However, whereas it might have been natural for men to kill men who seduced their wives as Bell did, his prior actions violated the very codes of masculine conduct on which he based his defence, thus rendering him an undeserving recipient of mercy.[67] According to the judge, Bell was 'much older than the girl, much more than old enough to be her father, and it was the height of folly to place all his happiness in such a match especially as he did not attempt to withdraw his Indian wife from the atmosphere of immorality which she must have perceived all around her.'[68]

A respectable and honourable man never would have married Annie – a much younger and Native woman – in the first place. But given that Bell did, he should have taken steps long before Datson's overtures to protect his young wife from the degrading environment of working-class Nanaimo. Had he done so, the tragedy never would have happened. In the light of his failure to fulfil his duties as a protector, Bell was left to hang.

More generally, the failure of Bell's story to secure a recommendation of mercy and a commutation, and the success of Qutlnoh's, stemmed from the intersection of the judge's social knowledge with the stories offered by the accused men. As a cultural insider – an Englishman – Begbie was able to understand the cultural codes that motivated Bell to act. While the social knowledge he shared with the accused man enabled him to understand his actions in killing Datson, it was not extensive enough to allow Begbie to empathize with Bell completely. Solidly middle class, Begbie might not have been favourably disposed to the plight of a working-class man who, in his eyes, was of questionable respectability. Bell's fate might be read as an example of familiarity breeding contempt and of John Donne's warning that a little knowledge was a dangerous thing: Begbie was familiar enough with Bell's kind to be able to criticize it, which, unfortunately for the Lancashire man, had fatal consequences.

Neither Begbie nor Crease was similarly situated to mount corresponding challenges to cultural defences put forward by Native peoples. As complete cultural outsiders, both judges and the executive lacked the kind of social knowledge about indigenous 'laws' that they possessed in cases where the accused was European. But this did not mean they lacked any framework of judgment with which to measure stories that involved Native peoples. In fact, they had a very sturdy one, which was provided by popularly shared ideas about Indians, ideas that had biblical origins and had been disseminated through art and literature, and by the nineteenth century, the popular press. Despite their long genealogy and the variety of media used to convey them, these ideas had changed very little in the four hundred years since Columbus and the first Europeans made contact with the indigenous peoples of the Americas. To Europeans, Indians were, first and foremost, different. They embodied the characteristics of natural man, and were either 'good' or 'bad,' leading lives characterized by liberty, simplicity, or innocence, on the one hand, or by licence, harshness, and deceit, on the other – depending, as Robert Berkhofer pointed out, 'on the observer's feelings about his own society and the use to which he wanted to put the image.'[69]

By the time Begbie and Crease were riding their circuits, European British Columbians were feeling decidedly positive about their own society and negative about the indigenous people who surrounded them. As settlement progressed and Native peoples became economically marginal, they were increasingly portrayed as savage, suspicious, superstitious, fickle, cunning, and covetous children given to acting on their emotions and perpetuating unspeakable barbarisms, from prostituting their women to eating human flesh.[70] Though these images had persisted for centuries, in the nineteenth century evolutionary theory gave them a patina of scientific authority they had not possessed before, laying the foundations for the new science of anthropology. According to the anthropologists, Indians represented an earlier stage of human development, the savage antecedents of European civilization. At once familiar but always different and inferior, Indians embodied all that white society was not.[71]

This ethnographic imagination coloured British expectations and their subsequent perceptions of life on the distant edges of empire, animating reports of indigenous uprisings in India and New Zealand, for instance, and less spectacularly, travel accounts and missionary tracts. Anyone seeking information about British Columbia in such literature would be confronted with the requisite chapter on 'The Indians,' a potted ethnography of the region's most numerous inhabitants. Duncan George Forbes Macdonald's *British Columbia and Vancouver Island* is a good example. Though its subtitle proclaimed it to be a 'description' of life in the colonies, its table of contents revealed none of the neutrality that one might expect of mere description. Instead, what Marianna Torgovnick calls a 'primitivist discourse' dominated.[72] Macdonald began chapter five with a discussion of the 'Human Species,' but moved in quick succession to describe the indigenous peoples of British Columbia, and by his choice of topics, simultaneously located them in a hierarchy of humanity: 'The Human Species – The Aborigines of British North America – Prominent Features in the Life and Character of the Indians – Slaves Horribly Abused – The 'Medicine Man' and the Dead – Mode of Scalping – Young Indians More Savage than the Old – Horrible Modes of Torture – Barbarous Conduct of an Old Squaw – Shocking Cruelties to an Old Man and Instance of Cannibalism – Horrible Massacre of Emigrants – Cruel Custom of Getting Rid of the Aged.[73]

Readers whose appetites were whetted by these fantastic and grotesque but all-too-brief 'descriptions' could sate themselves with entire books that put them *In the Wake of the War Canoe* or in other vantage points from which they were introduced to the *Scenes and Studies of Savage Life,* the ways of the *Ancient Warriors of the North Pacific,* or life *Among the An-ko-me-nums or Flathead Tribes of Indians of the Pacific Coast.*[74]

The fundamentally racial way of perceiving British Columbia embedded in this literature was also evident among its judges, particularly Matthew Baillie Begbie, for it was in his writing that the ethnographic and the legal imaginations were most clearly joined. The chief justice used his circuits through the colony and the province as opportunities to research its natural and human history. His observations were published in the proceedings of the Royal Geographical Society, and his report on the Indians of British Columbia was included in a larger Dominion government publication on the new province.[75] That report is worth quoting at length, for it reveals the kind of ethnographic sensibility that the chief justice possessed and was characteristic of the nineteenth century. 'The habits of the Indians are exceedingly simple,' the judge observed,

> probably such as are common to almost all societies in a low degree of organization. They appear to live very much on the 'village community' system, as described in 'Mayne's [Maine's] Ancient Law,' at least as regards land and its produce, and their fishing grounds. The chiefs owe their pre-eminence partly to birth or family connections, partly to personal attributes and the choice of the tribal family or tribe. The chiefs appear to acquire their predominance of wealth by voluntary contributions, or 'benevolences,' from those who admit their authority, offered sometimes from fear, sometimes from flattery, sometimes perhaps from motives of attachment. They preserve their influence by measures of recklessness and severity, or of wisdom, but principally perhaps by the generosity or lavishness with which they redistribute the wealth they have acquired; in fact, all this part of their polity very much resembles that of the Plantagenet Kings of England.[76]

Just as an anthropologist would, Begbie then went on to relate information about Indian dwellings, manufactures, marital practices, and religious notions.

That his ethnographer's eye was turned specifically towards capital cases is evident in his post-trial reports to the minister of justice. In explaining the actions of Attoo, a Native man found guilty of killing toll keeper George Jenkinson in 1879, the chief justice noted that Jenkinson was in the wrong place at the wrong time, having the misfortune of coming between a Native man bent on killing his unfaithful wife. In his experience, he wrote,

> the law of conjugal honor is very severe among the fishing tribes of the north west coast. Nothing prevents the wife from prostituting herself: in fact, it is rather a duty expected from her to do so, provided she brings the price to her husband. But it is a breach of duty to have relations with another man, gratis and still more, if she prostitute herself for money, and give the money to a favored lover. Then, there is not only dishonor, but loss. And in such a case the irritation of the husband is so great, that he often punishes the offence with death. I believe such was the provocation in the present case.[77]

Begbie was not exceptional in his joining of anthropology and law, for his fellow judge, Henry Crease, did the same thing. In explaining the actions of one Native man accused of killing another in a drunken rage, the well-educated and well-travelled Henry Crease made an analogy to 'Malays' 'running amok.'[78] If the custom in question had no parallels in his experience or reading, as was the case with Ha-at, Crease had no hesitations about conducting his own 'fieldwork,' making inquiries among the locals as to what constituted customary behaviour.[79]

Given the centrality of anthropology in the way judges saw the world, it did not require much of a leap of their ethnographic imaginations for them to believe that principles of vengeance or a fear of witchcraft could impel Native peoples to kill, particularly with the definition of culture that operated in the courts. When defence counsel and judges talked or wrote about culture, they tended to see it in positivistic terms: a set of rules that determined an individual's actions in a given set of circumstances. So for instance, when no compensation was forthcoming from Amos Youmans to the family of the man who had died while in his charge, Gitksan culture prescribed the proper course of action for the family – namely, the father – to take. Similarly, the principles of vengeance held that Dick had to kill a Squamish person to avenge the death of a relative who had met his end at the hands of another member of the Squamish Nation some years earlier. For British Columbia's lawmen there was an unproblematic, direct, and almost mechanical relationship between culture and action, between rules and outcomes. As such, the understanding of culture that animated nineteenth-century legal pluralism reduced Indians to little more than animals, portraying their actions as a set of reflexive responses chosen from a set repertoire of essential imperatives.

Ha-at and Qutlnoh escaped the noose, then, because the defences they offered were consistent with broadly shared, ethnocentric assumptions about how 'savages' would act, and because, presumably, they simply looked like Indians and their 'Indian-ness' was not at issue. Their otherness was confirmed by their criminal acts and reinforced by the culture that mandated them. Because of this consistency between their appearance, their actions, and the explanations offered for them, the cultural defences put forward for Qutlnoh and Ha-at resonated with the stories about Indians both the judge and executive possessed as part of their common sense. Their stories cohered in a way that George Bell's did not. In Bell's case, there was no such consistency between identity, action, and explanation. Bell was not, on first appearances, an 'other'; rather he was, from the judge and jury's perspective, 'one of us.' His actions, however, were definitely not those of a respectable white man, who should have had more sense not to get into such a situation in the first place, and to have more self-control when he did. There was thus a gap between the standard of responsibility set for white men and the behaviour of the particular white man who found himself in the dock. George Bell's murder of Thomas Datson might have been customary behaviour for a man under certain circumstances, but because he violated male codes of conduct in other aspects of his life, there was some doubt about the authenticity of his cultural affiliation; hence his cultural defence failed.

In *The Legal Imagination* (1973), James Boyd White asked his readers to 'think of law as ... a way of talking about people and their relationships' rather than focusing on how it talked to them.[80] One of the ways in which the law talks about people, whether it be through its rules or its personnel, is as caricatures rather than characters. Whereas 'character is the successful rendition of personality: believable, full, complex, living and breathing ... caricature is the reverse: it is a way of talking about people that reduces them to single, exaggerated aspects, to labels, roles, moments from their lives; it is narrow, two-dimensional, and unconvincing.'[81] But it is precisely because caricature simplifies that it is so effective as a rhetorical device in the law: caricature makes human actions and choices seem straightforward and uncomplicated, and in doing so, it makes the choices that judges and jurors must make about the guilt or innocence of an accused person much easier. While there is no doubt about the instrumental power of caricature, White wonders what the larger implications of talking about people in this way are.

If the caricatures of Native people that informed the exercise of mercy are any indication, talking about people that way sustained the racial ideology that underpinned colonization. The ethnographic eye that perceived cultural differences and hence saved some Indians from the noose did so by constructing them as exotic and inferior, as creatures of diminished responsibility who represented an earlier stage of human evolution. Ethnography was not without ideology – or, as many anthropologists have argued, ethnography *was* ideology: it was an expression of European colonial power, reinforcing 'an imperial sense of epistemic superiority.'[82] Thus, whether in the courtroom addresses of counsel or the written recommendations of the judge, British Columbia's lawmen were engaged in encoding and recoding difference. Every decision to commute that was based on cultural factors embedded racism into the very practice of the law. Exercising mercy thus reproduced relations of power even as it allowed a select few to escape them. As Catherine MacKinnon argued (albeit in a different context), the legal recognition of difference reproduces dominance.[83] Far from undermining racism, the savage mercy dispensed in British Columbia reinforced it.

Acknowledgments

An earlier version of this paper was presented to the Law and Society Association Conference in Toronto, Ontario, 1-4 June 1995. Research funding was provided by a President's Research Grant from Simon Fraser University. Thanks to the editor of this volume, Carolyn Strange, and the other contributors for their comments, and to Andy Parnaby for research assistance.

Notes

1 See Paul J. Magnarella, 'Justice in a Culturally Pluralistic Society: The Cultural Defense on Trial,' *Journal of Ethnic Studies* 19 (1991):65-84; Julia P. Sams, 'The Availability of the "Cultural Defense" as an Excuse for Criminal Behavior,' *Georgia Journal of International and Comparative Law* 16 (1986):335-54; and 'The Cultural Defense in the Criminal Law,' *Harvard Law Review* 99 (1986):1293-1311.
2 Sams, 'Availability of the "Cultural Defense,"' 342-3. Also see Magnarella, 'Justice in a Culturally Pluralistic Society,' 71-2.
3 *R. v. Ly* (1987), 33 C.C.C. (3d), 31-40.
4 Ibid., 35.
5 Ibid., 34.
6 Ibid., 35-9.
7 Sams, 'Availability of the "Cultural Defense,"' 335 and 352.
8 Keith Ralston, 'Jaded Justice' [a review of David Williams, *'The Man for a New Country': Sir Matthew Baillie Begbie* (Victoria, BC: Gray's Publishing 1977)], *Vancouver Sun* 2 December 1977, 37. In 1871, Native peoples constituted 70.8 per cent of the population of British Columbia.
9 Alfred Waddington, *Judicial Murder* (Victoria, BC: Alfred Waddington 1860).
10 See Michel Foucault, *Discipline and Punish: The Birth of the Prison* (New York: Pantheon Books 1977); Norbert Elias, *The Civilizing Process*, volumes 1 and 2 (1939; reprint, Oxford: Oxford University Press 1982) and Pieter Spierenburg, *The Spectacle of Suffering. Executions*

and the Evolution of Repression: From a Preindustrial Metropolis to the European Experience (Cambridge: Cambridge University Press 1984). For a very good introduction to all three, see David Garland, *Punishment and Modern Society: A Study in Social Theory* (Chicago: University of Chicago Press 1990), chs. 6 and 10.

11 Nikolas Rose, *Governing the Soul: The Shaping of the Private Self* (London: Routledge 1990).

12 On mercy as an expression of power, see Douglas Hay, 'Property, Authority and the Criminal Law,' in *Albion's Fatal Tree: Crime and Society in Eighteenth-Century England,* ed. Douglas Hay, Peter Linebaugh, John G. Rule, E.P. Thompson, and Cal Winslow, 17-63 (London: Allen Lane 1975); and Natalie Zemon Davis, *Fiction in the Archives: Pardon Tales and Their Tellers in Sixteenth-Century France* (Stanford, CA: Stanford University Press 1987).

13 Tina Loo, 'The Road from Bute Inlet: Crime and Colonial Identity in British Columbia,' in *Essays in the History of Canadian Law,* vol. 5: *Crime and Criminal Justice,* ed. Jim Phillips, Tina Loo, and Susan Lewthwaite, 112-42 (Toronto: Osgoode Society 1994). This theme is also developed in David Neal, *The Rule of Law in a Penal Colony: Law and Power in Early New South Wales* (Cambridge: Cambridge University Press 1991). See ch. 3 particularly. Also consult Greg Marquis, 'Doing Justice to "British Justice": Law, Ideology, and Canadian Historiography,' in *Canadian Perspectives on Law and Society: Issues in Legal History,* ed. W. Wesley Pue and Barry Wright, 43-70 (Ottawa: Carleton University Press 1988).

14 See Robin Fisher, *Contact and Conflict: Indian-European Relations in British Columbia, 1774-1890* (Vancouver: UBC Press 1977), ch. 4; George Stocking, *Victorian Anthropology* (New York: Free Press 1987); and Nicholas Thomas, *Colonialism's Culture: Anthropology, Travel, and Government* (London: Polity Press 1994).

15 See Thomas, *Colonialism's Culture,* chs. 4 and 5. On the appeal of the primitive, see Marianna Torgovnick, *Gone Primitive: Savage Intellects, Modern Lives* (Chicago: University of Chicago Press 1991). John Urry, *The Tourist Gaze* (London: Sage 1990), 142-4, touches briefly on 'ethnic tourism' and the racial aspects of tourism in general.

16 Thomas, *Colonialism's Culture,* 4.

17 George Stocking, ed. *Colonial Situations: Essays on the Contextualization of Ethnographic Knowledge* (Madison, WI: University of Wisconsin Press 1991), introduction; and Edward W. Said, *Orientalism* (1978; reprint, New York: Vintage 1994).

18 In petitioning the minister of justice on behalf of George Bell, whose case will be discussed below, Edwin Pimbury ended by quoting Portia from Shakespeare's *Merchant of Venice,* act 4, sc. 1, l. 182: 'An earthly power doth then show likest God's / When mercy seasons justice.' See National Archives of Canada [hereinafter NAC], RG 13, vol. 1409, file 56A, Edwin Pimbury to Dufferin, Victoria, July 1872, in the Capital Case File for George William Bell.

19 NAC, RG 13, vol. 1421, file 190A, Notes of Trial, 8 December 1884, Capital Case File for Haatq (or Aht).

20 Ibid.

21 Testimony of Itonia W. Diveria, *British Colonist,* 9 December 1884.

22 For an introduction to the issues in the Canadian context, see Timothy Macklem, 'Provocation and the Ordinary Person,' *Dalhousie Law Journal* 11 (1987):126-56.

23 See T. Loo, 'The Road from Bute Inlet.'

24 Bowser quote. In Tina Loo, 'Tonto's Due: Law, Culture, and Colonization in British Columbia,' in *Essays in the History of Canadian Law,* vol. 6: *British Columbia and the Yukon,* ed. Hamar Foster and John McLaren (Toronto: Osgoode Society 1995).

25 John Phillip Reid, 'Principles of Vengeance: Fur Trappers, Indians, and Retaliation for Homicide in the Transboundary North American West,' *Western Historical Quarterly,* 24, 1 (1993):21-43; and Hamar Foster, '"The Queen's Law Is Better than Yours": International Homicide in Early British Columbia,' in *Essays in the History of Canadian Law,* vol. 5: *Crime and Criminal Justice,* ed., Jim Phillips, Tina Loo, and Susan Lewthwaite, 49-60 (Toronto: Osgoode Society 1994).

26 On British Columbia's judges, see David R. Verchere, *A Progression of Judges: A History of the Supreme Court of British Columbia* (Vancouver: University of British Columbia Press 1988). On David Cameron, see *Dictionary of Canadian Biography* (Toronto: University of Toronto Press 1972), 10:115-18; on Henry Crease, see *Dictionary of Canadian Biography* (Toronto:

University of Toronto Press 1994), 13:228-31; and on Matthew Begbie, see *Dictionary of Canadian Biography* (Toronto: University of Toronto Press 1990), 12:77-81, and David R. Williams, *'The Man for a New Country': Sir Matthew Baillie Begbie* (Victoria, BC: Gray's Publishing 1977).

27 *British Colonist,* 8 November 1861.
28 Cameron to Kennedy, Victoria, 12 August 1864. Great Britain, Colonial Office, Correspondence Relating to Vancouver Island. CO 305/23, 87-90.
29 Capital Case File for Haatq or Aht, Drake's closing address, Notes of Trial, 8 December 1884 (emphasis added).
30 Ibid., Crease to secretary of state, Victoria, 15 December 1884.
31 NAC, RG 13, vol. 1409, file 57A, Petition on behalf of Qutlnoh, unsigned and undated in Capital Case File for Qutlnoh.
32 'Capital Punishment,' *British Columbian,* 23 May 1863.
33 Ibid.
34 On the importance to the state of making a good death and the limited amount of control they had in doing so, see especially Kathy Laster, 'Famous Last Words: Criminals on the Scaffold, Victoria, Australia, 1842-1967,' *International Journal of the Sociology of Law* 22 (1994):1-18; as well as Thomas Laqueur, 'Crowds, Carnival, and the State in English Executions, 1604-1868,' in *The First Modern Society: Essays in English History in Honour of Lawrence Stone,* ed. A.L. Beier, David Cannadine, and James M. Rosenheim, 305-56 (Cambridge: Cambridge University Press 1989); and Peter Linebaugh, 'The Tyburn Riot against the Surgeons,' in *Albion's Fatal Tree: Crime and Society in Eighteenth-Century England,* ed. Douglas Hay, Peter Linebaugh, John G. Rule, E.P. Thompson, and Cal Winslow, 65-118 (London: Allen Lane 1975).
35 *British Colonist,* 11 December 1878 (emphasis added).
36 Judge's Report, *R. v. Tattaguna,* 11 December 1885, enclosed in NAC, RG 13, vol. 1423, file 208A, Crease to secretary of state, Victoria, 11 December 1885, Capital Case File for Tattaguna.
37 Hay, 'Property, Authority and the Criminal Law.'
38 Tolmie's petition, Victoria, 15 July 1872, Capital Case File for Qutlnoh.
39 Capital Case File for Haatq or Aht, Drake's closing address, Notes of Trial, 8 December 1884.
40 This was how O.C. Bass, deputy attorney-general of British Columbia characterized Native peoples. NAC, RG 10, vol. 7472, file 19153-7, Bass to Williams, Victoria, 14 August 1929, in New Westminster Agency, murder of Lee Kee High by James Wallace, 1929.
41 James Boyd White, 'Telling Stories in the Law and in Ordinary Life: the *Oresteia* and "Noon Wine,"' in *Heracles' Bow: Essays in the Rhetoric and Poetics of the Law,* ed. James Boyd White, 168-91 (Madison, WI: University of Wisconsin Press 1985).
42 For an introduction, see the special issue of the *Michigan Law Review* 87 (1989) edited by Kim Lane Scheppele; M. Lance Bennett and Martha S. Feldman, *Reconstructing Reality in the Courtroom* (New Brunswick, NJ: Rutgers University Press 1981); and James Boyd White, *Heracles' Bow* and his *Legal Imagination: Studies in the Nature of Legal Thought and Expression,* abridged edition (1973; reprint, Chicago: University of Chicago Press 1985).
43 On *Kimura,* see Magnarella, 'Justice in a Culturally Pluralistic Society,' 72; on *Ly,* see *R. v. Ly* (1987), 33 C.C.C. (3d), 33; and on anthropologists in modern British Columbian courtrooms, see Dara Culhane, 'Adding Insult to Injury: Her Majesty's Loyal Anthropologist,' *BC Studies* 95 (1992):66-92.
44 For details, see Capital Case File for Qutlnoh.
45 Prisoner's Statement taken on H.M.S. *Sparrowhawk* by H.W. Mist JP, 24 November 1871, ibid.
46 On Duncan, see Jean Usher, *William Duncan of Metlakatla* (Ottawa: National Museums of Canada 1974).
47 Notes of Trial, *R. v. Qutlnoh,* Victoria Assizes, 5 July 1872, Begbie and Crease JJ. Capital Case File for Qutlnoh.
48 H.W. Mist, RN, W.H. McNeill, W.F. Tolmie, and William Duncan, Victoria, to the governor general of Canada, 8 July 1872, ibid.

49 On the '*John Bright* affair' see Barry Gough, *Gunboat Frontier: British Maritime Authority and the Northwest Coast Indians, 1846-1890* (Vancouver: UBC Press 1984), 125-8.
50 On Tolmie, see *Dictionary of Canadian Biography* (Toronto: University of Toronto Press 1982), 11:885-8.
51 Petition from W.F. Tolmie, Victoria, 15 July 1872, Capital Case File for Qutlnoh.
52 Charles Aubrey Angelo, *Idaho: A Descriptive Tour and Review of Its Resources and Route, with a Sketch of British Misrule in Victoria, V.I.* (San Francisco: H.H. Bancroft 1865), 8-9, cited in Tina Loo, *Making Law, Order, and Authority in British Columbia, 1821-1871* (Toronto: University of Toronto Press 1994), 34.
53 Lionel H. Laing, 'The Family-Company-Compact,' *Washington Historical Quarterly* 22 (1931):117-28.
54 On the lingering influence of the colonial bench, see Hamar Foster's essay in *Law and Justice in a New Land: Essays in Western Canadian Legal History*, ed. Louis Knafla (Toronto: Carswell 1986).
55 See Fisher, *Contact and Conflict*, ch. 6; and more generally J.R. Miller, *The Skyscrapers Hide the Heavens: Indian-White Relations in Canada* (Toronto: University of Toronto Press 1991) and John Webster Grant, *Moon of Wintertime: Missionaries and Indians in Encounter since 1534* (Toronto: University of Toronto Press 1984).
56 On the management of capital punishment in Canada, see Carolyn Strange, 'The Lottery of Death: Capital Punishment in Canada, 1867-1976,' *Manitoba Law Journal*, 23, 3 (1996):594-619.
57 On the importance of 'character' (which includes race, class, gender, age, and a variety of other factors) in legal decision-making, see J.M. Beattie, *Crime and the Courts in England, 1660-1800* (Princeton, NJ: Princeton University Press 1986), 440-9; and Peter King, 'Decision-Makers and Decision-Making in the English Criminal Law, 1750-1800,' *Historical Journal* 27 (1984):25-58; and Carolyn Strange, 'Patriarchy Modified: The Criminal Prosecution of Rape in York County, Ontario, 1880-1930,' in *Essays in the History of Canadian Law*, vol. 5, ed. Phillips et al., 207-51. On the importance of these factors in capital punishment cases specifically, see K.L. Avio, 'The Quality of Mercy: Exercise of the Royal Prerogative in Canada,' *Canadian Public Policy* 13 (1987):366-79; Constance Backhouse, *Petticoats and Prejudice: Women and Law in Nineteenth-Century Canada* (Toronto: Osgoode Society 1991), 119-24; and Strange, 'The Lottery of Death: Capital Punishment in Canada, 1867-1976.'
58 Bennett and Feldman, *Reconstructing Reality*, 3.
59 'Social knowledge' from Bernard S. Jackson, *Law, Fact, and Narrative Coherence* (Merseyside: Deborah Charles Publications 1988), 61.
60 Ibid.
61 Ibid., 62.
62 Bennett and Feldman, *Reconstructing Reality*, ch. 3.
63 Notes of Evidence taken at the trial *R. v. Bell*, for the murder of Thomas Datson. Nanaimo Assizes, 11 July 1872. Capital Case File for George Bell.
64 Petition, n.d., signed by forty-eight men asking that Bell's sentence be commuted. Enclosed in Bishop to Howe, Victoria, 26 July 1872, ibid.
65 Petition, n.d. signed by sixty-two men asking that Bell's sentence be commuted, Ibid.
66 Note attached to Notes of Trial, *R. v. Bell*, Capital Case File for George Bell.
67 This point is developed by Strange in 'Patriarchy Modified,' in *Essays in the History of Canadian Law*, vol. 5, ed. Phillips et al.
68 Note attached to Notes of Trial, *R. v. Bell*, Capital Case File for George Bell.
69 Robert F. Berkhofer, Jr., *The White Man's Indian: Images of the American Indian from Columbus to the Present* (New York: Alfred A. Knopf 1978), 27-8. Also see Peter Mason, *Deconstructing America: Representations of the Other* (New York: Routledge 1990); and Anthony Pagden, *The Fall of Natural Man: The American Indian and the Origins of Comparative Ethnology* (Cambridge: Cambridge University Press 1982).
70 Fisher, *Contact and Conflict*, ch. 4; and Loo, 'The Road from Bute Inlet.' On the image of the Indian in Canada generally, see Daniel Francis, *The Imaginary Indian: The Image of the Indian in Canadian Culture* (Vancouver: Arsenal Pulp Press 1992).

71 Berkhofer, 49-55; also see Stocking, *Victorian Anthropology*, ch. 3.
72 Torgovnick, *Gone Primitive*, Introduction.
73 Duncan George Forbes Macdonald, *British Columbia and Vancouver's Island* ... (London: Longmans 1862), Table of Contents.
74 W.H. Collison, *In the Wake of the War Canoe* (London: E.P. Dutton 1915); Gilbert Malcolm Sproat, *Scenes and Studies of Savage Life* (London: Smith, Elder 1868); Charles Harrison, *Ancient Warriors of the North Pacific; the Haidas, Their Laws, Customs, and Legends, with Some Historical Account of the Queen Charlotte Islands* (London: H.F. and G. Witherby 1925); and Thomas Crosby, *Among the An-ko-me-nums, or Flathead Tribes of the Pacific Coast* (Toronto: W. Briggs 1907).
75 Matthew Baillie Begbie, 'Journey into the Interior of British Columbia,' *Journal of the Royal Geographical Society*, 1861; and 'A Paper on the "Benches" or Valley Terraces of British Columbia,' *Journal of the Royal Geographical Society*, 1871; and Hector Louis Langevin, *Report of the Hon. H.L. Langevin, C.B., Minister of Public Works* (Ottawa: I.B. Taylor 1872). Also see Williams, 'The Man for a New Country,' ch. 4.
76 Langevin, *Report of the Hon. H.L. Langevin, C.B., Minister of Public Works*, 25.
77 Notes of Trial, *R. v. Johnson alias Attoo (Indian)*, for the murder of George Jenkinson, before Begbie at the Glenora Assizes, Cassiar, 25 August 1879. NAC, RG 13, vol. 1417, file 137A, Capital Case File for Attoo alias Johnson.
78 Crease to secretary of state, Victoria, 10 December 1878. NAC, RG 13, vol. 1416, file 132A, Capital Case file for Jacob.
79 Crease to secretary of state, 15 December 1884. Capital Case File for Haatq.
80 White, *The Legal Imagination*, abridged edition, 109, and ch. 3 generally.
81 Ibid., 113.
82 Thomas, *Colonialism's Culture*, 7. For an oft-cited influential critique of anthropology, see James Clifford and George E. Marcus, *Writing Culture: The Politics and Poetics of Ethnography* (Berkeley: University of California Press 1984).
83 Catherine MacKinnon, 'Difference and Dominance: On Sex Discrimination,' in *Feminism Unmodified: Discourses on Life and Law*, ed. Catherine MacKinnon, 32-45 (Cambridge, MA: Harvard University Press 1987).

5

Discretionary Justice: Political Culture and the Death Penalty in New South Wales and Ontario, 1890-1920

Carolyn Strange

Although justice and discretion have coexisted for centuries, their relationship in modern bureaucratic settings is uneasy. To legal minds trained in the precepts of formal rationality, justice is associated with precise rules and strict measurement, whereas discretion connotes idiosyncratic modes of governance typical of premodern polities. Since the Enlightenment, successive waves of reformers have tried to bind law to the stiff logic of rules, but discretionary administrative procedures have persistently bedevilled their projects. Even the most ruthlessly legalistic regimes allow scope, often unintentionally, for individualized judgments and the modification or annulment of punishment. Apparently the chief difference between traditional forms of legal decision-making, where Justice's eyes remain wide open, and modern bureaucratic procedures, where that noble lady is blind, is that formalistic, rule-bound justice aims to constrain discretion, yet never completely contains it.[1]

Pockets of discretionary decision-making linger in bureaucratic settings in spite of formally articulated procedural rules. Keith Hawkins observes that in modern democratic states 'discretion tends to be squeezed out to, or effectively assumed by, the periphery, where it may be exercised largely invisibly and immune from organizational control.'[2] Whenever critics discover pools of discretion they demand that administrators mop them up, either by restricting the scope of discretion or by reducing the number of discretionary actors. But discretion has a habit of bubbling up through the substratum of legal rules, placing modern administrators in the uncomfortable position of defending apparently unregulated forms of decision-making in the same breath as they extol the virtue of the rule of law. Where discretion persists, politicians and legal actors attempt to legitimate its more obvious expressions by connecting it to broader political goals and cultural forms. How their delicate balancing act – playing the rule of law against discretionary justice – is performed, and whether or not it appears credible to critical observers, depends both on the skills of legal actors and on the political and cultural context of decision-making.

Nowhere is this uneasy equilibrium more apparent than in executive disposition of capital cases. If discretion tends to be 'squeezed out' to the capillaries of bureaucracies, to the activities of unsupervised minor players, it also remains at their heart, in the form of executive justice. Whereas recent studies of discretion in the criminal justice context have analyzed judicial sentencing, prosecutorial charging, or police arrest proclivities, the administration of the death penalty has received comparatively little attention, especially in countries such as Canada and Australia, where abolitionists triumphed a generation ago.[3] Not surprisingly, social scientists and legal scholars have lost interest in capital case discretion, instead favouring more pressing concerns that capture current headlines.

Until the mid-twentieth century, when the death penalty was still in effect, Australian and Canadian academics, politicians, and public petitioners closely questioned capital case review practices.[4] Recent attempts to reintroduce the death penalty in these and other countries suggest that scholars might well return to the debates that once animated discussions about capital punishment. In fact, arguments about the anomalously discretionary character of capital punishment administration ultimately pushed liberal democratic nations to abolish the death penalty. Tenderhearted objections to killing criminals played a relatively minor role.[5] By the 1960s and 1970s most Western states, faced with a barrage of accusations that executive justice was unfair and unaccountable, eventually found the old balancing act too difficult to sustain.[6]

Uncovering the history of capital punishment and its administration leads to the juncture of politics, culture, and the law – a territory best charted with a variety of methodological approaches. Looking at discretionary justice in an historical context grounds the high-ranging view of political, anthropological, and legal theorists in the terrain of specific political cultures and legal forms.[7] Here, my focus on turn-of-the-century New South Wales (NSW) and Ontario scrutinizes discretionary justice from angles unavailable to contemporary onlookers, since the public was never fully apprised of the secret bureaucratic and cabinet procedures that lay behind executive decisions. Besides tabulating the trends in case dispositions, I recount some of the political disputes that fed into individual case outcomes. Only through examining public discussions and private correspondence concerning capital cases can one begin to place discretionary legal acts in the larger realm of political culture in these two jurisdictions.[8] If, as Modris Eksteins argues, nations at war tend to reveal their core values, it is also arguable that executives, faced with the unpalatable decision whether to execute or to commute, articulate the central cultural tenets of their polity.[9] Thus, analyzing capital case dispositions as expressions of political culture means concentrating less on the legal rules governing capital crime and the death penalty in favour of examining the political values expressed in the course of discretionary executive justice.

Executive Justice: Contrasting Pictures

Patterns of NSW and Ontario capital case dispositions at the turn of the century clearly indicate that the executive in Australia's most populous state was more inclined to mercy than its Canadian counterpart. To explore what accounts for this contrast leads us to differences in law but, more significantly, to the unique histories and political cultures of two polities founded on British precepts of justice. First, it is clear that dissimilar state forms, with Australian states retaining the right to formulate and administer criminal law, and Canadian provinces, left merely to administer federal policy, produced contrasting styles of executive justice. In both contexts, cabinet members, led by ministers of justice, bore the responsibility to make life and death decisions, but Canada's more elaborate federal justice bureaucracy mediated between the executive and potential sources for emotive appeals to mercy.

The other obvious distinction between the frameworks of executive decision-making in NSW and Canada was the scope of capital statutes. In contrast to the Canadian Criminal Code, which restricted the death penalty essentially to murder and treason, NSW's capital statutes remained broader than either Canada's or England's because legislators stubbornly refused to strike attempted murder, rape, and carnal knowledge of a girl younger than ten off the roster of capital crimes.[10] With so many more cases to consider, particularly ones that did not so readily inspire eye-for-an-eye retributivism, the NSW executive could afford to be merciful more often. Execution and commutation statistics confirm that, in practice, the NSW executive, like its common law counterparts elsewhere, essentially restricted capital punishment to murderers. State politicians evidently preferred to maintain the symbolic terror of the law, even if they rarely had the nerve to execute.

But these institutional differences only go part way to explaining why condemned persons in NSW were more likely to live than were those who faced the gallows in Ontario. To explore further, we need to probe the differences between these polities' political cultures. As Edward Lehman argued, the legal and political institutions that guide and govern decision-making do not on their own determine how actions will be legitimated or questioned. Rather, political culture is also produced through collective symbols (such as flags or anthems) and 'the doctrines for integrating and rendering them plausible' (such as democracy or liberalism).[11] Ontario and NSW shared legal and political institutional forms, and they were both governed according to formal precepts of parliamentary democracy, but they did not share a common history. Although the concept of British justice was officially vaunted as a vital component in the foundation of both jurisdictions, the former penal colony of NSW provided less fertile ground than Ontario for its unquestioned celebration. The infamous larrikinism in the Australian character emerged in explicit challenges to the executive's authority to dispense capital justice. Whereas the NSW Labor party became the chief exponent of formal abolitionist rhetoric, Ontarians did not develop a collective voice against the death penalty and its administration. Rooted in their proud, counter-revolutionary heritage, Ontarians were more deferential towards the executive arm of government and less inclined to question the merits of capital punishment as a crime-fighting measure. If the snap of the lash and the clang of convict chains still rang in the ears of Australian Labor men, the image of abortive rebellions rightly put down by authorities lingered in the minds of Ontarians. Put simply, in NSW, political culture bolstered expressions of executive mercy; in Ontario, the political culture supported the Canadian executive's relative ill-disposition to lenience (Table 5.1).

This is not to suggest that the Australian cabinet was uniformly merciful, nor the Canadian cabinet unremittingly severe. In fact, in considering cases arising from Ontario courts between 1890 and 1920, the Canadian executive commuted almost half. At the same time, its NSW counterpart commuted eight cases out of ten. What these statistics do suggest is that differences in commutation patterns are traceable not only to the peculiar features of colonial history, but to racial, gender, and class politics, all of which made up the mosaic of political culture in NSW and Ontario. These factors help explain the inclination of executives to commute some condemned and not others. For instance, in neither Ontario nor NSW was a single woman executed during this period. Condemned Aboriginals were likely to end up on the gallows in Ontario whereas their counterparts in NSW were frequently subjects of mercy. In contrast, foreigners did not do well when seeking mercy from NSW cabinets, yet their rates of commuta-

Table 5.1

Overall commutation rates in New South Wales and Ontario, 1890-1920

Jurisdiction	Number of capital cases	% commuted
New South Wales	221	79.6
New South Wales (murder only)	122	71.3
Ontario	121	46.3

Note: Cases modified on appeal not included.
Sources: See Tables 5.2 and 5.3.

tion were actually higher than that of Anglo-Celts in Ontario. And in both jurisdictions, the propensity towards mercifulness rose sharply by the 1910s, as a host of other countries and states wiped the death penalty off their statute books.[12] Global statistics on case dispositions outline important contrasts in the picture of executive justice in NSW and Ontario cases; these statistics give the impression of one jurisdiction dispensing mercy more generously than another. But they also mask the complex processes through which legal and political actors struggled to find a coherent fit between law, politics, and culture.

British Justice and Cultural Values

The master concept of British justice has, since the establishment of constitutional monarchy in the late seventeenth century, been invoked both in the adjudication of legal disputes and at a broader level of collective identity in common law jurisdictions. British subjects were 'British' not as an accident of geography and history, but as a result of living under the benign rule of British justice. As Canadian historian Greg Marquis puts it, 'British justice and British liberty were not simply pillars of elite ideology or state hegemony, but concepts deeply enshrined in popular culture.'[13] This 'potent fiction' of fairness inspired popular faith in the law as a remedy for injustice, even as the law legitimated and perpetuated class (not to mention race and gender) inequality.[14] Though they might not enjoy power or wealth, the most benighted of colonial settlers could reassure themselves that they possessed something – access to British justice – that less civilized peoples could only envy. British Virgin Islanders, for instance, continue to construct 'national' identity by honouring their position as law-abiding beneficiaries of British justice.[15] Bundled with this concept are allied political values, including democracy, freedom, and equality. But above all, British justice signifies fair play. Maintaining the credibility of discretionary justice accordingly depends on its consistency with these cultural concepts. As we will see, turn-of-the-century politicians in NSW and Canada could not appeal to democracy to legitimate executive justice in capital case dispositions; fair play was another story. As an ideal allied to natural equity – the welcome friend against the rule of law's cold embrace – fair play provided a defensible, though increasingly contestable, niche for discretionary justice to operate over this period.

Although both Australians and Canadians adapted English laws to local conditions and adhered to the principles of British justice, the contrasts in Canadian and Australian history produced distinct political cultures and, as it transpired, stark differences in ways that executive justice was represented and understood by its detractors and defenders. In Australia, and NSW in particular, those who had made fortunes in grazing or the gold-rush gloried in the new country's miraculous progress and made a conscious effort to forget the convict past, whereas Labor leaders, who spoke for ordinary blokes, refused to forget that British justice had historically manifested itself in terror. As well, the greater concentration of Irish Catholics in the Australian population fed a further current of bitterness towards British laws and institutions into the mix of Australian political culture.[16] In Canada, especially Orange-dominated and overtly Loyalist Ontario, the idealist rendition of British justice was more tenable.[17] Not only had the British preserved Ontarians from the encroachment of Americans in the War of 1812, but British military might had conquered Ontario's nearest rival: French, Catholic Quebec. Ontario's dominant political values of conservatism and deference were forged in this context of anti-Americanism and frostiness towards Quebec Catholic culture.[18] Disputes over the merits and demerits of the death penalty in NSW and Ontario were influenced by these contrasting views on British justice as it had manifested itself in distinct colonial histories.

Outwardly, NSW and Ontario shared many similarities by the turn of the twentieth century: white settlers had claimed a vast wilderness and had successfully tamed it, not only through land cultivation and the dispossession and subjugation of Native peoples, but by establishing the rule of law – British-style. Both jurisdictions were leading players in newly federated unions which, in turn, were stars among the so-called white dominions of the British Empire.[19] But the indelible difference between Ontario and NSW political culture remained their histories. In school texts and songs of Empire, Ontarians proudly traced their spiritual lineage to loyalism; in NSW, anglophiles might sing the same songs, but to drown out lingering doubts about the state's convict roots. British traditionalists had also to contend with the competing voices of Labor men and women, who preferred anti-authoritarian bush ballads to God Save the King.[20] In English Canada, puffed with pride over its imperial status at the turn of the century, the necessity to hold a strict line against criminals could be linked more persuasively with British justice than it could in NSW, the notorious penal colony where British justice had seemed anything but fair to those who suffered under its yoke. In NSW, petitioners who campaigned for the life of individuals, as well as abolitionists who opposed the death penalty on principle, could tap richer cultural resources. More than any other factor, the emergence of a vibrant labour movement in NSW (in contrast to the almost total absence of a labour voice in mainstream Canadian politics in the period) ensured that capital punishment retained a stronger whiff of tyranny in the Antipodes. The Australian propensity to question the state's right to inflict violence underwrote the NSW executive's readiness to commute; in Ontarian political culture, the less contentious virtues of British justice preserved the Canadian cabinet from serious challenges to its stingier commutation practices.

Still, harmonizing executive decisions with political culture was never a simple matter, hastily disposed of. How then did Canadian and NSW politicians and bureaucrats maintain equilibrium between the rule of law and discretion when they disposed of capital cases? The short answer is: gingerly. A longer reply requires considering how politicians and the public perceived crime, justice, and punishment in these two jurisdictions founded on English criminal law and the ideal of British justice. Just as power relations are central to political culture, so is the notion of justice central to legal culture. As legal anthropologist Lawrence Rosen argues in regard to Islamic justice, law and culture are intimately linked, not only by qadi judges, but through supposedly rational versions of Western jurisprudence and criminal justice bureaucracies. Thus the law, like any cultural form, amalgamates 'categories and concepts whose distinctive qualities must be carefully unpacked.'[21] Such values as truth and reason are common to all legal systems but they must be expressed in terms that conform to cultural logic to be considered authoritative. Few capital case dispositions in NSW or Ontario were undisputed in this period (at the very least by condemned persons or relatives of victims), but in neither jurisdiction were decisions to execute or commute sufficiently controversial to topple an administration. More important, abolitionist sentiment in Canada and NSW failed to dismantle the practice of capital justice altogether. In spite of sporadic protests, or, in the case of NSW, concerted Labor party opposition, politicians managed to maintain the credibility not only of the death penalty but also its discretionary administration as consistent with British justice. In fact, once in power in 1910, even the Labor party preferred to retain the death penalty *de jure,* but to restrict its infliction through discretionary justice.

At the level of individual case dispositions, executive justice also expressed hierarchical notions of race, class, gender, and ethnic differences. Here again, distinctions in political culture between NSW and Ontario were evident. For the vast majority of Ontarians condemned to capital punishment – predominantly poor Anglo-Celts, francophones, and foreign-born men – petitioners had little to trade on when it came to presenting pleas for mercy. When Ontario judges and Canadian Executive Councils looked at the characters of the condemned, they observed men (and the occasional woman) whose cultural assets left them with little in their favour. Fearful of the growing numbers of 'foreign' immigrants who had not yet benefited from the civilizing influence of British justice, Anglo-Celtic jurymen were easily convinced to convict non-British citizens on capital charges. Yet the values of British justice also prompted Canadian cabinets to look closely at the rank unfairness that typically occurred in foreigners' trials. Ironically, foreign nationals' supporters could shame Canadian cabinets for failing to uphold those very values. Although federal politicians publicly fulminated against the dangers posed by foreigners, and declared that Canada must retain the death penalty on that account, if no other, the executive quietly weeded out many cases that smacked of injustice.

In turn-of-the-century NSW, the burden of class, more than ethnicity or race, emerged as the principal argument against capital punishment. While Labor men provided a formal parliamentary voice for criticism of executive justice, they were not the only New South Welshmen who valued battling against the odds over the abstract and historically hollow concept of British justice. Even before the tragedy at Gallipoli inspired the ANZAC legend of the Australian fighting spirit, the 'Aussie battler,' the quintessential little guy, was adored in bush legends.[22] In campaigns for commutation, he often made an effective stand-in for the poor and rough men who typically faced capital charges. Foreigners, in contrast, inspired no such champions. Prior to the introduction of the infamous 'White Australia' policy in 1901, the immigration of people other than English-speaking, Christian Anglo-Celts had slowed to a trickle after the gold boom gave way to the uncertainties of agricultural and industrial production. Foreign nationals had fewer communal resources to tap than their Ontario counterparts when they faced the gallows. Racism was enshrined as official Australian policy, espoused by Labor men no less passionately than by Liberal politicians. Indeed, 'White Australia' was so appealing an ideal because it promised to protect ordinary 'diggers' against competition and to give working-class Australians a greater stake in the national wealth.[23]

Racial hierarchies bore a different character when it came to Aboriginals, as opposed to European foreigners who were not so readily identified as 'savages' (as Tina Loo discusses in her chapter). In both Canada and Australia, it was not unusual at the turn of the century for authorities to predict that indigenous peoples would, through disease and inferior constitutions, eventually die out.[24] In Canada, however, there were far more Native peoples who belied that prediction by surviving the encroachment of whites, particularly in the Prairies, the West, and the far north. In Ontario, a sizeable population of Ojibwa and Six Nations peoples lived in the province, albeit primarily in the north and on reserves distant from the principal cities. Twin federal policies of containment and assimilation had been effectively imposed since the 1870s, and Native peoples in Ontario were among the most integrated in white economic, religious, and political life. Hence, Ontarians had less reason than Maritimers to assume that Aboriginals would soon disappear, and they differed from Westerners whose memories of the North West Rebellion fuelled fears of 'savage' reprisals.[25] Cultural defences for Ontario Natives were rarely voiced and singularly unsuccessful.

In NSW, where predictions of Aboriginal extinction were authoritatively asserted, there was more scope for the brand of patronizing mercy that was often demonstrated in British Columbia in the same period. When European ethnographers and journalists studied Aboriginal peoples in turn-of-the-century NSW, their reports were filled with accounts of their being remnants of an ancient race, doomed to peter out. In 1910, the NSW Aboriginal Protection Board was established to see that their passing was supervised in an (allegedly) humanitarian manner. It was not until the mid-twentieth century that the persistence of the Aboriginal population and its drift to towns and cities inspired a concerted shift to assimilationist policies.[26] At the turn of the century it was still possible for white Australians to view Aboriginals with a combination of pity and contempt, and thereby to see them as less than fully culpable beings. Only a small number of Aboriginals, notably Jimmy Governor and his two accomplices in a spate of brutal murders of whites, were judged fully responsible for their actions. In most cases, even ones where Aboriginal men were convicted of capital crimes against whites, they reaped the meagre trade-offs of colonization and white racism.

Disposing of capital cases involving female defendants also required men to evaluate persons they presumed to be inferior to, or at the very least substantially different from, themselves. Feminists assumed a critical role in ensuring that women's murders would be understood differently from the vast majority of capital cases that concerned men's violence. Although suffragists in Canada and Australia argued for the right to participate equally in politics and the professions, calls for equality in the ballot booth did not translate into cries for strictly equal justice. Indeed, most suffragists agreed with their conservative critics that women, labouring under biological, historical, and socio-economic handicaps, deserved special consideration because they could not be held fully accountable for their actions.[27] Mainstream feminists at the turn of the century stressed the complementarity of the sexes, not their strict equality. As suggested by the notorious case of Angelina Napolitano, a pregnant woman condemned to death in 1911 for killing her abusive husband, the mainstream women's movement in Canada was primed to regard the capital conviction of a woman as a call to arms.[28] In NSW, the stronger voice of Labor women who demanded equal rights in the workplace seems to have rendered Australian feminists ambivalent about reconstructing their condemned sisters as victims.[29] Although many prominent feminists, such as NSW's Rose Scott, were abolitionists, campaigns to spare the lives of women were less enthusiastic than they were in Canada.[30] In either case, an appropriate representation of contrite victimhood was the price of public support: respectable women shrank from female criminals who seemed cold-hearted or unfeminine. But whether or not condemned women received help from feminist backers, it was men who bore the responsibility for sentencing women to death or deciding that they might be spared. Like white constructions of Aboriginal immaturity, male bureaucrats and cabinet members' perception of women as overgrown children – highly emotional, easily swayed, and victims rather than perpetrators – insulated them from the full force of the law. Feminists may have heightened public awareness of sexual difference, but men had their own reasons to treat condemned women mercifully.

Petitioners for the lives of condemned males faced a stiffer challenge, yet they too drew upon gendered concepts of culpability when they urged the executive to consider the particular disabilities of individual men. Whether they were untutored in Christian morality, ignorant of civilized customs, or besotted through excessive drinking, the most brutish criminals found advocates who transformed them into candidates for compensatory fair play. The absence of pressure from a comparable men's movement did not stop cabinet ministers from sympathizing with men who maintained that they had been cuckolded, spurned, or taunted into violence. Commuting men's sentences often depended on invoking less flattering images of womanhood – the adulteress, the temptress, the shrew. Thus gender stereotypes, like reflexive notions of Aboriginal savagery and childlikeness, served double duty: they could just as easily inculpate as exculpate.

To all but outright abolitionists, discretionary justice offered the surest possibility of relief from the doom of formal justice; consequently, petitioning for mercy typically translated into appeals for individualized, subjective justice. Although the royal prerogative of mercy was an anachronism from a procedural point of view, its administrators proudly defended it as an expression of fair play – the sober second look, the judicious consideration of factors beyond the frame of the law, a service provided to all, irrespective of status or representation. Members of the public certainly rebelled against specific executive decisions, and backbenchers, clerics, and editorialists periodically challenged the death penalty per se, but in both jurisdictions politicians maintained an uneasy accord between the rule of law and discretion because they managed to keep executive justice more or less in tune with political culture.

Managing Death

At the level of day-to-day practice, the broad scope of capital statutes meant that NSW cabinets frequently met with their minds made up to commute, whereas the narrower range of capital crimes in Canada rendered case outcomes less predictable. In NSW, cabinets often dealt with cases of attempted murder, rape, and carnal knowledge. Only four cases, two involving robbers' assaults on peace officers and two arising from savage rapes of children, provoked the executive to order executions (the last one taking place in 1902). In contrast, Canadian executive members knew that they could count on a murder case whenever they met; and they regularly faced tougher decisions than their counterparts in NSW because every case involved the most serious offence (second only to treason) in the criminal calendar. Dealing exclusively with murder offences meant that unique case features assumed greater significance for the Canadian executive than did formal legal charges. The pressure on decision-makers was amplified by their increased workload over this period. As purblind justice bureaucrats complained, processing more than a score of cases each year required working night and day.[31] However, the Canadian executive's preparedness to commute increased as the Justice Department's case-load became bloated in the 1910s. The growing number of cases, a quarter of which originated in Ontario courts, encouraged federal cabinet ministers and their departmental assistants to develop common-sense notions of typical mitigating and aggravating factors. Bureaucratic modes of decision-making were 'situationally rational' in that rules of thumb determined case dispositions. As Keith Hawkins argues of legal decision-making, 'discretion is heavily influenced by conceptions of precedent, by understandings of the "normal ways" of acting and deciding.' Case outcomes were therefore predictable but not predetermined. Although no one could prophesy whether Canadian cabinet members would commute or execute in individual cases (as could observers of NSW cases involving offences other than murder), Justice bureaucrats developed routine strategies to typify and dispose of cases.[32]

An organizational culture of discretionary justice emerged from the quotidian practices of a bureaucracy charged with handling all capital cases. Shortly after Confederation, the Canadian government established a Remissions Branch as a wing of the Department of Justice devoted to sentence remissions of all sorts. It assumed the task, formerly performed by the undersecretary of state, of collecting information considered necessary to dispose of capital cases. From the beginning, a standard roster of evidence was gathered, including trial transcripts and judges' reports. From this and any other relevant material (typically petitions, news clippings, and lawyers' correspondence), Remissions Branch officers prepared summaries for the justice minister's consideration. In most cases, officers included a recommendation to commute or execute, and it was rare for ministers to contradict their trusted assistants' advice. Besides, ministers of justice came and went with the tides of political fortune: remissions officers often held on for twenty years and more. It was they, not transitory politicians, who developed expertise in reading cases for possible reasons to execute or commute.

Although the Canadian public associated final decisions with the minister of justice or solicitor-general, the invisible bureaucracy exerted procedural control over the process of decision-making. As a result, Canadian cabinet ministers were cocooned from heart-wrenching appeals for mercy. Furthermore, it was easier for them than for their NSW counterparts to discount local commutation campaigns since they often considered cases from the farthest reaches of the country, remote from the centre of political power.[33] Thus bureaucratic dispersal of responsibilities, combined with physical and emotional distance from local petitioners, encouraged the Canadian executive to focus more clearly on the incontrovertible fact of convictions than on the debatable merits of appeals to mercy.

The mechanisms for assessing capital cases were less formal in NSW, and the executive there was more directly involved in decision-making. Until Federation in 1901, the colonial secretary acted as the chief administrator of capital cases, and his undersecretary was responsible for overseeing case preparations based on judges' accounts of trials and police reports on the condemned. Because ministries flipped so frequently in this pre-party era, a tradition arose for the whole cabinet, led by the premier, to debate the merits of capital punishment in each case. After Federation, the undersecretary of justice, who reported to the cabinet minister, assumed responsibility for the administration of capital cases, but the practice of protracted executive debates continued. The lieutenant governor-in-council theoretically retained the power to veto cabinet decisions, but appointees had long respected elected politicians' prerogative to set the standards of justice.[34] Relatively unmediated ministerial responsibility augmented an already close relationship between politicians and public opinion.

In NSW's state-run justice system, unlike in Canada's federal system, every case concerned crimes committed within a territory from which at least one cabinet member was likely to hail; thus, there was always a strong possibility that cabinet ministers would be well aware of local feelings about crimes and their aftermath. Rather than relying on bureaucrats' dry summaries, elected ministers kept their ears closer to the ground of public sentiment. And public sentiment in turn-of-the-century NSW waxed in favour of mercy, particularly in cases of attempted murder and sexual assault. But strong feelings were also expressed whenever death seemed too severe a penalty for particular murderers. In modifying the punishment in four-fifths of the cases they considered, the NSW executive members undermined the terror of the law, but they bolstered their image as Australian-style democrats every time they gave ordinary blokes a 'fair go.' At the same time, they could rationalize less popular commutations with assertions that they were leading the state from its barbarous past into a civilized future. On the one hand, retaining a broad range of capital statutes underlined the state's continuing commitment to law and order; on the other, commuting so many cases suggested that putting state violence into play had become well-nigh unnecessary. It was not a perfect balance, and critics frequently pointed to unjust anomalies, but it was a compromise that allowed the NSW executive to deal in the symbolism of death without often having to bear the responsibility to execute.

The Contours of Discretionary Justice

Between 1890 and 1920, the average execution rate of 53.7 per cent for those sentenced to capital punishment in Ontario was more than twice as high as it was in NSW, which had an extraordinarily low rate averaging 21.4 per cent. In both jurisdictions, the influence of worldwide abolitionist agitation was visible in the declining rate of executions over the period, but a more dramatic dip was recorded in NSW, where the Labor administration came close to abolishing capital punishment. Whereas the proportion of persons convicted of capital punishment in Ontario who were executed sank from 69 per cent in the 1890s to 38 per cent in the 1910s, the proportion in NSW plunged from 31.5 per cent to 6.2 per cent over the same period. The translation of these rates into numbers of persons hanged should also be noted since even a single execution is a potent reminder of state power and the terror of the law. The NSW executive's dwindling willingness to execute was obvious, since only five persons were hanged in the 1910s, whereas twenty-three had been executed in the 1890s (Table 5.3). In Canada, the rate of executions changed but the number of persons executed remained remarkably stable, varying from twenty to nineteen to twenty-two between 1890 and 1920 (Table 5.2).

Although informal rules of thumb allowed capital case reviewers in NSW and Canada to recognize typical case features and to act accordingly, the results of those decisions were remarkable. The most obvious practice in both jurisdictions was the transposition of women killers into pitiful creatures worthy of mercy. Less obvious patterns also emerged in the disposition of cases involving foreign-born men. In Canada, foreigners (mainly non-English-speaking European men) undoubtedly suffered from racism at the trial level in Ontario. Convictions of Italians, Russians, Bulgarians, Greeks, and other non-British immigrants largely accounted for the mush-

Table 5.2

Capital case dispostions in Ontario, 1890-1920

	1890-1900	1901-10	1911-20
No. of cases	29	34	58
No. of executions	20	19	22
No. commuted	8	12	36
New trial or quashed*	1	3	0
Commutation rate	27.6%	35.3%	62.1%

* Minister's order for a new trial, retried and found innocent or guilty of a non-capital offence, or conviction quashed on appeal.
Source: Data extrapolated from Lorraine Gadoury and Antonio Lechasseur, *Persons Sentenced to Death in Canada, 1867-1976: An Inventory of Case Files in the Records of the Department of Justice (RG 13)* (Ottawa: Government Archives Division, National Archives of Canada, 1992).

Table 5.3

Capital case dispositions in New South Wales, 1890-1920

	1890-1900	1901-10	1911-20
No. of cases	73	66	82
No. of executions	23	11	5
No. commuted	49	55	72
New trial or quashed*	1	0	5
Commutation rate	67.1%	83.3%	87.8%

* Minister's order for a new trial, retried and found innocent or guilty of a non-capital offence, conviction quashed on appeal, or conviction reversed through s. 475 of the Crimes Act.
Source: NSW, Comptroller General of Prisons, 'Death Sentence Register,' 1839-1968.

rooming of cases decided by the Canadian executive in the 1910s. Yet 48.6 per cent of these men (only one 'foreigner' was a woman) saw their death sentences commuted by the executive, whereas only 39.7 per cent of Anglo-Celtic men were spared (Table 5.4). In NSW, this tendency towards compensatory justice was reversed. Anglo-Celtic New South Welshmen were by far the most likely ethnic group to benefit from executive discretion. Foreign men and Aboriginals fared worse, and the few condemned Chinese were the least likely to be shown mercy. Although these profiles of commutation proclivities have been reconstructed from extant archival records, even casual contemporary observers appreciated that sparing some people but not others revealed the hand of discretionary justice at work at the very centre of state power.

Distinctions between commutation practices in Canada and NSW are also attributable to contrasts in the scope of capital statutes in the two juris-

Table 5.4

Men's cases commuted* in Ontario and New South Wales, by ethnicity and race, 1890-1920

	Ontario		New South Wales	
	%	No.	%	No.
Anglo-Celtic	39.7	25	81.7	143
Foreign	48.6	17	66.7	10
Aboriginal	0	0	72.7	8
Black	33	2	0	0
Chinese	100	1	63.6	7
Francophone	42.9	3	n/a	n/a

* Ontario: Three cases decided on appeal not included (two Anglo-Celts and one Native). Commutations exclude three suicides: two foreign and one Anglo-Celtic man. New South Wales: Six cases decided on appeal (all Anglo-Celts) not included, no suicides confirmed.
Sources: See Tables 5.2 and 5.3.

dictions. Almost one-half of the cases that came before the NSW executive concerned capital convictions for non-fatal acts of violence. Between 1890 and 1920, NSW cabinets considered forty-four cases of rape and carnal knowledge, as well as fifty-four cases of attempted murder, and commuted all but four of them. Thus, it seems that the commutation rate in NSW was extraordinarily high because virtually everyone accused of non-fatal offences was spared. But when murder cases are removed, the rate slips only slightly, from 74.5 per cent to 71.3 per cent. In other words, even if one restricts analysis of executive discretion in NSW to the same sorts of cases that came before the Canadian cabinet, NSW's commutation rate is still substantially higher than Ontario's rate of 46.3 per cent. The symbolic merits of the death penalty in NSW evidently far outweighed the political will to punish. Talk circulated in the legislature and the press about the prospect of formalizing customary commutation practices by striking attempted murder, sexual offences, and murders committed by women from the Crimes Act, but it remained just that – talk. Nevertheless, for all its readiness to find excuses to commute, not even the Labor party could resist either the threat of the death penalty or the occasional demonstration of state violence in this period. To NSW politicians, administering the death penalty was a painful exercise in coming to terms with their cultural ambivalence over the legitimacy of state violence.

The uncertainties of executive discretion were less obvious in Canada because the federal cabinet executed more consistently and also because the scope of capital punishment was much narrower. Like NSW, Canada maintained the death penalty for rape long after England had reduced the penalty to imprisonment. After 1873, however, Canadian judges were given the option to substitute a prison sentence in lieu of the death penalty. Although Ontario judges continued to sentence rapists to death for several years after 1873, the executive commuted all such sentences. By the 1890s, the Canadian executive no longer had to perform the charade of reviewing rapists' death sentences. Likewise, attempted murder and carnal knowledge of a girl younger than ten years old became a non-capital offence after 1887, when the maximum penalty of life imprisonment was introduced.[35] Because the remaining capital offences of treason and piracy were rarely tried, the Canadian executive considered nothing but murder cases.

The great exceptions to this pattern were the cases of Louis Riel and other rebels for treason in the aftermath of the North West Rebellion.[36] After Riel's execution, along with that of eight Native men in 1885, no other person was executed in Canada for a crime other than murder. By the time that the Canadian Criminal Code was introduced in 1892, a general consensus had emerged that murderers were the only criminals who actually deserved the death penalty. Convicted traitors could have faced the hangman too, but no further Riel figures emerged on the political land-scape to test Canadian politicians' mettle. This hardly made the federal executive's work easier than the NSW cabinet's; rather the scope of executive discretion was narrowed statutorily in Canada, whereas an informal political culture of mercifulness played a greater role in informing decisions to commute in NSW.

History, Culture, and Politics

In a curious way, blending extraordinary severity and extraordinary mercy made sense in a state that owed its origins to the penal policy of a distant imperial power. A century after English explorers 'discovered' Australia, England decided that it would be an appropriately desolate, out-of-the-way dumping ground for its excess criminal population. Convicts were granted the possibility of earning their freedom, but the system provided more facilities to punish than to reform. Overseers administered frightful flog-gings and governors regularly ordered men, women, and children publicly hanged in order to terrorize other miscreants into obedience. In 1830 alone, at a time when convicts and emancipated convicts constituted over 60 per cent of the colony's population, fifty people were executed in public squares.[37] Legislative means to restrain severe imperial policies were absent until the 1840s, when elected and appointed legislators began to gain a measure of control over colonial affairs. Although transportation had been all but dismantled by that point, the colony had absorbed 80,000 convicts and the infamous convict stigma lingered for generations.[38] Emancipated convicts and the children of former convicts had a stake in forgetting the past, but free settlers, who began to make up the bulk of the population by the 1860s, were not so quick to forget that their neighbours, or their neigh-bours' parents, had reached Australia's shores in chains. From this crucible of convictry, ambivalent attitudes were forged into NSW's political culture: in one respect, the colony's progress buoyed legal reformers' confidence because England's castoffs had triumphed against the odds; in another, conservatives wondered if the draconian criminal justice system had not been the key to progress.[39] The first assumption suggested that NSW could safely dispense with the death penalty; the second inspired arguments that it be maintained at all costs.

When it came to governing their own colony after the introduction of responsible government in 1856, New South Welshmen began what was to be an enduring strategy of retaining wide-ranging capital statutes but rarely calling upon the hangman's services. Over the second half of the nineteenth century, only an average of 3.5 executions took place each year, and several years passed without a single execution. The Criminal Law Amendment Act (1883) and the Crimes Act (1900) narrowed the range of capital crimes, but as critics charged, NSW maintained wider scope for the death penalty than did other British colonies and the mother country itself. Justifications for statutory severity varied with the times but the laws remained in place until 1955, when capital punishment was finally abolished. At the turn of the twentieth century, however, the state government periodically referred to the unruliness of foreign fortune hunters in NSW, its isolated and backward outback, periodic depressions, labour radicalism, and the remote threat of Aboriginals – all to justify the death penalty and its broad application.

Ironically, the colony's troubled history was invoked more often by opponents of capital punishment than by its supporters. During legislative debates in 1888 over the prospect of hanging Louisa Collins (who would become the last woman to be executed in NSW), one member declared that it would be a 'disgrace to us to retain this heritage handed down to us from the early days of sin, sweat, and sorrow.' Instead of marking NSW's centenary with an execution, he urged his fellow MLAs to abolish capital punishment, 'or otherwise let us acknowledge that our boasted civilization was nothing but a sham.'[40] Taunting opponents into abandoning a relic of the past was Labor man John Haynes's favourite strategy. When he introduced his 1896 abolition bill, the first of four over the following six years, he reminded his colleagues that NSW lagged behind the mother country, which had narrowed the scope of the death penalty. Even more embarrassing was the fact that NSW was 'on all fours' with countries such as China, Persia, Abyssinia, 'and other countries which have little regard for human life.' Haynes and his supporters regarded NSW as a great democratic experiment for which the abolition of capital punishment would be the crowning symbol. Another Labor party man complimented Haynes's campaign, maintaining that it was one more move to 'strike off, one by one, the old links and fetters, the old traces of the leg-irons, shackles, flogging, hanging, and everything else that has degraded this country.' Thus, abolishing the death penalty would announce to the world that NSW had 'at last made a step out of the old bloodthirsty days.'[41] Haynes's bill went down to defeat, as did the three that followed, but the power of his message, at once denouncing the past while goading his fellow politicians to pave the way towards a humane future, echoed in cabinet chambers when executive members faced difficult decisions. Commuting four out of every five individuals who received a capital conviction appealed to the prevailing sentiment that the advance of civilization depended on moderation over cruelty. The seeming illogic of condemning people to death and sparing all but a few was consistent with the ambivalent political mood of NSW and the cultural logic of mercy.

In contrast, Canadian abolitionists could not exploit history to such rhetorical advantage. Parliamentary opposition to the death penalty was expressed, as it was in most Western countries, in the language of Christian humanism and progressive penology. For instance, John Bickerdike, the leader of the Canadian abolition movement in the 1910s, asserted that Canada ought to keep in step with 'the marked growth of humanitarian sentiment' throughout the civilized world. To support his cause, he aired predictable quotes from the Bible and up-to-the-minute criminological texts. However, when he tried to put history to work, he stumbled. Because liberal ideology is founded on the notion of moral and economic progress, the history of hanging in Canada provided an uncomfortable fit for arguments that equated abolition with the advancement of civilization. Bickerdike maintained that in the twenty years following the execution of fifteen rebels in 1838, 'no government of Canada would allow a man to be hanged.' First, he was wrong: in the united Province of Canada at least three were executed in the 1850s.[42] Second, he glossed over the increasing regularity of hangings after the 1860s. If the colonies had been more capable of enlightened restraint in the 1840s than was the young Dominion in the 1910s, was he hinting that Canadian civilization had declined? His appeals to English heritage were off-key as well. While he argued that Canada's legacy of British 'freedom, fairplay, justice, and mercy' laid the groundwork for abolition, his opponents cooly replied that if the death penalty was good enough for the mother country, it was good enough for Canada.[43] Thus, colonial history and British heritage, the trump cards in NSW abolitionists' hands, were liabilities to the cause of abolition in Canadian politics.

If anything, the infamous adherence of Canadians to the principles of peace, order, and good government created a cultural disinclination to mercifulness. Upper Canada had begun its move away from capital punishment by reducing capital statutes in the 1820s and 1830s (while half a world away, scores of convicts and those emancipated were hanged every year in the city squares of Sydney and Hobart). By 1833, only eleven capital statutes remained, and hangings for murder and robbery accounted for the bulk of executions. As Barry Wright discusses in his essay, in the aftermath of the rebellions, during which fifteen men were executed for their treasonous actions, the Upper Canadian executive made better use of transportation and the new Kingston penitentiary than the noose, in part to reassure colonials that imperial rule could be temperate and enlightened.[44] The granting of responsible government in 1848 attracted many former rebels back to the fold, and a conservative, anti-republican culture took firm hold of the colony.[45] When the border state of Michigan abolished capital punishment in 1846, for instance, the United Canadas did not budge. Legislators dutifully followed England's lead in criminal justice, and cautiously at that. When England removed rape from its capital statutes in

1841, Canada stood fast until 1955. Bold experimentation was alien in this political milieu: whereas abolition smacked of republicanism, executive review maintained monarchical traditions.

The only threat to the flowering of conservative political culture in Ontario was the rise of organized labour in the 1870s and 1880s. Ontario, along with Quebec, became the chief beneficiary of industrial progress, but it also became a centre of vocal labour protest. As post-Confederation labour radicalism threatened to disrupt class hierarchy, Prime Minister John A. Macdonald's Conservative party managed to convince trade union leaders that their best bet for improvements lay in cooperation rather than confrontation. Once the short-lived triumph of the Knights of Labor faded in the 1890s, the radical critique of capitalism was muffled in the relatively conservative guise of craft unionism.[46] Thus Ontario was left without a strong, united voice on behalf of the working poor and the indigent – the sorts of men and women who most often found themselves at the executive's mercy. The keenest critics of classist injustice (socialists, anarchists, and Wobblies) were relegated to the fringes of political culture where their efforts failed to make a positive impression on cabinets that were distrustful of their radical agendas. In neither Ontario nor the rest of Canada did a force comparable to the NSW Labor party pressure the executive into abolishing the death penalty or, failing that, adopting a *de facto* policy of mercy.

The Logics of Commutation in Ontario Cases

In keeping with the precepts of British justice, judges and justice ministers frequently congratulated themselves on the class- and colour-blind quality of justice in Canada, particularly in contrast to the inferior brand of justice in the republic to the south. It was customary in capital cases for assize judges to commend court-appointed lawyers for their unstinting service to clients who otherwise would have faced capital charges without legal representation. To underline the justice of convictions, judges often uttered the phrase 'You have been ably defended' in the same breath as they announced: 'It is the decision of the court that you be hanged by the neck until dead.' However, genuflecting to the Union Jack did not erase the fact that the poor were at the greatest risk of execution, largely because their court-appointed lawyers rarely had more than a day or two to prepare their cases. But leftist criticism of classist injustice in Canada was never as forthright nor as effective as it was in NSW.[47]

Given the rank injustice meted out to indigent accused, it is somewhat surprising that petitions for mercy in cases involving racial and ethnic minorities were more successful in Ontario than in NSW. Those least integrated into formal structures of political power – women and foreign nationals – fared better than those whose principal misfortune was poverty.

Virtually disenfranchised citizens, foreigners and women were more likely than poor Anglo-Celts or francophones to find effective advocates. Supporters of foreign-born men were remarkably well organized and effective in making political capital out of the injustices these men suffered. Although their advocates did not enjoy the perfect record of women's petitioners, they saved more than half of their compatriots from the gallows. Feminists who found particularly poignant cases of injustice also lobbied vigorously to save their condemned sisters, particularly when their crimes could be linked to sexual exploitation. Their work was made easier, however, because assumptions about female frailty and irresponsibility were widely held, and most important, by powerful *men*. In both NSW and Ontario, male cabinet members were easily persuaded during the heyday of the women's movement that women merited a modified form of justice, whether or not condemned women were adopted as feminist causes.

In the Canadian criminal justice system, foreignness and racial difference were simultaneously liabilities and loopholes for men accused of capital crimes. Unlike the white, native-born poor, who suffered inordinately from injustice, foreign status provided leverage at the commutation stage since international pressure and the threat of national embarrassment could eclipse anti-foreign and racist prejudice. Although cabinets spared two of six black Ontario men whose cases came before them in this period, everyone involved, including witnesses, prosecutors, judges, Remissions Branch officers, ministers, and even their own advocates, deployed racist stereotypes of black animality and sensuality either to condemn or to excuse their actions. While southern and eastern Europeans were dismissively labelled 'foreigners,' blacks and mixed-race persons were deemed virtually subhuman.[48]

Ironically, non-Canadian black men could use their foreignness at the executive phase of the justice process to offset racist prosecutorial practices and jurors' prejudice. When Judge Kelly charged the jury in the 1904 murder trial of Edward Slaughter, he noted gratuitously that in the US, 'prejudice too often prevail[ed] to the injury and damage of justice.' However, 'in a Canadian Court,' he proudly predicted that jurors would be swayed solely by the evidence, 'though this man belongs to a foreign country and is a coloured man.'[49] Although the local legal fraternity thought that the case had, at the most, amounted to manslaughter, the man received a capital conviction. The fact that Slaughter was a US citizen, not the vaunted fairness of Canadian justice, likely saved him from the gallows. Was the Canadian executive going to outdo its former slave-holder neighbours, petitioners cried? As one Detroit doctor urged his friend, a southwestern Ontario MP, 'For the honor of the fair name of Canada cannot something be done to save this man?' The American asked the MP to speak to the minister of justice, stressing that a reprieve would 'be to the honor of the Dominion.' Mindful that the story had been picked up in the Michigan papers (a state without the death penalty) the cabinet decided to commute Slaughter's sentence.[50]

The Canadian executive was also aware that Italy and several other European countries had abolished capital punishment. By the early twentieth century, Italians were the single largest non-Anglo-Celtic ethnic group in the province and they regularly rallied workers, neighbours, priests, and even diplomats together when one of their own faced the gallows. During a 1914 debate on abolition, Justice Minister Doherty mentioned Italy's abolitionist status while arguing Canada's need to retain the death penalty. On the basis of his statistics that twenty-seven of thirty-eight foreigners convicted of capital crimes hailed from countries without capital punishment, he argued that Canada had become a killing field: 'We are getting flooded with a population who are accustomed to think that you can kill your neighbour but that your life is so sacred that the state will never touch you.'[51] In spite of his parliamentary grandstanding, he and other executive members knew that foreigners accounted for a disproportionate share of capital cases because they were prejudicially processed at lower levels of the justice hierarchy. Consequently, Italians were often beneficiaries of executive mercy – small recompense for prejudicial trial proceedings, but a welcome respite from the gallows.

Although a wide array of southern and eastern European immigrants to Ontario found themselves convicted on capital charges, Italians were the most numerous. Lobbyists for Italian convicts became skilled at the life-and-death game of petitioning because they practised more often than they would have wished. Like most of the foreigners tried for murder, Italian criminals were typically convicted for assaults sparked by jealousy, insults, or physical provocation. Prosecutorial discretion allowed for such homicides to be considered manslaughter, but foreign men were more vulnerable than Anglo-Celtic Ontarians to be charged with and convicted of murder. Nick Scarfo's case was typical. He was sentenced to death in 1914 for shooting another Italian in Fort William, a northern industrial town that was home to a large 'colony' of Italians. Witnesses testified that a group of men had been arguing on the street and that one of them, allegedly Scarfo, had fired a gun and fled. Judge Lennox half-heartedly charged the jury on the possibility of a manslaughter conviction and Scarfo, like many other non-English speakers, sat dumbly through the trial, mystified by the proceedings, until a court interpreter whispered that he was to be hanged. Stunned, the man relayed his reply to Lennox's standard inquiry as to whether he had anything to say: 'I only have to say that I am innocent, my Lord.'

While many defence lawyers in this period resorted to cultural defences (as Tina Loo discusses in her article), experienced trial advocate Frank Keefer saw Scarfo's conviction as a travesty of justice. The rush was on to save the condemned man, and Keefer had no trouble, with the help of Scarfo's parish priest, in gathering 880 signatures over several weeks. One month before Scarfo's scheduled execution, the vice-consul of Italy wrote to the minister of justice, Charles Doherty, to urge commutation and to advise him that another petition was on the way. The minister of justice refused to make the requested decision to order a new trial but a compromise was reached by commuting his death sentence. Even after the executive's decision, prompted by Judge Lennox's extraordinary suggestion that Scarfo might be innocent, Italian consular agents continued to petition for his release. The real murderer, it was discovered, was Scarfo's brother-in-law, whom Scarfo had lied to protect. Had consular agents not maintained pressure to have him deported to Italy, Scarfo would likely have spent many more than nine years in prison.[52]

Between 1890 and 1920 only six women were sentenced to death in Ontario, compared with thirty-five foreign men. All but one of these women, Angelina Napolitano, were Anglo-Celtic.[53] Although women's supporters had less practice than the churches, workers' organizations, and diplomatic agents who came to the aid of foreign men, they were successful in each commutation campaign for women convicted of murder. It certainly helped that four out of the six had been accused of infanticide, a crime that Canadian cabinet members had long considered less serious than adult homicides. It also helped that the arguments used to spare women tapped broad cultural values that appealed to men as well as women. Indeed, feminists sometimes shied away from condemned women whom chivalrous men harboured fewer reservations about defending. Olive Sternaman, the first person convicted of a capital crime in Canadian history to have her conviction set aside by the minister of justice (rather than have her sentence commuted to a term of imprisonment), inspired only lukewarm support from women.[54] She was tried in 1897 for poisoning her husband (and suspected of, but not tried for, the murder of her first husband, who had died several years earlier). The conviction depended on circumstantial evidence and on suggestions that this had been Mrs. Sternaman's second attempt to collect life insurance by despatching a husband. The men of the jury reached their guilty verdict reluctantly but attached a recommendation for mercy. Chief Justice Armour sourly reported to the minister of justice, attributing the jurors' recommendation to 'moral cowardice and mistaken compassion,' and not to want of evidence. Other men and women were overtaken by compassion as well. According to one petition (signed by 250 Torontonians and 630 citizens from the Cayuga area where Sternaman lived), ordering a 'mother of a family' to her death was 'repugnant to the natural feelings of a Christian civilization.' Dr. J. Baxter, the MPP for Cayuga, advised Minister of Justice David Mills that local opinion had turned sharply in her favour since all but two jurors stated they would have declared her not guilty if they had known she might be executed. Fellow Liberal MP John Charlton reminded Mills of the potential political fallout: 'I would be sorry to see the first execution during your official career as Minister of Justice, that of a woman.' Mills evidently decided that executive reversal of a court verdict, although unprecedented, was less politically risky than hanging this woman.[55] He protested that gender had nothing to do with his decision, however. As he explained to Baxter, 'The executive department of the Government could hardly undertake to administer the law in such a way as practically to repeal it with regard to one-half of the community.'[56] Yet that is precisely what he and his successors did. Executive-decreed 'gendered justice' reflected dominant notions of femininity and masculinity, but because it would have violated the concept of equality before the law, legislators did not exempt women statutorily from the death penalty.[57] Executive mercy – in this case, ordering a new trial – was the perfect compromise.

Women who were condemned for committing infanticide were the most sympathetic figures in commutation campaigns, particularly if the man responsible for the pregnancy could be painted as a villain. In Annie Robinson's case, this characterization required little imagination. After her husband had repeatedly raped her daughters, Robinson delivered three, and suffocated two, of his incestuous offspring. Even the minister of justice, Sir Allen Aylesworth, described the man as an 'unnatural monster.' Bowing to public pressure, he commuted her sentence to ten years, but he failed to satisfy the scores of supporters who called for her release. After she had served only three months of her sentence, her MPP tried to convince Aylesworth that 'she was guilty of her crime only through possible threats from her brutal Husband.' Besides, a pardon, he predicted, 'would be very popular with the people of this section and others as well.' Faced with so many persuasive appeals, from Christian ministers to suffragists and members of Parliament, Aylesworth caved in and made the extraordinary decision to issue an unconditional pardon. Although no other Ontario woman at the turn of the century was condemned to death for killing more than one person, this murderer of two, recast as a victim in the post-conviction phase of her case, was the only one to be pardoned.[58]

Unless well-organized commutation campaigns, such as Robinson's, disturbed the steady rhythm of case management, the Canadian executive was under less pressure than that of NSW to demonstrate the law's merciful aspects through frequent commutations. Instead, an informal recognition of the public's tolerance of state violence seems to have tempered the federal executive's actions, since the number of persons executed remained remarkably stable at about two per annum. And calculated mathematically, what could have appeared fairer than a commutation rate of almost 50 per cent? When public figures argued about the appropriateness of capital punishment, they were less likely to bring up history than their differing interpretations of British justice and Christian civilization. As long as Ontarians perceived executive decisions as upholding British fair play, they conformed to the grammar of political culture. For Ontarians, unlike the case of New South Welshmen, the history of Ontario and its prominent role in the nation's founding was something not to overcome but to live up to.

The Logics of Commutation in NSW

In NSW, Labor politicians ensured that executive discretion was politicized as a class issue. In the course of critiquing classist injustice, however, legislative debates put the spotlight on the broader political dynamics of executive discretion. Unlike in Canada, where political opposition to the death penalty did not surface until the 1910s, in NSW regular legislative battles raged from the 1880s. The execution of four youths for rape in 1889 and the double hanging of men charged with attempted murder in 1894 galvanized critics and set the stage for frequent debates over the politics of mercy and severity: the rich, it seemed, could buy their way to freedom whereas the poor were sacrificed, just as they had been in the convict days. But ambivalence over NSW's status as a civilized colony lingered in the defence of the death penalty. Outside Sydney and Newcastle, almost half the population lived in small country towns and out-of-the-way sheep stations where justice was remote and the uncivilizing lure of the bush strong. While the wide-open port city of Sydney attracted both the rough and the respectable from across the globe, non-British foreigners accounted for a much smaller proportion of the state's population than they did in Ontario. When race played a role, it was expressed through resentment of resident Chinese and, in the outback, latent fear of Aboriginals. After 1899, when five white women, children, and men were viciously murdered by Jimmy Governor and two fellow Aboriginals, conservatives had only to mention the 'Breelong Blacks' to topple abolitionist arguments. But just as official posturing in Canada against the 'foreign threat' was undercut by the executive's preparedness to commute, so the NSW cabinet did not adopt a uniform policy of executing Aboriginals, including those who had raped white women.

NSW cabinet members seemed to have required little prodding to deal mercifully with women, since most were spared without the benefit of commutation campaigns that were regularly mounted on behalf of condemned Ontario women. Instead, men who made executive decisions were inspired by pity and a gender-based sense of superiority. Even the most conservative NSW parliamentarians were known to wheeze assurances that chivalrous white men were there to protect women and children: after all, this was why the state retained the death penalty for rape and carnal knowledge. Feminists were not so sure about their self-proclaimed protectors' intentions, particularly after those same men balked at raising the age of consent for girls. For their part, suffragists in NSW concentrated on saving women whose crimes appeared to be the product of seduction. As happened in Canada with Ontario cases, the plight of women facing the death penalty aroused sympathy from all corners, but most important, from cabinet chambers.

The NSW executive was more reluctant to commute in cases in which foreign-born and Aboriginal men faced the death penalty. Like women, they were exceptions to the rule about the typical sorts of men left to the mercy of executive justice. Although over two-thirds of foreigners and Aboriginals were spared, their commutation rates were lower than those of Anglo-Celtic New South Welshmen. Labor politicians spoke feelingly of the injustice suffered by poor defendants, but parliamentarians did not speak up for non-British accused, most of whom were even more destitute than the men of British background. Furthermore, their small numbers among the NSW population meant that foreigners could not so readily count on community resources, which saved so many foreign men in Ontario. A more ambivalent attitude was evident towards Aboriginal men. While the Governor murders provided a gruesome reminder that Aboriginals were 'savages,' their decimation and expected demise lent an air of forbearance to cabinet deliberations. In sum, the gender, race, and ethnic patterns of discretionary justice suggest that in NSW executing non-Anglo-Celts and non-whites was less politically risky than sacrificing errant 'Aussie battlers' or emotionally overwrought females.

Executions for attempted murder or sexual offences never formed a large proportion of hangings in NSW, but men were put to death for these offences as late as 1902. Public tolerance for severity in such cases dwindled over the 1890s and early post-Federation years, largely as a result of vocal objections from Laborite men. The most controversial executions for attempted murder in this period were those of Charles Montgomery and Thomas Williams, two men who had been convicted of assaulting a police officer.[59] Hounded by deputations and snowed under by 28,000 petitions, Premier Sir George Dibbs stood his ground: considering that the whole country was gripped in an unprecedented economic crisis at the time, daring robberies of this nature would not abate unless the law took its course. The petition countered that commuting their death sentence would do more to deter crime because it would discourage the 'criminal class' from murdering in the course of robbery. Furthermore, mercy would 'convince the rest of the civilized world that the section under which they were convicted was the result of an oversight on the part of our Legislature rather than a desire to cause this Colony to stand invidiously from the whole of the English-speaking world.'[60] According to Dibbs's government, the merits of law and order outweighed mercy, however. Montgomery and Williams were executed, as was another man who was convicted of attempting to murder a nightwatchman in 1895. As the depression dragged on, conservative coalition governments veered away from mercy, executing fifteen men between 1893 and 1897 when the colony endured the bleakest period of economic and social strife in Australia prior to the Great Depression.[61] After prosperity slowly returned, cabinets no longer seriously considered putting men to death unless they had actually murdered. All subsequent sentences for attempted murder were commuted.

The execution of the 'Mount Rennie rapists' in 1889 continued to exercise influence over the politics of discretion at the turn of the century. Although politicians often explained that rape remained a capital offence because Australian womanhood was vulnerable to Aboriginals and uncouth swagmen, the Mount Rennie 'outrage' took place in suburban Sydney and local working-class lads, not 'savages,' had been convicted of the brutal gang rape. The grossly botched hanging of the principal offenders, several still in their teens, fuelled rage that was skilfully channelled into a critique of executive discretion. Because the executed men were members of inner city youth gangs, Labor men argued that the alleged protection of Australian womanhood was merely a mask for class terror.[62]

Every time that a man stood convicted of rape, the Mount Rennie martyrs were used to good effect. In the course of a debate on abolition in 1899, Labor members chided their opponents that gentlemen seducers ought to be held more accountable than brutish men overtaken by sudden, animalistic lust. As one member bleated, 'What about the thousands of men in this country, and every other country – some of them leading citizens – who have seduced girls under all kinds of promises, and left them on the streets. Is there any punishment for such men? No.'[63] Discounting the trauma of rape was a by-product of class-based politics. As John Haynes believed, rape, 'as a crime, is nothing compared to the moral death of a girl seduced by artifice, by men who are never reached by the law.'[64] Of course, he did not mean to suggest that seducers ought to be hanged; rather his remarks emphasized the law's replication of class distinctions between different forms of male lust.

Commutation patterns suggest that the executive, even before Labor was elected in 1910, was well-disposed to accept sudden rage, drunkenness, or unrequited love as credible reasons to commute, especially if crimes involved male violence towards women. As earlier noted, the NSW executive extended a virtual amnesty for men convicted of sexual offences. Aside from one man who had repeatedly raped all three of his daughters, and another, a drifter who had abducted and raped two young girls, none of the ninety-eight men convicted of sexual crimes against women and girls was executed.[65] So indulgent were juries, judges, and the executive towards violent spurned men that the chief justice thought it was time to take a stand.

Edward Connoughton was the unfortunate example. He was a US sailor who refused to take no for an answer after he repeatedly asked a Sydney barmaid to marry him in 1903. On hearing that she was to marry another man, an accusation she denied, he shot her, saying that if she did not marry him, she would marry no one. The jury recommended mercy 'on the ground that he was led away by passion at the time he committed the crime.' Sympathetic Judge Rogers exercised his option to *record* the sentence of death, rather than pronounce it. This formality was a recognized signal to the executive that the judge regarded commutation more appropriate than execution. Chief Justice Darley wanted none of this sympathy for a murderous man. Speaking in his capacity as the lieutenant governor, he bristled: 'Cases of men shooting women who do not comply with their wishes have of late become so numerous that it was time some example was made and with all due respect to the learned and experienced Judge who tried the case, I think it is unfortunate he did not sentence the prisoner to *Death,* leaving it to the executive to say whether the extreme penalty of the law should or should not be carried out.' The executive took Darley's advice but did not go so far as to execute the man. Gendered justice did not automatically translate into absolution but it did demand the modification of punishment to maintain the image of fair play. Glumly contemplating spending the remainder of his days behind bars, Connoughton confided to his brother that his modified sentence seemed anything but fair: 'Its [*sic*] true the Law is very square but what can you expect from Imposters that has it all cut an dry to get one man off light an all cut an dry to get me for life.'[66] Had the bitter man's sentiments been politicized (as in Ontario where foreign nationals' cases were frequently fashioned into national embarrassments), Premier Wade's government might have been in trouble. As it stood, the commuted life sentence satisfied the NSW public, if not the convict, that justice was served.

When NSW politicians had to decide the fate of eight women convicted of capital offences, the ghost of Louisa Collins, as tangible a spirit as the Mount Rennie rapists, hovered over cabinet deliberations. Not one of them was executed, even though three had apparently carried out premeditated plans to kill adults (two husbands and a woman lover). Feminists preferred to lobby in cases such as Ethel Herring's, a woman who had been seduced by a hotelkeeper and abandoned once she told him she was pregnant. Although Herring was tried for murder, the judge had charged the jury on both manslaughter and murder, and the jurymen had convicted her on the lesser charge. Since Rose Scott of the Women's Political Education League was trying to push the Girls Protection Act through the legislature at the time, Herring's was a perfect case for its cause. On 28 August 1903, Scott, accompanied by J.R. Holman, the future Labor minister of justice, presented a petition signed by 5,000 people from Herring's home district requesting that she be released to care for her newborn twins. Although the Liberal premier would not be moved to further commutation in Herring's case, the universal commutation of women's death sentences, even by the most conservative administrations, suggests that in NSW, as in Ontario, the broadly held assumptions about women's lesser culpability informed capital case deliberations.

A trans-colonial consensus over the inferiority of indigenous peoples was evident in the political management of Aboriginals' cases in NSW. While the state Aboriginal Protection Board assumed a 'caretaking' role towards a doomed race, the executive frequently slipped into a similarly paternalistic pose towards condemned Aboriginals. The Governor murders in 1900 certainly provoked vitriolic threats from members of the NSW legislature that those offenders ought to be burned alive or boiled in oil, but more mundane Aboriginal offenders inspired a patronizing brand of racism. One of Labor's most controversial commutations was that of Jack Lacey, a 'full-blooded Aboriginal' who broke into an inner-city home in Sydney in 1912 and raped a ninety-four-year-old white woman, who later died. 'As to his intelligence,' the government medical officer testified at his trial, 'he seems to me to be about the average of the aboriginal individuals. I do not, of course, look upon them as a high type.' It was not so much that he had been drinking, but that he was a drunken *Aboriginal* that diminished his responsibility for the crime: 'My experiences of the effect of alcohol on the aboriginals of low type is, they bear it very badly as a rule. They are apt to become mere animals.' Lacey turned out to be brighter than the doctor imagined. He was sharp enough to realize that he was unlikely to be executed because the Labor government had recently commuted the death penalty for a white man who had raped and killed his daughter. On his arrest, Lacey confidently chirped: 'Anyhow, they did not hang Phillips, the fellow who murdered his own child.'[67]

By the turn of the century, commuting condemned Aboriginals was less a matter of the government's abolitionist tendencies than the opinion of educated authorities that blacks could not be measured against the same standards of civilization as whites. When sixteen-year-old 'George' was convicted of raping a white twelve-year-old girl in a remote station, the jury strongly recommended that he be granted mercy 'on account of his age and color.' As the convicting judge reported, George had been 'seized with a Paroxysm of sexual passion.' On the one hand, he behaved like any other man in the outback, untutored in civilized dealings with women; on the other, he was prone to the animalistic drives of his race. On both counts he might be a fit subject for mercy.[68] Indeed, none of the Aboriginal men convicted for rape in this period was executed, an extraordinary fact given the frequent lynchings and judicial hangings of US blacks in the same period (and given the readiness of Canadian cabinets to execute two of the three Natives condemned in Ontario in this period). The difference, of course, was white Australians' assumption that Aboriginals were less threatening than freed North American slaves or the Aboriginal population in Ontario because indigenous Australians were shrinking in number and largely scattered in the remote areas of the state. As abolitionist Labor man John Haynes explained, executing Aboriginals as a deterrent for others was unnecessary since their time was running out. As he advised his legislative colleagues, Native violence 'will only end, as in Tasmania, when the last aboriginal has gone.'[69]

Although juries could find plenty of reasons for recommending mercy, and judges could concoct justifications for recording death sentences, it was the executive branch of the reigning administration that faced the keenest scrutiny of the secret decision-making process. Opposition politicians tried to prod governments into explaining their reasoning process but conservatives and Labor men alike stalwartly guarded executive discretion from the realm of legislative interference. One Liberal member, during a 1900 abolition debate, let the cat out of the bag by admitting that unfettered executive discretion compensated for the rigidity of the rule of law. As MLA Ewing put it, 'Capital punishment is the only portion of the law that is not administered, if I can use the term, in accordance with the law.'[70] Why abolish the death penalty, he reasoned, when juries, judges, and ultimately the cabinet acted as safeguards against the possibility of injustice? In life-sentenced Edward Connoughton's opinion, those safeguards were hardly foolproof since commuted sentences could feel as cruel as the prospect of execution. But this compromise between the rule of law and discretion is precisely the balance that turn-of-the-century NSW executive members successfully maintained, between dramatic but contained bouts of severity, with a liberal dose of mercy.

Conclusion

By the late nineteenth century, sovereigns were far removed from the commutation process, particularly in colonies where executive members of elected legislatures had been delegated the power to decide the fate of condemned persons. Formal petitions were still addressed to royally appointed governors, but petitioners in-the-know realized that ministers of justice and the executive rendered final decisions. Although they were commoners elected by the people, cabinet members were as free as kings and queens to condemn or spare without having to explain or justify their decisions. Thus, justice ministers wore two hats: in their parliamentary role, they sported umpires' caps to oversee the equal application of laws to every citizen; in cabinet chambers with their fellow executive members, they switched to their qadi fezzes, evaluating each capital case on its own merits.[71] The executive's dual roles of impartial lawmaker and subjective adjudicator were difficult to reconcile because its combined duties exposed the central paradox of liberal legal orders – like cases are to be treated alike except when unique cases are to be treated differently.

The disposition of capital cases in these two jurisdictions, barely out from under the shadow of colonial rule, illustrates that ancient forms of discretionary justice persisted well into the period associated with the rule of law. As Michael Ignatieff observed, equating modernization with rationalization arises from confusing intent and substance. If we focus on the administration of justice as it actually operates, we see that 'modernity is the site of a recurring battle between rationalizing intention and institutions, interests, and communities which resist, often with persistent success.'[72] Discretion was not confined to executive review of capital cases: to this day, it marks every stage of the criminal justice process, from reporting, policing, and charging to sentencing and parole. However, the drama and publicity of capital cases cast a spotlight on discretionary forms of justice, illuminating the fact that executives rendered life-and-death decisions without having to be accountable. But to conclude that the executive was literally unaccountable would imply a naïve reading of capital case administration. The procedural nature of the death penalty meant that the men who made these decisions were *politically* accountable. Unpopular decisions that violated tenets of political culture always had the potential to bring governments down. As each of the essays in this collection affirms, when decisions about the death penalty conflicted with prevailing political sentiments and cultural sensibilities, governing powers searched for alternative means of meting out justice.

At the turn of the twentieth century, when many Western nations considered abolishing capital punishment and several removed capital statutes, questions about discretionary justice began to flavour political culture. Mixed with questions about the meanings of Christianity, civilization, and democracy, public debates in legislatures and the press turned to the death penalty and its administration. Each time a convicted felon faced the gallows, mini-referenda were conducted on the question of capital punishment in democratic states that were governed according to the rule of law and founded on the bedrock of British justice. Whether or not politicians earned approval for their decisions in individual cases, the *process* of executive decision-making was increasingly contentious. Both retentionists and abolitionists found themselves asking: How could states founded on the notion of the rule of law justify executive modifications of punishment?

Exploring this question through the history of capital punishment in Australia and Canada during the first wave of abolitionism focuses on the contingency of discretionary justice. While it is useful to analyze discretion at an abstract level, it is best understood in context, where real actors made difficult decisions in never-ideal circumstances. Sometimes, as in the case of Louis Riel, the executive failed to defend its capital case decisions convincingly, throwing the government into a precarious state of illegitimacy. In other cases, such as those involving police killings or infanticide, both executions and commutations could garner popular approval for the government of the day. Unlike other states in this period, Canada and NSW did not resolve this awkward balancing act legalistically, by placing a moratorium on executions or by abolishing capital punishment. Politicians in NSW came close after the first victory of the Labor party in 1910, but abolition did not take place until 1955. Canadian politicians took even longer: the death penalty remained in the Criminal Code until 1976. In the interim, retaining capital punishment expressed governmental desires to appear tough on crime even if executions were rarely carried out.

Both NSW and Canadian politicians were moved by the death penalty's seductive symbolic association with law and order. But by managing the death penalty, rather than abolishing it, politicians also trafficked in the figurative appeal of British justice and fair play.[73] In commuting sentences, they were suggesting that only those who *really* deserved the death penalty would be actually executed, while those who *truly* merited mercy would be spared. In the interest of fairness, they were prepared to lift judicially sanctioned penalties and to revise sanctions according to the principles of natural justice. By stating that they weighed all possible factors, that every case was reviewed (no matter how horrible the crime, or how poor or brutish the perpetrator), and that every potential mitigating factor was considered, the executive tried to justify a secret, highly discretionary process of case disposition as fair – arguably fairer than trials themselves. In the eyes of the men who had to make the decisions, executive review was an opportunity for considered second thought, free from the passions and prejudices of the courtroom, and receptive to arguments and evidence ruled out by the law.

The compatibility of British justice and the death penalty was challenged by outspoken abolitionists who pointed to the possibility of wrongful convictions and the unfairness of poor legal defences. However, when lobbyists pleaded for the lives of condemned individuals, they rarely framed their arguments in frankly abolitionist terms. What they called for were discrete acts of fair play – decisions to spare *this* man or *this* woman for *these* reasons, under *these* circumstances. Thus the political culture of British justice tutored colonials and their elected representatives in the values of restraint even as it rationalized the death penalty itself.[74] In soul-searching moments, cabinet ministers may have convinced themselves that they were doing justice when they sent some to prison and others to hang, but popular acceptance of discretionary justice was never guaranteed. Rather, political, cultural, legal, and historical factors modulated capital case outcomes, rendering discretionary justice volatile, partial, and inevitably contingent.

Acknowledgments

I would like to thank Camilla Jenkins, who cast her critical eye on an earlier draft and pointed me towards several shortcomings. Thanks also to Julie Stacker and Ashley Hogan for her research and advice.

Notes

1 On the mythic qualities and social force of supposedly rational Western legal forms, see Peter Fitzpatrick, *The Mythology of Modern Law* (London: Routledge 1992).
2 Keith Hawkins, 'The Use of Legal Discretion: Perspectives from Law and Social Science,' in *The Uses of Discretion*, ed. Hawkins (Oxford: Oxford University Press 1992), 34.
3 Thirty-nine US states currently retain the death penalty. New York state reinstated the death penalty in September 1995. The eleven states that do not have the death penalty are North Dakota, Minnesota, Wisconsin, Iowa, Michigan, West Virginia, Vermont, Massachusetts, Maine, Hawaii, and Alaska.
4 The death penalty was abolished in Canada in 1976. In Australia, the last state to abolish capital punishment was Western Australia in 1984, but no hangings were performed there after 1964. Ivan Potas and John Walker, 'Capital Punishment,' *Trends and Issues in Crime and Criminal Justice*, 3 (Feb. 1987).
5 This argument is elaborated in Carolyn Strange, 'The Lottery of Death: Capital Punishment in Canada, 1867-1976,' *Manitoba Law Journal*, 23, 3 (1996):594-619.
6 In June 1995, the South African Constitutional Court ruled that the death penalty constitutes cruel and unusual punishment. Prior to this ruling, South Africa was the only 'democratic' state in the 1980s to execute more of its citizens than the US did.
7 Recent examples of seminal works include Peter Fitzpatrick, *The Mythology of Modern Law*; Peter Just, 'History, Power, Ideology, and Culture: Current Directions in the Anthropology of Law,' *Law and Society Review* 26, 2 (1992):373-412; and Susan Hirsch and Mindie Lazarus-Black, eds., *Contested States: Law, Hegemony, and Resistance* (New York: Routledge 1994).
8 In speaking of political culture, I rely on David V.J. Bell's definition of the term, which includes 'beliefs and values related to politics, attitudes to the political system and to political issues, and commonly accepted standards of political behaviour.' Bell, 'Political Culture in Canada,' in *Canadian Politics in the 1980s* (2nd ed.), ed. Michael S. Whitington and Glen Williams, 155-74 (Toronto: Methuen 1986), 155. Bell and other political writers are influenced by Gabriel A. Almond and Sidney Verba's *Civic Culture: Political Attitudes and Democracy in Five Nations* (Princeton, NJ: Princeton University Press 1963). Those authors referred to political culture as a set of 'specifically political orientations – attitudes towards the political system and its various parts, and attitudes towards the role of the self in the system.' *The Civic Culture*, 13.
9 On this issue, Eksteins quotes Nicholas Berdyaev, who argued that war 'revealed the personality of our civilization.' Modris Eksteins, 'The Great War: Ritual, Symbol, and Meaning,' in *Main Trends in Cultural History*, ed. Willem Melching and Wyger Velema, 204-21 (Amsterdam: Rodopi 1994), 205.
10 The Criminal Code of Canada (1892) included rape and piracy along with murder and treason as capital offences. Several men were convicted for piracy (but not executed). However, the charge, like treason, was extremely rare. It does not appear that any Ontario men were sentenced to death for rape after 1880.

11 Edward Lehman, *Political Society: A Macrosociology of Politics* (New York: Columbia University Press 1977), 24-5, 42.

12 John F. Galliher, Gregory Ray, and Brent Cook, 'Abolition and Reinstatement of Capital Punishment during the Progressive Era and Early 20th Century,' *The Journal of Criminal Law and Criminology* 83, 3 (1992):538-76. By the 1930s, eight of the ten states had repealed abolition statutes. Among the first countries to abolish capital punishment were Brazil, Colombia, Iceland, Italy, the Netherlands, Norway, Portugal, Switzerland, Sweden, and the Soviet Union. Most reinstated the death penalty over the course of the twentieth century. Amnesty International, *When the State Kills ... The Death Penalty: A Human Rights Issue* (New York: Amnesty International 1989).

13 Greg Marquis, 'Doing Justice to "British Justice": Law, Ideology, and Canadian Historiography,' in *Canadian Perspectives on Law and Society, Issues in Legal History,* ed. W. Wesley Pue and Barry Wright, 43-70 (Ottawa: Carleton University Press 1988), 70.

14 John Brewer and John Styles, eds., *An Ungovernable People: The English and Their Law in the Seventeenth and Eighteenth Centuries* (London: Hutchinson 1980), 14.

15 Bill Maurer, 'Writing Law, Making a "Nation": History, Modernity, and Paradoxes of Self-Rule in the British Virgin Islands,' *Law and Society Review* 29, 2 (1995):255-86.

16 On the contribution of the Irish to Australian national culture, see Patrick O'Farrell, *The Irish in Australia* (Kensington, NSW: University of New South Wales Press 1987). O'Farrell's thesis is that the Irish did not produce the irreverent strains of anti-Britishness in Australian culture, but that they were 'central to their championing.' (p. 13). The proportion of Irish-born immigrants in the total population of Ontario was actually substantially higher than it was in NSW: between 1901 and 1921, it averaged 24 per cent in Ontario, and 3.34 per cent in NSW. For exact figures in Ontario, see Canada, *Census*, vol. 1, 1921, 354-5. For NSW, see NSW, *NSW Statistical Register* (1903 and 1914). On wider contrasts between Australian and Canadian political culture, see Henry S. Albinski, *Canadian and Australian Politics in Comparative Perspective* (New York: Oxford 1973), 4, 14-15.

17 For a classic appraisal of the ties between Ontario's conservative value system and its democratic elements, see S.F. Wise, 'The Ontario Political Culture: A Study in Complexities,' in *The Government and Politics of Ontario* (4th ed.), ed. Graham White, 44-59 (Scarborough, ON: Nelson 1990).

18 Allan Greer and Ian Radforth, eds., *Colonial Leviathan* (Toronto: University of Toronto Press 1992); Robert Fraser, '"All the Privileges Which Englishmen Possess": Order, Rights and Constitutionalism in Upper Canada,' in *Provincial Justice: Upper Canadian Legal Portraits from the Dictionary of Canadian Biography,* ed. Robert Fraser (Toronto: Osgoode Society 1992); Paul Romney, 'From Constitutionalism to Legalism: Trial by Jury, Responsible Government, and the Role of Law in the Canadian Political Culture,' *Law and History Review* 7, 1 (1989):121-74.

19 John Eddy and Deryck Schreuder, *The Rise of Colonial Nationalism* (Sydney: Allen and Unwin 1988).

20 On the enduring tension between Loyalist and anti-authoritarian strains in Australian political culture, see S. Alomes, *A Nation at Last? The Changing Character of Australian Nationalism, 1880-1988* (North Ryde, NSW: Angus and Robertson 1988).

21 Lawrence Rosen, *The Anthropology of Justice: Law as Culture in Islamic Society* (Cambridge: Cambridge University Press 1989), 12.

22 Richard White, 'Bohemians and the Bush,' in *Inventing Australia* (Sydney: Allen and Unwin, 1981).

23 As an editorialist in the Brisbane *Worker* warned in 1901, 'Australia is to be saved from the coloured curse ... or else to be a mongrel nation torn with racial dissension, blighted by industrial war, permeated with pauperism.' Quoted in Manning Clark, *A Short History of Australia* (New York: Penguin 1987), 197.

24 For an example of this sentiment, see B. Hopkins, ed., *Canada: An Encyclopaedia of the Country* (Toronto: Linscott Publishing 1898). I am grateful to one of the anonymous readers of the manuscript for this reference.

25 For an overview of Aboriginal population shifts, see Olive Patricia Dickason, *Canada's First*

Nations: A History of Founding Peoples from Earliest Times (Toronto: McClelland and Stewart 1992).

26 Patricia Grimshaw, Marilyn Lake, Ann McGrath, and Marian Quartly, eds., *Creating a Nation, 1788-1990*, 146-7, 292. In 1959, J.A. La Nauze wrote, 'Unlike the Maori, the American Indian, or the South African Bantu, the Australian aboriginal is noticed in our history only in a melancholy footnote.' La Nauze, 'The Study of Australian History, 1929-1959,' *Historical Studies* 9, 33 (1959):11, quoted in Brian H. Fletcher, *Australian History in New South Wales, 1888-1938* (Kensington, NSW: New South Wales University Press 1993), 176.

27 For general overviews of the women's movement in both jurisdictions, see Carol Lee Bacchi, *Liberation Deferred? The Ideas of the English-Canadian Suffragists, 1877-1918* (Toronto: University of Toronto Press 1983) and Olive Lawson, *The First Voice of Australian Feminism: Excerpts from Louisa Lawson's 'The Dawn,' 1888-1895* (Sydney: Simon and Schuster 1990).

28 Karen Dubinsky and Franca Iacovetta, 'Murder, Womanly Virtue, and Motherhood: The Case of Angelina Napolitano, 1911-1922,' *Canadian Historical Review* 72, 4 (1991):505-31. Napolitano's sentence was commuted to life in prison.

29 Patricia Grimshaw, 'The "equals and comrades of men"? Labour and "the woman question" in Melbourne,' in *Debutante Nation: Feminism Contests the 1890s*, ed. S. Magarey, S. Rowley, and S. Sheriden (Sydney: Allen and Unwin 1993).

30 Judith A. Allen, *Rose Scott: Vision and Revision in Feminism* (Melbourne: Oxford University Press 1994). Although women signed petitions against executions of women, they also signed in protest against executions of men in NSW. I have as yet uncovered no evidence of a concerted women's campaign on behalf of a condemned woman in NSW in this period.

31 In the 1890s, 32.2 per cent of Canadian capital cases originated in Ontario; in the 1900s, 27.6 per cent; in the 1910s, 24.1 per cent. The decline was due, in large part, to the population boom in the west during this period.

32 Keith Hawkins argues that in bureaucratic contexts, informal rules 'dictate what information is relevant and how each case should be dealt with.' Hawkins, *The Uses of Discretion*, 40.

33 Jonathan Swainger, 'A Distant Edge of Authority: Capital Punishment and the Prerogative of Mercy in British Columbia, 1872-1880,' in *Essays in the History of Canadian Law*, vol. 6: *British Columbia and the Yukon*, ed. Hamar Foster and John Maclaren, 204-41 (Toronto: Osgoode Society 1995).

34 In 1887, Lord Carrington, the governor of NSW, had disagreed violently with the Legislative Council's decision to execute four youths for the Mount Rennie gang rape but he did not exercise his right to overrule. NSW State Archives, Colonial Secretary, Special Bundle 218095.3.

35 Desmond H. Brown, *The Genesis of the Canadian Criminal Code of 1892* (Toronto: University of Toronto Press for the Osgoode Society 1989), Table 3, 169.

36 Riel was hanged for high treason; the Native men were hanged for treason felony. See Cyril Greenland, 'The Last Public Execution in Canada: Eight Skeletons in the Closet of the Canadian Criminal Justice System,' *Criminal Law Quarterly* 29, 4 (September 1987):415-20.

37 In NSW, the colony that received the bulk of the Australian convict population, over 900 executions were carried out during the transportation era. Satyanshu K. Mukherjee, Anita Scandia, Dianne Dagger, and Wendy Mathews, *Source Book of Australian Criminal and Social Statistics, 1804-1988* (Canberra: Australian Institute of Criminology 1989), 651-9.

38 As late as 1841, free immigrants made up only 13 per cent of NSW's population. David Neal, *The Rule of Law in a Penal Colony: Law and Power in Early New South Wales* (Cambridge: Cambridge University Press 1991), 200-1.

39 On Australia's ambivalent attitudes towards British heritage and native nationalism, see Stuart Macintyre, *The Oxford History of Australia*, vol. 4: *1901-41, 'The Succeeding Age'* (Melbourne: Oxford University Press 1987), 123.

40 NSW, *Legislative Debates*, 19 December 1888, Hassall, 1338.

41 Ibid., 9 June 1896, Cotton, 686.

42 Claude Deslauniers, 'La Peine de Mort dans la Législation Criminelle de 1760 à 1892,'

Revue Générale de Droit 8, 2 (1977):156-7, 141-84. Deslauniers maintains that this was the first execution since the *patriotes'* and that it was followed by a double hanging in 1858 and another execution in 1865. Each of these took place in Canada East.

43   Canada, *Parliamentary Debates,* 14 January 1914, Bickerdike, 484, 487.

44   Deslauniers, 'La Peine de Mort,' 159. The throne speech in 1850 expressed the government's belief that 'la discipline établié dans le pénitenciare provincial et les prisons, soit autant que possible efficace pour arrêter le crime et arrêter les coupables' (p. 157). Nonetheless, the executive allowed the execution of a man, Longuedoc, the same year.

45   This interpretation is a matter of debate among Canadian historians. For an argument outlining the instrumentality of elite political culture, and a response to his critics, see Paul Romney, 'Very Late Loyalist Fantasies: Nostalgic Tory "History" and the Rule of Law in Upper Canada,' in *Canadian Perspectives on Law and Society,* 119-48.

46   The presence of trade union leaders on the 1886 Royal Commission on the Relations of Labour and Capital was typical of Macdonald's co-optation tactics. See Gregory S. Kealey, *Toronto's Workers Respond to Industrial Capitalism, 1867-1892* (Toronto: University of Toronto Press 1980), 160-2, 241-3. On the rise and decline of the Knights of Labor, see Gregory S. Kealey and Bryan Palmer, *Dreaming of What Might Be: The Knights of Labor in Ontario, 1880-1900* (Toronto: University of Toronto Press 1982).

47   In 1919, Canadian labour radicals supported Frank McCullough, a man who alleged that he had shot a police officer accidently. The executive ordered his execution in spite of a threatened 'Bolshevik' revolt. National Archives of Canada [hereinafter NAC], RG 13, vols. 1497 and 1498, file 619A/CC101. For an overview of leftist political criticism, see Peter Weinrich, *Social Protest from the Left in Canada, 1870-1970* (Toronto: University of Toronto Press 1982).

48   For a typically racist construction of inferiority, see Jones, NAC, RG 13, vol. 1545, file 267. Quoted in Michael Boudreau, 'Blacks, Chinese, and "Foreigners": The Ethnic Dimensions of Halifax's Criminal Underworld, 1918-1935,' paper presented to the Atlantic Law and History Workshop, Dalhousie University, March 1995.

49   In response to a drunken man's racist slurs and, some said, threats, Slaughter struck him on the head. No one attended the victim, who died a month later after having had an operation and while he was suffering from typhoid. Nevertheless, it took only two hours and fifteen minutes for the all-white jury to convict Slaughter for murder. Slaughter, NAC, RG 13, vol. 1447, file 362A.

50   Ibid. Roderick Park to Alexander Maclaren, MP, 10 October 1904. Slaughter's respectable father, a Baptist minister, undoubtedly influenced the outcome of his son's case.

51   Doherty, *Parliamentary Debates,* 18 February 1914, 270.

52   NAC, RG 13, vol. 1483, file 512A. By the 1920s, deportation was a common solution in the case of foreigners whose sentences had been commuted.

53   For a fuller discussion of the impact of ethnicity in this case, see Dubinsky and Iacovetta, 'Murder, Womanly Virtue, and Motherhood.'

54   Although the campaign to support Napolitano split the Canadian women's movement, it attracted support from women and men worldwide. Ibid., 516-17. Sternaman did inspire sympathy among some women (for instance, 'Kit' of the *Globe and Mail,* as well as twenty-nine 'lady' petitioners from Lindsay, Ontario), but most of her public supporters were men. NAC, RG 13, vol. 1431, file 286A.

55   The first woman executed after the Liberals' victory in 1896 was Hilda Blake, a young Barnardo girl convicted of killing her mistress in Brandon, Manitoba. She was hanged in 1899. Tom Mitchell, '"Blood with the Taint of Cain": Immigrant Labouring Children, Manitoba Politics, and the Execution of Emily Hilda Blake,' *Journal of Canadian Studies* 30 (Winter 1993):30.

56   NAC, RG 13, vol. 1431, file 286A.

57   Once the organized women's movement waned at the close of the First World War, executions of women resumed, the first hanging taking place in 1922. Strange, 'The Lottery of Death.'

58   NAC, RG 13, vol. 1484, file 417A.

59   The pair had robbed a householder in a wealthy suburb of Sydney, then set about to rob

the Union Steamship Company in the central city when they were disturbed by several constables who gave chase. Montgomery had a loaded revolver, which he threatened to use, but he and his accomplice used iron bars to ward off the policemen. NSW State Archives, Colonial Secretary, Special Bundle, 4/1081-2 and 4/909.1.

60 NSW, State Archives, Special Bundle 4/1081, May 1894.

61 Bank failures in 1893, combined with protracted strikes and drought, crippled the economies of the eastern states. See Beverley Kingston, *The Oxford History of Australia,* vol. 3: *Glad, Confident Morning* (Melbourne: Oxford University Press 1993), 45.

62 David Walker, 'Youth on Trial: The Mt. Rennie Case,' *Labour History* 50 (May 1986): 28-41.

63 NSW, *Debates,* 28 November 1899, Ferguson, 2653.

64 Ibid., 12 August 1902, Haynes, 1811. He added: 'An unfortunate brute, suddenly yielding to passion, and assaulting a woman, is not nearly as bad a man as he who continuously gives himself to plan the moral destruction of women.'

65 Charles Hines was executed for incest rapes in 1897, and Joseph Campbell was executed in 1902. Numerous petitions were sent to request Hines's reprieve, including one from Scone district police who reported that 'outside matters of morality, nothing could be alleged against the condemned man, as he was honest in business matters and paid his way.' NSW State Archives, Colonial Secretary, Special Bundle, 4/924.2.

66 NSW State Archives, Attorney General and Justice Correspondence, 7/5490, file 1915/7749.

67 Ibid., 7/5465.

68 His death sentence was commuted to fourteen years. NSW State Archives, Premier's Office, Special Bundle, official papers, 1892-07, 2/8396.

69 NSW, *Legislative Debates,* John Haynes, 24 July 1900, 1222.

70 Ibid., 24 July 1900, Ewing, 1228.

71 The fez is not a standard feature of qadi garb, but is sometimes worn by qadis in Morocco, where Lawrence Rosen conducted his case study.

72 Michael Ignatieff, 'State, Civil Society, and Total Institutions,' in *Social Control and the State: Historical and Comparative Essays,* ed. Stanley Cohen and Andrew Scull, 75-105 (Oxford: Basil Blackwell 1983), 83.

73 Clifford D. Shearing and Richard V. Ericson, 'Culture as Figurative Action,' *British Journal of Sociology* 42, 4 (December 1991):481-505. In applying the authors' analysis, I would argue that British justice was a meta-narrative in which different stories, generated over the course of distinct colonial histories, were given meaning.

74 On punishment as both a reflection and signifier of colonial political culture, see John Pratt, 'Penal History in Colonial Society: New Issues in the Sociology of Punishment,' *Australian Journal of Law and Society* 11 (1995):3-31.

Punishment in Late-Twentieth-Century Canada: An Afterword

Anthony N. Doob

For a criminologist like me, who is interested in the way we impose punishments, reading this book can be either a depressing or a reassuring experience. It is depressing in that, at a certain level of abstraction, there is little *now* that is different from earlier periods of Canadian, Australian, and English history described in this book. The problems that governments faced in meting out punishments and dispensing mercy are remarkably similar to those we are facing in Canada today. We 'invent' new punishments from time to time, but they do not appear to accomplish much. There is, however, some reason to be happy about the parallels between other times and places and our current situation: we have not been remarkably successful in finding new ways to be brutal, and an afterword like this one will not quickly go out of date.

There is a very important lesson in these chapters for anyone interested in current criminal justice policy: any policy that appears to create harsh punishments will have the effect of generating strong pressures to mitigate these harsh punishments in some cases. The cases that will benefit from this mercy will not be predictable from a sensible set of publicly acceptable principles. The principles governing the dispensing of mercy are more likely to resemble the process Carolyn Strange described for commutations of the death sentence in Canada.[1] Although commutations were fairly common, the cabinet followed no obvious principles in making these decisions. Instead, whether a person was executed or not appeared to be determined by a combination of factors related to the offender, the offence, public campaigns for or against execution of the offender, and an assessment of the political ramifications of the decision.

The essays in this volume can, however, be used to illustrate a somewhat broader set of suggestions for current policy-makers. These include the following:

- the necessity of deciding what we are we trying to accomplish in the sentencing of offenders
- the futility, in the absence of a coherent 'theory' of punishment, of searching for the 'ideal' punishment
- the problems inherent in the public dispensing of mercy
- the inevitable tension between harsh punishments and mercy.

Lack of Coherence in Policies Governing Punishment and the Necessity of Mercy

Parliament has given Canadian judges very little guidance on how sentences should be handed down. Court decisions constantly refer to the importance of each of the 'standard' purposes of sentencing: denunciation, individual and general deterrence, incapacitation, and rehabilitation. Courts often cite a Saskatchewan Court of Appeal case[2] that listed these general purposes but gave no guidance on how penalties should be determined. Courts appeal to deterrence as justification for increasing a penalty, and to the need for rehabilitation as justification for reducing a sentence. They seldom explain how a heavier sentence will deter, given that most offenders do not commit acts assuming that they will be apprehended and sentenced. Nor do courts explain why a lighter sentence would automatically be more rehabilitating.

Deterrence is currently the most popular justification for harsh sentences.[3] Hence attempts are made to use offenders, at sentencing, as resources to prevent further crime. A typical case involved a twenty-one-year-old female gospel singer from Halifax who was apprehended carrying what the police described as half a million dollars worth of cocaine into Canada. She and a friend were each to have been paid $2,000 for their work. The woman's sentence was raised by the Ontario Court of Appeal from three years to five years because 'it falls to the courts to warn would-be couriers, in no uncertain terms, that they will pay a heavy price for choosing to import large quantities of drugs.' Unfortunately the judges did not explain how they had determined that three years would provide an inadequate warning. A short article on page five of the *Globe and Mail* that described the new five-year sentence presumably warned potential couriers of the dangers of mixing with the justice system. The couriers themselves were described by the judges as 'weak and vulnerable,' but other potential couriers, the judges would have us believe, supposedly read Canada's national newspaper regularly enough to get the warning.[4] The difficulty, of course, is that where deterrence is just one principle that can be invoked, and 'assisting in the rehabilitation of offenders' and 'promoting a sense of responsibility in offenders' are others,[5] the 'deserving' are likely to be seen as candidates for rehabilitation and the 'less deserving' used in an attempt to make the rest of us safe.

We have, then, two quite separate views. Judges and politicians, more often than not, appear to believe that harsher sentences deter crime more effectively. However, almost all those who have reviewed the evidence on deterrence conclude that judges cannot reduce crime by raising the severity of their sentences. The common criminological wisdom is that crime control efforts should be focused elsewhere. As the Canadian Sentencing Commission noted, 'Intuitively, at least, one would rather resort to a security guard than to a sentencing judge to protect one's home.'[6]

The conflict, then, between what policy advisers 'know,' and what is actually 'done' in the criminal justice system has carried through to the present day. The Canadian Sentencing Commission in 1987 summarized the evidence on the deterrent impact of sentencing and concluded that harsher penalties would not deter. Very occasionally, trial or appeal judges write carefully documented arguments suggesting that extremely harsh penalties are no more effective in deterring than merely moderately harsh penalties. Typically, these will be dissenting opinions at the appeal level[7] or overturned opinions at the trial level. Even a Conservative-dominated House of Commons committee in 1993, only a few months before the general election in which the Progressive Conservatives were almost completely removed from the federal political scene,[8] noted, 'If locking up those who violate the law contributed to safer societies, then the United States should be the safest country in the world. In fact, the United States affords a glaring example of the limited impact that criminal justice responses may have on crime.'[9]

The committee that wrote that statement appears to have understood the criminological literature. Those responsible for shaping criminal justice policy, however, appear to act in blissful ignorance of what is known. It appears to be politically attractive, though intellectually bankrupt, to suggest that simple legal or administrative changes in sentencing policy can reduce crime. Such approaches are no more effective today than they were two centuries ago. Our inability to develop a sensible and coherent purpose of sentencing is, of course, not new. Simon Devereaux notes that during the late eighteenth and early nineteenth centuries, there was no consensus about penal purposes, but at the same time he points out that commentators of the day saw transportation as an all purpose punishment, adaptable to a number of penal objectives.

Punishment in the Absence of a Coherent Purpose

The search for new punishments (for example, boot camps, electronic monitoring of offenders in the community, conditional sentences) appears to be pursued with more enthusiasm than the examination of the purposes of these punishments. Governments appear to be enthusiastic about the technology of punishment, but less interested in addressing the complex question of what punishment is supposed to accomplish. The Canadian Sentencing Commission stands alone in its explicit recommendation for a coherent, and limiting, statement of purpose and principles of sentencing. The first legislative statement on sentencing principles in Canada became law only in late 1996.[10] Predictably, it contained a smorgasbord of justifications for punishment (deterrence, incapacitation, reparations for harm done to victims, etc.) with no direction to judges as to how to match punishment purposes with offenders.

In effect, then, the Canadian Parliament of the day might be seen as having avoided difficult decisions in much the same way as the United States Sentencing Commission had done almost ten years earlier when it stated:

> Most observers of the criminal law agree that the ultimate aim of the law itself, and of punishment in particular, is the control of crime. Beyond this point, however, the consensus seems to break down. Some argue that the appropriate punishment should be defined primarily on the basis of the moral principle of 'just deserts' ... Others argue that punishment should be imposed primarily on the basis of practical 'crime control' considerations ...
>
> Adherents of these points of view have urged the Commission to choose between them, to accord one primacy over the other. Such a choice would be profoundly difficult ... As a practical matter, in most sentencing decisions both philosophies may prove consistent with the same result.[11]

The United States Sentencing Commission may have been right that 'purposes' did not matter since the commissioners' apparent goal – to increase the size of the federal prison population – was determined by the commission's published 'guidelines' quite independent of any stated purpose. Similarly, if the English Home Office's goal in the eighteenth century was simply to 'get rid of' offenders, the niceties of why offenders were being transported to Australia did not matter. The modern Canadian punishment policy, like its American counterpart or like transportation in eighteenth-century England, usually devolves to a familiar tune: 'If you have the capacity to punish, use it, and don't worry about why you are doing it.' The result is that in recent years our prison population has increased quite dramatically. When governments do seem interested in reducing the use of imprisonment, they appear to be responding primarily to budgetary concerns. Recently, for example, two provinces (Quebec and Alberta) have announced their intention to reduce imprisonment, more to contain costs than to comply with reasoned arguments that certain types of offenders should not be imprisoned.[12]

Mercy and Discretion

In spite of the growing movement towards severity, Canada has maintained its official belief in discretion, particularly at the sentencing stage of proceedings. Recent amendments to the Criminal Code make it explicit that aggravating and mitigating factors *relating to the offence or the offender* can be used to increase or decrease sentences.[13] More interesting, perhaps, is the special recognition of the problem of Aboriginal offenders in the criminal justice system. Tina Loo points out that the dispensing of mercy in nineteenth-century British Columbia was affected by cultural beliefs about the relative impact of different sanctions. She notes that some judges believed that to execute an Aboriginal offender was to show mercy since, in their opinion, Native people saw imprisonment as a punishment more cruel than execution. With capital punishment removed from the arsenal of punishments, one assumes the minister of justice was suggesting that an extra measure of mercy be shown to Aboriginal people when he introduced legislation, since passed into law, stating, 'All appropriate sanctions other than imprisonment that are reasonable in the circumstances [should] be considered for all offenders, with particular attention to the circumstances of aboriginal offenders.'[14] With a highly disproportionate number of Aboriginal people in our prisons,[15] the issue of how to deal with Aboriginal offenders, addressed in Tina Loo's chapter, is certainly still with us.

The problem we are faced with is much the same as that described in this book. We still do not have a coherent structure for punishment. Lack of coherence leads, inevitably, to the type of arbitrariness described in many parts of this book. But, from a practical perspective, there are some very real problems with harsh penalties. We have learned that executing large numbers of people was not seen as being a very effective way of dealing with crime. The goal was always to find an 'intermediate' punishment – something between doing little or nothing, on the one hand, and executing the offender, on the other. Our modern-day search for intermediate punishments is different only in the sense that we are typically looking for something 'between prison and probation.'[16]

One of the problems with our present sentencing structure is that it appears to assume harsh penalties, with everything less than 'harsh' being seen as showing mercy. Thus for the most part the Criminal Code specifies maximum sentences, and nothing more. No wonder many people are upset with the courts' decisions typically not to use maximum penalties.[17] Since the courts tell us that they can deter crime, why wouldn't any reasonable person ask them to raise the penalty and reduce crime a bit more?

Seeing the maximum penalty as a 'standard' has another rather unfortunate effect: when an accused person pleads guilty, it is permissible for the court to reduce the sentence but, by logical gymnastics that one needs a law degree to understand, this does not mean that there is a penalty for pleading not guilty.

Greg Smith points out that in the early nineteenth century, the exercise of mercy led to a shift away from physical punishments of the body to punishments of the soul. The ambivalence of 'what' we punish is still with us, and becomes salient when the soul-punishing experience of imprisonment becomes too expensive for the middle class taxpayer. American punishers, faced with high costs and overcrowded prisons have created punishment regimes based more on movie images of soul-changing experiences than on principled thought: the boot camp.[18] In understanding the popularity of these facilities among the American punitive elite, one must remember that often a 'short' stay in a boot camp is substituted for a much longer stay in a state prison. Mercy, then, comes with a price, as it always has: in this case it is the substitution of a short punishment of body and soul for a longer punishment solely of the soul. The Ontario Conservative government, smitten with the idea of returning to core values of punishing the body as well as the soul, announced in late 1995 that it will be setting up boot camps for Ontario's young offenders. In a 'punish first' and 'think later' approach, however, it first announced the creation of boot camps and then created a task force to design them and recommend what type of offender should be sent to them.

How Public Can the Dispensing of Mercy Be?

The chapters in this book raise – and I think, answer – an important question: How is it that governments can 'get away with' dispensing mercy? The answer may be a simple one: punishments are usually determined by one branch of government (typically, now, the legislature) and imposed by another (the judiciary). Mercy, on the other hand, is exercised by the third branch of government: the executive. It is also important, perhaps, that the reasoning behind decisions concerning mercy take place in private. Reasons without principles might not stand up to public scrutiny.

In our current system of punishment, the most commonly used form of 'mercy' is dispensed by correctional authorities and by parole boards. For the most part, these decisions are invisible. Individual offenders are allowed out on passes; and prisoners are released on parole. Little publicity is given to these individual decisions. As long as we do not have a coherent theory of sentencing and mercy can be dispensed privately, we have a plausible chance of getting away with punishing less than the original sentence required.

It is also easier to be 'tough' on the one hand (for example, by imposing harsh mandatory penalties) and show mercy on the other if two different branches of government are doing this under different guises. As Carolyn Strange points out in her introduction, mercy allows harshness to exist. If a system still allows mercy to be dispensed, then one can separate the deserving offenders from the non-deserving.

We are, however, ambivalent about the exercise of mercy. The jury has traditionally exercised mercy in acquitting those for whom the laws were not 'meant to apply.' To ensure that the basis of jury decisions remain private, in 1972 Canada made it an offence for anyone to disclose jury proceedings,[19] apparently to keep the public from understanding the process by which juries arrive at their decisions.

Judges do not show much enthusiasm for letting people know that juries have the right to dispense mercy. In the 1970s, the Law Reform Commission of Canada asked Canadian citizens, jurors in Canadian cases, and judges who had the jurisdiction to hear jury cases whether jurors should be informed of their right to show mercy if it were the best way of achieving justice.[20] Both members of the public and jurors (before and after they had served on a jury) were very much in favour of such instructions being given. Judges, on the other hand, were strongly against such instructions being given.[21] The Supreme Court of Canada also felt that juries should not be openly encouraged to show mercy and criticized a lawyer for suggesting that it was their right.[22]

One wonders, in the light of recent jury acquittals in the United States, whether the exercise of discretion by a jury to acquit might not also have come into disrepute with the public. The acquittal of Los Angeles police officers in the videotaped beating of Rodney King created controversy in large part because millions of people were able to view the crucial evidence that showed King being hit by the police. Football star O.J. Simpson's entire trial was watched by millions on live television. Many viewers and television commentators concluded – on the basis of evidence that differed somewhat from that heard by the jurors – that Simpson was guilty. The jury acquitted him. It is one thing for a jury to acquit quietly and relatively privately; it is quite another when the acquittal is shown on live television. Publicizing decisions that are made in the absence of principles may not show the criminal justice system in a favourable light.

It is possible, therefore, that one of the reasons that mercy was tolerated in the places and periods described in this book is that mercy was seen as the exception rather than the rule. If nobody was 'keeping score' on what cabinet was doing (until twentieth-century historians came along), people may not have worried as much about the overall impact of decisions to dispense mercy as they did about the appropriateness of individual decisions. Focusing on individual decisions does not necessarily involve questioning the legitimacy of the process itself.

The process of modifying punishments could, in the past, be separated quite effectively from the imposition of punishments. Hence, one could easily imagine a judge imposing, for denunciatory or deterrence purposes, a very harsh sentence. This same sentence, after examination by the executive, might be modified, but the 'rule' was untouched: the exception constituted an instance of the dispensing of mercy. Our current system does not allow such separation to take place so easily. Newspaper, radio, and television reports of sentencing routinely refer to the date when the sentence can be 'modified': the parole eligibility date. When Karla Homolka was sentenced (for manslaughter) to twelve years in prison for her part in the killing of two young girls, news reports regularly referred to her being eligible for (day) parole after three and a half years.

The decision to parole an offender, then, has shifted in the public's mind from the dispensation of mercy to a routine and 'soft-headed' modification of the punishment. In addition, individual members of the parole board can be disciplined when they have 'failed in the due execution of the member's office.'[23] It is no wonder, then, that fewer people are released on parole now than were released a few years ago when day-to-day decisions were not as visible. It is hard to argue against the principle of holding decision-makers responsible for their decisions, but if dispensing mercy through the parole system is an integral part of the punishment system, the effect will almost certainly be to reduce the number of people who will be released on parole.

The Irresolvable Tension between Harsh Penalties and Mercy

There are times when legislatures appear – at least for a while – to be successful in eliminating all hope for mercy. The United States federal sentencing guidelines provide an opportunity to examine the impact of a dramatic increase in the severity of punishment being handed out. The first, and most obvious, impact was to strengthen the power of the prosecutor, largely in terms of the prosecutor's power to plea bargain effectively. Judges, however, were not given the power to sentence in a way that they regarded as sensible, and were not allowed the flexibility to be merciful in exceptional cases. The effect is that there has been widespread dissatisfaction with the sentencing process among judges, and one judge has even refused to hear certain types of cases. After referring to two people he had sentenced in the previous week, one judge notified his colleagues that he would no longer hear drug cases, saying: 'These two cases confirm my sense of depression about much of the cruelty I have been party to in connection with the "war on drugs" ... I need a rest from the oppressive sense of futility that these drug cases leave ... This resolution leaves me uncomfortable since it shifts the "dirty work" to other judges. At the moment, however, I simply cannot sentence another impoverished person whose destruction has no discernible effect on the drug trade ... I am just a tired old judge who has temporarily filled his quota of remorselessness.'[24]

In Canada as well, we appear to be better at eliminating opportunities for the exercise of mercy than we are at creating sensible penalties. Parliament legislated that 'an offender should not be deprived of liberty, if less restrictive sanctions may be appropriate in the circumstances'[25] at almost the same time that a large number of mandatory minimum sentences of four years have been imposed for offences involving a firearm.[26] The fact that it will be difficult for the court to ignore the presence of the weapon in an offence means that it is almost inevitable that those wishing to exercise mercy will be unable to do so or will have to be unusually creative. Presumably, however, 'deserving' offenders will benefit from a merciful finding of facts by the prosecutor or the court.

The historical accounts contained in the earlier chapters of this book make it clear that it is almost inevitable that mandatory harsh penalties will give rise to great pressure to find a way of dispensing mercy for deserving offenders. The trial of Saskatchewan farmer Robert Latimer is a case in point. He was found guilty of second degree murder in the killing of his severely disabled and chronically suffering daughter. It appears to be accepted that his sole motivation was to put her out of her pain.[27] The elimination of most avenues for the exercise of mercy in cases where a person is found guilty of murder and sentenced to life in prison with parole ineligibility for ten years created a controversy that has not yet been resolved.[28] A similar case, tried in the same year, where a plea of manslaughter was accepted and a suspended sentence and probation was imposed, resulted in almost no controversy.[29]

Perhaps the lesson we should learn from reading the essays in this volume is a simple one: when strict punishments are imposed on a system, there will be very strong pressures to find ways to dispense mercy when those punishments 'do not fit the crime' or when society cannot afford to impose those punishments. Accomplishing 'justice' through the private dispensing of 'mercy' may be impossible. If mercy has historically been a 'lottery' as Carolyn Strange suggests,[30] perhaps we would do well to find a new model for criminal justice policy.

Notes

1 Carolyn Strange, 'The Lottery of Death: Capital Punishment in Canada, 1867-1976,' *Manitoba Law Journal* 23, 3 (1996):594-619.
2 *R. v. Morrisette and two others* (1970), 1 C.C.C. (2d) 207.
3 Canadian Sentencing Commission, *Sentencing Reform: A Canadian Approach,* (Ottawa: Supply and Services Canada 1987), 135.
4 Thomas Claridge, 'Appeal court increases drug sentence,' *Globe and Mail*, 14 February 1996, A5.
5 Criminal Code, section 718 (as amended 1996).

6 See note 3 above, 148.

7 See, for example, the dissent of Vancise J.A. in *R.* v. *McGinn* (1989), 49 C.C.C. (3d) 137.

8 No political commentators that I am aware of have suggested that the Progressive Conservatives were annihilated because of their criminal justice policy. It is more likely that 'progressive' statements like that made by the committee were noticed only by a small number of academics.

9 Canada, House of Commons, Standing Committee on Justice and the Solicitor General (Dr. Bob Horner, Chairman), twelfth report, *Crime Prevention in Canada: Toward a National Strategy* (Ottawa: February 1993) 2.

10 An Act to amend the Criminal Code (sentencing) and other Acts in consequence thereof, 1995 (Bill C-41). Proclaimed into force in late 1996.

11 United States Sentencing Commission, *Federal Sentencing Guidelines Manual (1988), 1.3-1.4.*

12 Brian Lagni, 'Alberta to free up jail space; keep violent criminals in longer, *Globe and Mail*, 19 April 1996, A4. Rhéal Séguin, 'Quebec launches prison reforms: Measures include six closings, fewer jailings of non-violent criminals, *Globe and Mail*, 3 April 1996, A1.

13 Criminal Code, section 718.2(a), legislated in 1996 as part of Bill C-41.

14 Ibid., section 718.2(e), legislated in 1996 as part of Bill C-41.

15 See Julian V. Roberts and Anthony N. Doob, 'Race, Ethnicity, and Criminal Justice in Canada,' in *Crime and Justice: A Review of Research,* ed. Michael Tonry (Chicago: University of Chicago Press, forthcoming).

16 See Norval Morris and Michael Tonry, *Between Prison and Probation: Intermediate Punishments in a Rational Sentencing System* (New York: Oxford University Press 1990).

17 See, for example, Anthony N. Doob and Julian V. Roberts, 'Public Punitiveness and Public Knowledge of the Facts: Some Canadian Surveys,' in *Public Attitudes to Sentencing: Surveys from Five Countries,* ed. Nigel Walker and Mike Hough, 111-33 (Aldershot: Gower 1988).

18 See Jonathan Simon, 'They Died with Their Boots On: The Boot Camp and the Limits of Modern Penalty,' *Social Justice* 22, 2 (1995):25-48.

19 Criminal Code, section 649.

20 See Anthony N. Doob, 'The Public's View of the Criminal Jury Trial'; Doob, 'The Canadian Juror's View of the Criminal Jury Trial'; Doob, 'Canadian Trial Judges' Views of the Criminal Jury Trial,' in *Studies on the Jury* (Ottawa: Law Reform Commission of Canada 1979).

21 Judges in British Columbia would not even let potential jurors be asked the question. See A.N. Doob, 'The Canadian Juror's View of the Criminal Jury Trial', ibid., 66.

22 *R.* v. *Morgentaler, Smoling and Scott* (1988), 37 C.C.C. (3d) 449.

23 Corrections and Conditional Release Act, section 155.2(2)(c), as amended 1995.

24 Eastern District of New York Judge Jack B. Weinstein, 'Memorandum,' reprinted in full in (1993) 5 *Federal Sentencing Reporter:*298.

25 Criminal Code, section 718.2(d), legislated in 1996 as part of Bill C-41.

26 As part of the 'firearms' legislation in 1995, minimum penalties of four years were imposed for each of a large number of offences, including robbery 'where a firearm is used in the commission of the offence.'

27 For a discussion of this case, see Peter MacKinnon, 'Reflections on Homicide.' *Criminal Law Forum* 6, 2 (1995):315-26.

28 The ultimate outcome of this case is not known at the time of writing since an appeal is still pending and, even in the absence of a successful appeal, a new trial has been ordered on quite separate grounds.

29 Rob Andrus, 'Sentence suspended in "mercy killing."' *Toronto Star*, 3 March 1995, 1.

30 Carolyn Strange, 'The Lottery of Death.'

Select Bibliography

Amnesty International. *When the State Kills ... The Death Penalty: A Human Rights Issue.* New York: Amnesty International 1989

Amussen, Susan Dwyer. 'Punishment, Discipline, and Power: The Social Meanings of Violence in Early Modern England.' *Journal of British Studies* 34 (1995):1-34

Beattie, J.M. *Crime and the Courts in England, 1660-1800.* Princeton, NJ: Princeton University Press 1986

–.'Violence and Society in Early-Modern England.' In *Perspectives in Criminal Law*, ed. Anthony N. Doob and Edward L. Greenspan. Aurora, ON: Canada Law Book 1985

Bennett, M. Lance, and Martha S. Feldman. *Reconstructing Reality in the Courtroom.* New Brunswick, NJ: Rutgers University Press 1981

Boissery, Beverley. *A Deep Sense of Wrong: The Treason Trials and Transportation of Lower Canadian Rebels to New South Wales after the 1838 Rebellion.* Toronto: Osgoode Society/Dundurn 1995

Braithwaite, John. *Crime, Shame, and Reintegration.* Cambridge: Cambridge University Press 1989

Buetow, Harold A. *The Scabbardless Sword: Criminal Justice and the Quality of Mercy.* Tarrytown, NY: Associated Faculty Press 1982

Cockburn, J.S. 'Punishment and Brutalization in the English Enlightenment.' *Law and History Review* 12, 1(Spring 1994):155-79

Davis, Natalie Zemon. *Fiction in the Archives: Pardon Tales and Their Tellers in Sixteenth-Century France.* Stanford, CA: Stanford University Press 1987

Duff, Antony, and David Garland, eds. *A Reader on Punishment.* Oxford: Oxford University Press 1994

Ekirch, A. Roger. *Bound for America: The Transportation of British Convicts to the Colonies, 1718-1775.* Oxford: Clarendon Press 1987

Elias, Norbert. *The Civilizing Process*, vol. 1: *The History of Manners.* vol. 2: *State Formation and Civilization.* Trans. Edmund Jephcott. 1939; reprint, Oxford: Blackwell 1994

Fitzpatrick, Peter. *The Mythology of Modern Law.* London: Routledge 1992

Foster, Hamar. '"The Queen's Law Is Better than Yours": International Homicide in Early British Columbia.' In *Essays in the History of Canadian Law*, vol. 5: *Crime and Criminal Justice*, ed. Jim Phillips, Tina Loo, and Susan Lewthwaite. Toronto: Osgoode Society 1994

Foucault, Michel. *Discipline and Punish: The Birth of the Prison.* New York: Vintage Books 1977

Galligan, David J. *Discretionary Powers: A Legal Study of Official Discretion.* Oxford: Oxford University Press 1986

Garland, David. *Punishment and Modern Society: A Study in Social Theory.* Chicago: University of Chicago Press 1990

Gatrell, V.A.C. *The Hanging Tree: Execution and the English People, 1770-1868*. Oxford: Oxford University Press 1994

Hartz, Louis. *The Founding of New Societies*. New York: Harcourt, Brace 1964

Hawkins, Keith, ed. *The Uses of Discretion*. Oxford: Oxford University Press 1992

Hay, Douglas. 'Property, Authority and the Criminal Law.' In *Albion's Fatal Tree: Crime and Society in Eighteenth-Century England*, ed. Douglas Hay, Peter Linebaugh, John G. Rule, E.P. Thompson, and Cal Winslow, 17-63. London: Allen Lane 1975

-.'Time, Inequality, and Law's Violence.' In *Law's Violence*, ed. Austin Sarat and Thomas Kearnes, 141-73. Ann Arbor: University of Michigan Press 1993

Ignatieff, Michael. *A Just Measure of Pain: The Penitentiary in the Industrial Revolution*. New York: Pantheon Books 1978

-.'State, Civil Society, and Total Institutions.' In *Social Control and the State: Historical and Comparative Essays*, ed. Stanley Cohen and Andrew Scull. Oxford: Basil Blackwell 1983

Laqueur, Thomas. 'Bodies, Details, and the Humanitarian Narrative.' In *The New Cultural History*, ed. Lynn Hunt. Berkeley: University of California Press 1989

Laster, Kathy. 'Famous Last Words: Criminals on the Scaffold, Victoria, Australia, 1842-1967.' *International Journal of the Sociology of the Law* 22 (1994):1-18

Linebaugh, Peter. *The London Hanged: Crime and Civil Society in the Eighteenth Century*. London: Allen Lane 1991

Macklem, Timothy. 'Provocation and the Ordinary Person.' *Dalhousie Law Journal* 11 (1987):126-56

Magnarella, Paul J. 'Justice in a Culturally Pluralistic Society: The Cultural Defense on Trial.' *Journal of Ethnic Studies* 19 (1991):65-84

Marquis, Greg. 'Doing Justice to "British Justice": Law, Ideology, and Canadian Historiography.' In *Canadian Perspectives on Law and Society: Issues in Legal History*, ed. W. Wesley Pue and Barry Wright, 43-70. Ottawa: Carleton University Press 1988

McGowen, Randall. 'The Body and Punishment in Eighteenth-Century England.' *Journal of Modern History* 59 (December 1987):651-79

-.'The Changing Face of God's Justice: The Debates over Divine and Human Punishment in Eighteenth-Century England.' *Criminal Justice History* 9 (1988):63-98

-.'The Image of Justice and Reform of the Criminal Law in Early Nineteenth Century England.' *Buffalo Law Review* 32 (1983):89-125

Moore, Kathleen D. *Pardons: Justice, Mercy, and the Public Interest*. New York: Oxford University Press 1989

Murphy, Jeffrie, and Jean Hampton. *Forgiveness and Mercy*. New York: Cambridge University Press 1988

Neal, David. *The Rule of Law in a Penal Colony: Law and Power in Early New South Wales*. Cambridge: Cambridge University Press 1991

Phillips, Jim. 'The Operation of the Royal Pardon in Nova Scotia, 1749-1815.' *University of Toronto Law Journal* 42 (1992):401-49

Pratt, John. 'Penal History in a Colonial Society: New Issues in the Sociology of Punishment.' *Australian Journal of Law and Society* 11 (1995):3-31

Reid, John Phillip. 'Principles of Vengeance: Fur Trappers, Indians, and Retaliation for Homicide in the Transboundary North American West.' *Western Historical Quarterly* 24 (1993):21-43

Rosen, Lawrence. *The Anthropology of Justice: Law as Culture in Islamic Society*. Cambridge: Cambridge University Press 1989

Sams, Julia P. 'The Availability of the "Cultural Defence" as an Excuse for Criminal Behaviour.' *Georgia Journal of International and Comparative Law* 16 (1986):335-54

Spierenburg, Pieter. *The Spectacle of Suffering. Executions and the Evolution of Repression: From a Preindustrial Metropolis to the European Experience*. Cambridge: Cambridge University Press 1984

Strange, Carolyn. 'The Lottery of Death: Capital Punishment in Canada, 1867-1976.' *Manitoba Law Journal* 23, 3 (1996):594-619

Thomas, Nicholas. *Colonialism's Culture: Anthropology, Travel, and Government*. Cambridge: Polity Press 1994

White, James Boyd. *Heracles' Bow: Essays in the Rhetoric and Poetics of the Law*. Madison, WI: University of Wisconsin Press 1985

Wiener, Martin J. *Reconstructing the Criminal: Culture, Law and Policy in England, 1830-1914*. New York: Cambridge University Press 1990

Wright, Barry. 'The Ideological Dimensions of the Law in Upper Canada: The Treason Proceedings of 1838.' *Criminal Justice: An International Annual* 10 (1989):131-78

Contributors

Simon Devereaux is a Junior Fellow at the Centre of Criminology, University of Toronto. He has published articles on the criminal trial and the press in late eighteenth-century London.

Anthony N. Doob is a Professor at the Centre of Criminology, University of Toronto. He was a member of the Canadian Sentencing Commission from 1984 to 1987 and has published widely on public attitudes about sentencing, crime and criminal justice in Aboriginal communities, victimization, and the youth justice system.

Douglas Hay teaches law and legal history at York University. He has contributed to *Albion's Fatal Tree: Crime and Society in Eighteenth-Century England* (1975), *Policing and Prosecution in Britain* (1989), and numerous other collections. His most recent book, with Nicholas Rogers, is *English Society in the Eighteenth Century* (1997).

Tina Loo is an Associate Professor in the Department of History, Simon Fraser University. She is the author of *Making Law, Order, and Authority in British Columbia, 1821-1871* (1994) and, with Carolyn Strange, the co-author of *Making Good: Law and Moral Regulation in Canada, 1867-1939* (1997).

Greg T. Smith is a Junior Fellow in the Centre of Criminology, University of Toronto. His dissertation examines violence in eighteenth- and early nineteenth-century England.

Carolyn Strange teaches at the Centre of Criminology, University of Toronto. She has published on the history of crime, justice, and moral regulation in Canada and Australia.

Barry Wright is an Associate Professor in the Department of Law, Carleton University. His most recent book, co-edited with Murray Greenwood, is *Canadian State Trials: Law, Politics, and Security Measures, 1608-1837* (1996).

Index

Abolition of punishment, Australia and Canada, 6, 148, 157-60. *See also* Capital punishment, abolition of
Aboriginal culture affecting judiciary decisions, 108-9, 157, 170. *See also* Cultural defence
Aboriginal laws, legitimacy in capital cases, 112
Aboriginal offenders, 6, 9, 107 (table), 133, 138, 153, 157
Aboriginal Protection Board, 138
Aboriginals: attitudes towards execution, 113, 170; colonization affecting justice for, 106-7, 114, 116, 121, 138; extinction of, 137-8; mercy shown towards, 110-12; remote threat to colonists, 146. *See also* Cultural defence; Justice, 'savage,' for Aboriginals
Alberta, 169
American Revolution (1776), 56, 60, 66
Amnesty: for political prisoners, 91-2, 96, 97; for sex offenders, 155
Anthropology, science of: and evolutionary theory, 121, 125; justifying European racial views, 109, 116, 121, 123
ANZAC legend of Australia, 137
Aristocrats, obligations to, 6
Arthur, Sir George, 84-6, 89-92, 94, 96, 97
Asian cultures, individual liberties in, 24
Attoo, trial of, 123
Australia, offenders transported to. *See* ANZAC legend; Transportation as punishment, to Australia; Van Diemen's Land
Australian Labor Party, 14
Australia's convict past, 7
Aylesworth, Sir Allen, 152

Bamford, Samuel, 61-2
Banishment, 6, 15, 63; from province to US, 81-2, 84, 86, 88-90, 91
Barbarism, 45
Bayley, Thomas, 67-8
Beamer, Jacob, 87, 91
Beattie, John, 7, 9, 10, 58-9
Beccaria, Cesare, 12, 14, 26
Begbie, Judge Matthew Baillie, 106, 108, 112, 115, 116, 120, 121, 122-5
Benevolence. *See* Discretionary mercy
Bennett, W. Lance, 119
Bentham, Jeremy, 12, 82
Berkhofer, Robert, 121
Bickerdike, John, 147
Black, Donald, 11
Blacks in US justice system, 10, 14, 157-8
Blackstone, William, 30
Bloody Assize (1685), 91
Bond Head, Sir Francis, 85
Boot camps, 14, 168, 171
Boswell, James, 28
Botany Bay (NSW), 60, 62
Braithwaite, John, 40
British government, intervening in Upper Canada trials, 88, 90, 91-2, 97, 166
British justice, 137; fair play in, 9, 134-5, 147, 153, 156, 160. *See also* Rule of law
Broughton, Lord Henry, 39, 40
Brutality, acts of, 26
Bryant, John, 110, 111
Burke, Edmund, 33

Cabinet members, 4, 150, 160. *See also* Executive Councils (Canadian); Executive discretion
Cameron, David, 112

Canada, justice in. *See* Criminal justice system, in Canada
Canada, province of: executions, 147
Canadian Sentencing Commission, 168, 169
Capital case dispositions: comparison of NSW and Ontario, 131-2, 136, 139-40, 159; in New South Wales, 143 (table); in Ontario, 142 (table)
Capital cases: changes in numbers, 79, 81, 82, 83, 98; codes of honour in, 119, 120; minor and corporal punishments for, 31; outcomes, 161
Capital punishment, 25, 52, 130, 132; abolition of, 146-8, 149, 150, 155, 157, 158, 159-60; in eighteenth century, 80, 107, 168-9; in England, 56; of Italians in Ontario, 150; move to reinstate, 14, 17, 21; in nineteenth-century British Columbia, 106-8, 111-14, 118, 119-20, 124, 170; of women and children, 15, 30-1, 151, 154. *See also* Death Penalty; Punishment; Transportation, as punishment
Capital statutes, comparison of NSW and Ontario, 132
Caricature, as a legal device, 124-5
Chandler, Samuel, 87, 91
Chilcotin Chiefs, 77
Civilizing process, general ethos of, 10, 24, 27, 46-7
Class inequalities. *See* Punishment, class inequality of
Clemency. *See* Pardons
Cochrane, Lord Thomas, 36
Cockburn, James, 33
'Cognitive dissonance,' in European settlers, 108
Collins, Louisa, 146, 156
Commercial trade: growth of, 22, 41-2; and street culture, 42; and street maintenance, 44
Commutations: by ethnicity and race, 143, 149, 153, 154; gender differences in, 15, 16; patterns, 9, 141, 148, 152, 155; rates of, 9, 10, 16, 133, 144, 146; of sentences, 6, 8, 108, 112, 156, 158, 160, 166. *See also* Death Penalty; Executions; Sentences
Compassion of citizens, 151
Conditional pardon. *See* Pardons, conditional
Corporal punishment, 21, 23-5, 38-9; move to restore, 14, 15, 17; shame and pain of, 40, 45
Corrections: authorities, 171; therapeutic, 12, 13

Courts martial, trials by, 84, 87, 92
Cranner, William, 37-8
Crease, Judge Henry, 110, 112-15, 120, 121, 123
Crime rates, viii, 13, 14, 22
Criminal Code of Canada, 144, 160, 170
Criminal justice system, vii-ix, 7, 12, 14-15, 18, 159; in Canada, 166-74; in New South Wales, 141, 145
Criminal law: administration of, 47, 77, 79-82, 93-5, 96-7; appearance of compassion, 7; campaigns to reform, 47; changes in North America, 104; procedural changes in, 80, 85, 86, 88, 98
Criminal Law Amendment Act (1883), 145
Criminality, ways to 'correct,' 12
Criminological literature, 11-14
Cultural defence, 104, 110, 115, 120, 124, 125, 149, 150; of Aboriginal offenders, 9; Gitksan law as, 111-12, 123; and governing diversity, 105-6, 108, 174; role of experts in, 116-19; success related to quality of story, 116, 118, 119
Cultural interpretation, example of, 24

Davis, Kenneth Culp, 12
Davis, Natalie Zemon, 8, 9
Death penalty, 6, 25, 83, 106 (table), 107 (table), 131-2, 136, 144-7; challenged, 139, 153, 159-60. *See also* Capital punishment, abolition of; Capital punishment, move to reinstate
Defoe, Daniel, 31, 36
DeLacy, Margaret, 58-9
Deterrence: justification for increasing penalties, 15, 167, 168, 169, 173; versus reform, 52, 54-5, 59, 61; role of cultural defence in, 114, 158. *See also* Capital punishment, move to reinstate
Discretion, judicial, 12, 16, 82, 130-1, 134, 139, 142-3, 159-61; authority of, 77, 80, 136; power of, 25, 70; role of, 112, 113, 171-3
Discretionary mercy: administrative, 12, 17, 114; ambivalence of government to, 172; benevolence, 7; cultural defence as appeal for, 104, 108-22, 112, 113, 114, 116, 118, 125; as form of social control, 107-8; judicial role in, 112, 113, 171, 172, 173; legislative, 78-9, 84, 170-1, 173-4; through parole system, 173; political objectives of, 6-7, 16, 17, 93-4, 97; theories of, 12-13, 14; unpredictable

decisions of, 12, 15, 166. *See also*
  Pardons
Doherty, Charles, 150-1
Drake, Montague, 111, 112-15
Drug cases, sentences for, 167, 173, 174
Duff, Antony, 13
Durham, Lord John George Lambton, 87,
  91-2, 96-7
Durkheim, Emile, 11
Dyott, William, 69

Economic inequality, of low-status
  persons, 11. *See also* Punishment, class
  inequality of
Eksteins, Modris, 131
Eldon, Lord Chancellor John Scott, 36,
  58
Elias, Norbert, 10, 23, 27, 34, 47, 107
Elites, role in justice system, 6, 8, 80, 81,
  83, 118. *See also* Family Compact
Emergency pardoning legislation in
  Upper Canada, 84-6, 88, 90, 92, 97
Ericson, Richard, 11
'Ethnographic imagination,' 109, 121-2,
  125
European immigrants in Ontario, 150
Europeans, racial views of Native peoples,
  106, 108, 121, 122, 125
Executions, 6-7, 87, 88 (table), 89, 91, 93,
  113, 147, 148; of aristocrats, 6; in
  centre of town, impropriety of, 41; in
  eighteenth-century London, 21-2, 26,
  27-31, 43; elimination of public, 21, 26,
  29, 31, 46; or imprisonment, 52, 158;
  for murder or sexual offences in NSW,
  154-5, 157; over-representation of
  Aboriginals, 106 (table), 107 (table),
  170; and pain, 26, 29; as a public act,
  21, 27-8, 29, 46; rates, 22, 57-8, 142,
  147; statistics in NSW and Ontario,
  132-4, 140, 158; in United States, 10,
  14, 17, 158. *See also* Capital case dispositions; Capital punishment;
  Commutations; Death Penalty;
  Punishment; Treason
Executive Councils (Canadian), 84, 87,
  89, 91, 92, 136, 139-40
Executive discretion, 108, 115, 118, 130-
  1, 153, 158-60, 166, 171-3; contrasting
  styles in NSW and Ontario, 132, 134,
  137, 141, 145-6, 149, 152, 158. *See also*
  Discretionary mercy
Exemplary punishment, 62, 80, 90, 93,
  94, 114. *See also* Punishment; Terror
Expert witnesses. *See* Cultural defence,
  role of experts in

Fair play. *See* British justice, fair play in
The Family Compact, 81-3, 95, 97-8
Fay, Michael, trial of, 23, 47
Fielding, Henry, 29
Fines as punishment, 6, 25, 45, 46
First Nations. *See* Aboriginals
Flogging: in Australia, 145; clemency from,
  38; military, 39; public, 6, 37, 38, 46
Foreign nationals, 153, 156; dispropor-
  tionate number in capital cases, 150-1,
  154; petitions for, 148-9
Foucault, Michel, 13, 16, 26-7, 107
Furman v. *Georgia* (1972), 10, 13

Garland, David, 5, 13, 22
Gatrell, V.A.C., 8
Gender-based justice. *See* Women, as
  defendants; Women, discrimination in
  punishment
George, Dorothy, 41
Glenelg, Lord Charles Grant, 85, 91
Goodman, Ellen, 24
Gordon Riots (1780), 44
Governing diversity. *See* Cultural defence,
  and governing diversity
Governments, role in administering
  justice, 166-9, 171-2
Governor, Jimmy, 138, 153-4, 157
Grenville, William, 31, 41
Guilty plea, in exchange for pardon. *See*
  Plea bargaining

Habeas corpus, suspension of, 85, 88
Hamilton, Alexander, 78
Hammett, Sir Benjamin, 30-1
The Hanging Judge. *See* Begbie, Judge
  Matthew Baillie
Hangings. *See* Executions
Hawkins, Keith, 130, 140
Hay, Douglas, 6-7, 8, 10, 15, 17, 70, 78,
  80, 93, 95, 98, 114
Haynes, John, 146, 155, 158
Heron, Sir Robert, 37
Historical literature, viii, 7-10
Homosexuality, 32
Honour, codes of, 104-5, 119-20, 124,
  151, 153
House of Commons Standing Committee
  on Justice and the Solicitor General, 168
Howard, John, 59, 67, 82
Hughes, Robert, 8
Hulks. *See* Prison hulks
Humanitarian trend, 22, 24-5, 47, 54,
  147. *See also* Reform, penal

Ignatieff, Michael, 159

Imprisonment, 6, 7, 14, 15, 25, 59, 82, 84, 171; and fining, 45; instead of death penalty, 108, 114; levels of, 15, 68; reducing, as cost-saving measure, 169-70; reformation of offenders, 52, 71
Inequalities in justice. *See* Punishment, class inequality of
Infanticide, 81, 151-2
Irish Catholics in Australia, 135
Irish Rebellion (1798), 86

Jackson, Bernard, 119
Jails: county, 66; overcrowding in London, 67
Jameson, Robert, 82, 89
Japanese culture, parent-child suicide in, 104
Jenkinson, George, 123
Johnson, Dr. Samuel, 32, 41, 59
Judgments, individualized, 130, 144
Judicial system, bloody, 29
The Judiciary: circuits and assizes of, 65-6, 69, 148; opinions about Aboriginals, 109, 170; recommending mercy, 108, 109, 170. *See also* Discretionary mercy, judicial role in
Juries, 70, 124; and cultural defence, 112, 118-20; exercising mercy, 151, 156, 172; recommending acquittals, 80, 82, 84
Justice, 15, 70, 148; discretionary, 12, 16, 82, 130-1, 134, 136, 139, 142-3, 159-61; qualities of, 3, 17; 'savage,' for BC Aboriginals, 106-10, 124, 125; tempered with mercy, 4, 94-7, 110, 152, 166-7, 170, 174. *See also* Discretionary mercy

Keefer, Frank, 150-1
King, Peter, 9
King's law and the community, 65
Kingston penitentiary, 82, 83, 89, 98, 147. *See also* Penitentiaries
Kirchheimer, Otto, 11
Knights of Labor, 148

Labour movement, comparison NSW and Ontario, 135, 148
Land claims cases, 116
Langbein, John, 8
Law Reform Commission of Canada, 172
Legal pluralism, 115, 124
Lehman, Edward, 132
Linebaugh, Peter, 8
Liverpool, Lord Robert Banks Jenkinson, 61, 63
Lount, Samuel, trial of, 87, 89, 91, 94-6

Macdonald, Duncan George Forbes, 121, 122
Mackenzie, William Lyon, 87, 96
Mackintosh, James, 55, 61
Manning, Preston, 15
Marks, Frederick, 113
Marquis, Greg, 134
Marx, Karl, 11
Matthews, Peter, trial of, 87, 89, 91, 94-6
McGowen, Randall, 28-9, 54, 56, 80
McNaught, Kenneth, 93
Men, 30, 39, 120, 138-9, 142-3, 148-9, 151, 153-5; gender-based sense of superiority, 15, 138-9, 152, 153, 155, 156. *See also* Honour, codes of
Mercy: as form of social control, 6, 107, 108; politics of, 6-7, 9, 10, 17, 155; qualities of, 3-4; racist character of, 10, 17, 136; recommendation for, 151, 156, 158; theoretical views of, 7-14. *See also* Discretionary mercy; Justice, tempered with mercy; Pardons
Military criminals, 10
Mills, David, 151-2
Ministers of justice and the executive, parliamentary role, 158
Missionaries, as experts in cultural defence cases, 117, 118
Mob justice, 34-6
Mollies of the Vere Street coterie, 33, 36
Montgomery, Charles, 154-5
Moore, Kathleen, 17
Morreau, James, 87, 91
'Mount Rennie rapists,' 155-6
Murphy, Jeffrie, 17

Napier, Charles, 39
Napoleonic Wars, 70
Native people. *See* Aboriginals
Needham, Joseph, 112
New South Wales. *See* Political culture, in NSW and Ontario
Newgate Prison, 28, 33, 66-7; relocation of the gallows to, 43-4, 57
North West Rebellion, treason trials in. *See* Treason, in North West Rebellion
Nova Scotia, pardon system in colonial, 10

Offenders, rehabilitation of, 78, 167; sentencing of (*see* Sentences)
Old Bailey trials, 25, 28, 37, 39, 43, 56
Oppressed and/or exploited people, 15
'Ordinary person,' standards of, 105

Pain in punishment, 9, 15, 17-18, 26, 29, 31-2, 40, 45, 67, 69

Pardon letters, 8

Pardons, 4, 10, 70; conditional, 5, 9, 38, 68, 80, 83-4, 86-7, 89, 91; granted according to political considerations, 6, 17, 78-9, 82, 85-7, 90, 91-7, 166; history, before Upper Canada rebellion, 77-80, 82-3; posthumous, 77, 97; studies about, 10, 17; unconditional, 152. *See also* Rebellion in Upper Canada, role of pardons in; Royal prerogative of mercy, in pardons

Parent-child suicide, 104

Parole, eligibility for, 159, 173, 174

Parole boards, 171, 173

'Patriot' raids, 78, 83, 85, 87, 90-2, 97

'Peace, order, and good government,' 147

'Peaceable kingdom,' Upper Canada as, 77, 82, 95

Peel, Sir Robert, 45, 58, 64-5, 69, 79, 81

Penal change. *See* Reform, penal

Penal codes and practices, 16, 21-3, 24

Penal colonies. *See* Transportation as punishment

Penitentiaries, 56, 59, 64, 67, 80, 98; nationwide system of, 72; private, 17; in Upper Canada, 81-2. *See also* Kingston penitentiary

Petitions for mercy, 8, 94, 96, 114, 148, 158

Phillips, Jim, 7, 10

Philosophers, Judeo-Christian, 4, 5

Pillory, 25, 32-3, 45; bill for removal of, 34, 37; and gentlemen, 36; and manslaughter, 33-4; and public whipping, 21, 44

Pitt, William Morton, 67-8, 70

Plea bargaining, 87-9, 90, 91, 98, 173

Pluralism. *See* Legal pluralism

'Political correctness,' 105

Political culture: differences influencing punishments, 5, 6, 8-9, 16, 159; in NSW and Ontario, 5, 131, 133, 135-6, 145, 146, 148, 153

Poverty: legal representation and, 8-9; mercy and, 148-9, 154. *See also* Punishment, class inequality of

Power, reinforcing legitimacy of authority, 6, 13, 78, 93, 95, 116

Prescott, battle in, 87, 92

Prince, Colonel John, 92

Prison hulks: convicts moved to, 68-9; discipline of, 64

Prisoners' rights, 13

Prosecutions, rising numbers influencing justice system, 17, 56, 94, 140

Provocation in cultural defence of Aboriginals, 111, 112

Public opinion, influencing justice system, vii, 6, 8, 11, 14, 79, 83-6, 93-5, 96-7, 109, 141, 166, 167, 171

Public order, concern for, 22

Public space and decorum, 31

Punishment, 21, 29; class inequality of, 6, 7, 10, 11, 13, 15-16, 36, 46, 137, 155; costly burden, 44; court decisions and, 167, 168, 170, 171, 174; fines as, 6, 25, 45, 46; lack of coherent policy for, 47, 167-72, 173, 174; modes of, 52, 69; modification in, 5-6, 7, 9, 10-12, 15-18, 22-4, 31, 130, 156, 173; and pain, 9, 15, 17-18, 26, 31-2, 67, 69; proportionality in, 14, 55; purposes of, 7, 53-4, 56, 60-1; reformative character of, 56, 61; scaffold expense, 43; shame and dishonour of, 32, 40-1; spectacle of, 26; theories of, 11-12; therapeutic model, 12-14; unanticipated consequences of, vii, 5, 27; uniformity and predictability of, 12, 70, 77, 82-3. *See also* Capital punishment; Corporal punishment; Pardons; Secondary punishment; Transportation, as punishment

Quebec, province of, 135, 148, 169

Racial stereotyping, through exercising mercy, 109-10, 112, 142, 149, 153. *See also* Cultural defence

Racism: in justice system, 13, 16, 17; official Australian policy, 137. *See also* Aboriginals; Blacks in US justice system; Foreign nationals

Rape, penalty for, 37, 147, 153, 155, 157

Read, Theodosius, 33

Rebellion in Upper Canada, role of pardons in, 5, 9, 83-7, 88 (table), 89-98

Recidivism rates, 13

Redemption, promise of, 56, 71

Reform, penal, 21, 24, 46-7, 52, 56, 70-2; in nineteenth century, 13, 36, 78-82, 96-8, 107; philosophy, 11-13, 45, 54, 64, 68, 145

Refugees, as experts, in cultural defence cases, 116

Repugnance, thresholds of, 23

Reputation and standing, 38

Retribution, vii, 35, 54-5, 56

Retributivist movement, viii, 12, 14, 17, 59

Riel, Louis, trial of, 77, 97, 144-5, 160

Robinson, Sir John Beverley, 81, 82, 86, 87, 90, 92, 94, 95

Robson, John, 113, 114
Romilly, Samuel, 36, 55, 63, 67, 70
Rosen, Lawrence, 136
Rousseau, Jean-Jacques, 11
Royal Navy, as experts, in cultural defence cases, 117, 118
Royal prerogative of mercy, in pardons, 4, 5, 8, 10, 12, 16, 17, 57, 78-80, 98, 112, 139; assumed by Upper Canada government, 84, 86, 90, 91, 97. *See also* Pardons
Rule of law, 12, 16, 94, 104, 108, 158-9; and discretion, 136, 139; virtue of, 130. *See also* Justice, tempered with mercy
Ruling class. *See* Elites, role in justice system; Punishment, class inequality of
Rusche, Georg, 11

Scott, Rose, 138, 156
Secondary punishment, 56, 64, 79, 83, 84, 90; non-capital, 25, 77. *See also* Transportation as punishment, secondary
Sentences, 167-70, 172-4; hard labour regimes, 46, 54, 56-7, 64; home detention, 17; modified, 156; non-capital, 25, 77
Short Hills (Ontario), skirmish, 87, 91, 92
Simond, Louis, 33-4
Singapore, corporal punishment in, 23
Smith, Sydney, 45
Smith, William, 33, 40
Social knowledge in trials. *See* Cultural defence, role of experts in; 'Ethnographic imagination'
Social science literature, 11
Society, polite and commercial, 43
Sodomy, 32-3, 37. *See also* Mollies of the Vere Street coterie
Soul, punishments of, 16, 107, 171
Southey, Robert, 55, 62
Spierenburg, Pieter, 107
'State formation' literature, 98
State-run justice system (NSW), 141
Stephen, James, 90, 92, 95
Suffragists in NSW, 154
Sydenham, Lord Charles Poulett Thomson, 93, 98

Talfourd, Thomas, 34, 36, 40-1
Taylor, C.J., 82, 83
Taylor, Michael Angelo, 32, 35-7
Terror, 3, 6, 53, 65, 93, 135; judicial, 29, 45, 72, 141-2, 145, 155. *See also* Exemplary punishment
Therapeutic punishment model, 12-14

Thompson, E.P., 6
Ticket of leave, 98
Tolmie, William Fraser, 115, 117-30
Torgovnick, Marianna, 121
'Tory image of justice,' 80, 98
'Total' institutions, 82, 98. *See also* Kingston penitentiary; Penitentiaries
Trade union leaders, in Ontario, 148
Transportation as punishment, 5, 6, 9, 16, 86, 93, 97, 168, 169; to Africa, 66; to America, 25, 60, 66; to Australia, 25, 53, 58, 71-2; banishment as alternative to, 81-2, 84, 86, 88-90, 91; convict stigma lingered, 145; deterrent value of, 63-5, 66-8, 72; for life, 63, 69; from metropolitan areas, 66-7; to New South Wales, 60-2, 64, 66; of political offenders, 62, 87-91, 96, 147; primary, for military, 81, 84; purpose of, 53-4, 59, 60-5, 67-8, 71-2, 168; reinstitution of, in eighteenth century, 58-60, 66; secondary, 45, 66, 79, 80-4, 89, 90; Upper Canada rebels to Australia, 87-91, 96; to the West Indies, 66
Treason, 30; in North West Rebellion, 144; in Upper Canada, 81, 83, 85, 87, 88 (table), 90, 94-6, 147
Tyburn procession and fair, 25, 28-9, 34, 41, 43-4, 56-7

United States, criminal justice system in, 14, 158, 168, 171, 172, 173
United States Sentencing Commission, 169
Upper Canada: capital offences in, 80, 82, 83, 85, 86, 147; rebellion in. *See* Rebellion in Upper Canada, role of pardons in; Treason, in Upper Canada
Utilitarian reform. *See* Reform, penal, in nineteenth century

Van den Haag, Ernest, 35
Van Diemen's Land (Australia), 84, 87, 88, 89, 96, 99. *See also* Transportation as punishment, to Australia
Victorian morality, 22
Violence, state-sanctioned, 34, 152
Von Hirsh, Andrew, 13-14

Wait, Benjamin, 87, 91, 96
Walpole, Horace, 42
War of 1812, 83
Wellington, Duke of, Arthur Wellesley, 55
'Whig image of justice,' 80, 81
Whipping. *See* Flogging
White, James Boyd, 115, 124

'White Australia' policy of 1901, 137
Whites, political dominance in British
   Columbia, 9, 110, 120
Wiener, Martin, 40
Wilberforce, William, 30
Williams, Thomas, 154-5
Willis, Judge John Walpole, 81
Windsor (Ontario), battle in, 87, 92
Women: burning of, 30-1; changes in
   punishment of, 30, 46; as defendants,
special consideration, 15, 16, 138-9,
142, 148-9, 151-2, 153, 156-7; discrimi-
nation in punishment, 13, 16, 138-9;
disorderly mob of, 34, 36; and physical
punishment, 22, 38-9, 133; public roles
of, 22, 29, 30, 139, 149, 152; punishment of elderly, 38, 39
Women and capital punishment. *See*
   Capital punishment, of women and
   children

Printed and bound in Canada by Friesens

Set in Stone by Michael Kelley

Copy-editor: Robyn Packard

Proofreader: Gail Copeland

Indexers: Margalo Whyte and Carol Graham